TAKING THE LEAD

Long track speed skating coach Xiuli Wang and multiple Olympic medallist Clara Hughes epitomize the coach/athlete relationship.

PHOTO: MIKE RIDEWOOD

TAKING THE LEAD

Strategies and Solutions from Female Coaches

EDITED BY SHEILA ROBERTSON

THE UNIVERSITY OF ALBERTA PRESS

Published by
The University of Alberta Press
Ring House 2
Edmonton, Alberta, Canada T6G 2E1

Copyright © 2010 The University of Alberta Press

LIBRARY AND ARCHIVES CANADA CATALOGUING IN PUBLICATION

       Taking the lead : strategies and solutions from
female coaches / edited by Sheila Robertson ; introduction
by Dru Marshall.

ISBN 978-0-88864-542-5

       1. Women coaches (Athletics). 2. Women coaches
(Athletics)--Social conditions. 3. Women coaches
(Athletics)--Conduct of life. 4. Leadership.
I. Robertson, Sheila

GV709.14.T35 2010   796'.082   C2009-906601-7

The University of Alberta Press is committed to protecting our natural environment. As part of our efforts,
this book is printed on Enviro Paper: it contains 100% post-consumer recycled fibres and is acid- and
chlorine-free.

The University of Alberta Press gratefully acknowledges the support received for its publishing program
from The Canada Council for the Arts. The University of Alberta Press also gratefully acknowledges
the financial support of the Government of Canada through the Book Publishing Industry Development
Program (BPIDP) and from the Alberta Foundation for the Arts for its publishing activities.

The University of Alberta Press gratefully acknowledges the financial support of the Coaching
Association of Canada for the publication of this book.

CONTENTS

Message from the Coaching Association of Canada   VII

Message from the Canadian Association for the
Advancement of Women and Sport and Physical Activity   IX

Preface *Sheila Robertson*   XI

Introduction *Dru Marshall*   XV

PART ONE—ISSUES

ONE

The Perils and Pleasures of Coaching and Motherhood
Sheila Robertson

3

TWO

Changing the Androcentric World of Sport: Is it Possible?
Penny Werthner, Diane Culver, and Rose Mercier

37

THREE

Female Coaches' Experience of Harassment and Bullying
Gretchen Kerr

57

FOUR

Homophobia in Sport: Fact of Life, Taboo Subject
Guylaine Demers

73

PART TWO—SKILLS

FIVE

Communicating with Clarity: Guidelines to Help Female
Coaches Succeed
Penny Werthner and Shaunna Taylor

101

SIX

Understanding Mentoring as a Development Tool
for Female Coaches
Dru Marshall and Dawn-Marie Sharp   117

SEVEN

Political Advocacy in Coaching: Why Engage?
Rose Mercier and Dru Marshall   147

PART THREE—ADVICE

EIGHT

Coaching as a Viable Career Path for Women
Penny Werthner and Bettina Callary   167

NINE

Developing the Next Generation of Female Coaches
Dru Marshall, Guylaine Demers, and Dawn-Marie Sharp   181

TEN

The Business of Greatness
Rose Mercier   203

ELEVEN

Contracts and Contract Negotiations
Hilary Findlay   217

Afterword *Dru Marshall*   243

Appendix 1 *A Five-Point Collaborative Strategy for Change*   245

Appendix 2 *Provincial and National Coaching Associations*   255

Appendix 3 *A Decade of Articles from the* Canadian Journal   259
            for Women in Coaching

Contributors   265

Index   271

MESSAGE

from the Coaching Association of Canada

THE COACHING ASSOCIATION of Canada (CAC) takes pride in supporting *Taking the Lead: Strategies and Solutions from Female Coaches.*

Our association strives to improve the effectiveness of coaching across all levels of Canada's sport system and to enhance the experiences of all Canadian athletes through quality coaching. We believe that *Taking the Lead* presents powerful arguments regarding the essential role female coaches can and should be playing to improve coaching in Canada. Through our Women in Coaching program, we are committed to developing and maintaining the partnerships, networks, resources, and strategies that are essential to increasing the numbers of female coaches and retaining women in the coaching field.

Taking the Lead is a strong and clear demonstration of the nationwide leadership role CAC's Women in Coaching program has taken since the late 1980s to increase coaching opportunities for women at all levels of sport. As well as publishing the online *Canadian Journal for Women in Coaching,* which provided the genesis for *Taking the Lead,* the program supports women in coaching by working toward solutions to issues that affect female coaches, and by profiling its endeavours nationally and internationally.

Specific initiatives include the National Team Apprenticeship Program and Canada Games Apprenticeship Program, an annual National Coach Workshop, and the Online Mentor Program. Our Grants and Scholarships program enables national sport organizations to organize programs for female coaches, offers professional development support, and provides scholarships to female coaches wishing to attend a National Coaching Institute. Best Practices are applauded and Groundbreakers—female coaches who, by their athletic and coaching successes, have brought honour to themselves, to their sport, and to Canada—are profiled online.

The authors of *Taking the Lead* are experienced sport leaders who have made important contributions to our association and to coaching development over many years. We know first-hand that they are passionately committed to implementing systemic change, and to uprooting the ingrained, traditional attitudes that hold back many female coaches. We believe that *Taking the Lead* shows individuals and organizations how to get to the heart of the matter because, after all, truly effective change happens from the inside out. Such change would benefit from more women's leadership, which is the ultimate goal of Women in Coaching and one that is strongly supported by the Coaching Association of Canada. Strengthening female coaching leadership is a critically important upward climb, and we believe that *Taking the Lead* details important steps in that direction.

—JOHN BALES, CHIEF EXECUTIVE OFFICER,
COACHING ASSOCIATION OF CANADA

MESSAGE

from the Canadian Association for the Advancement of Women and Sport and Physical Activity

THE CANADIAN ASSOCIATION FOR the Advancement of Women and Sport and Physical Activity (CAAWS) is very pleased to support *Taking the Lead: Strategies and Solutions from Female Coaches.* Bringing together issues and realities of women in coaching, this book provides guidance on how to make the sport community more welcoming, supportive, and respectful of female coaches. The information shared here supports CAAWS's mission to provide leadership and education and build capacity to foster equitable support, diverse opportunities, and positive experiences for girls and women in sport and physical activity.

Nearly thirty years after it was originally founded in 1981, CAAWS continues to be a vibrant force on the Canadian scene. Those original leaders of national, provincial, and local sport and physical activity groups saw CAAWS encouraging girls and women to become active in sport and physical activity both as participants and as leaders. This mandate continues today—with an even broader perspective. CAAWS's desire to see women and girls reap the benefits of a healthy, inclusive sport and physical activity system has led to a wider variety of activities and initiatives than ever before.

Over the last few years CAAWS has led the sporting community in opening up discussion on addressing homophobia in sport. The CAAWS

Women and Leadership program was developed for women by women who understood the unique challenges women faced—from volunteers working on amateur boards to administrators running complex organizations. CAAWS has successfully partnered with Aboriginal leaders and communities to engage young girls in physical activity and to provide professional development opportunities for Aboriginal women to increase their skills and confidence.

Resources to assist a wide range of practitioners, coaches, and sport leaders on a variety of issues are available through the CAAWS website. Many partnerships with government and non-government organizations have been developed, leading to various activities and initiatives that advocate for positive change for girls and women in the sport and physical activity communities.

Canada is a country where CAAWS has been able to make its voice heard, and we value the opportunity to lend our expertise, knowledge, and resources beyond our borders. Recognized internationally for advocating and ensuring girls and women have increased opportunities, CAAWS shares the experiences and successes from Canada with countries where girls and women do not yet have the same freedom to pursue participation in sport and physical activity.

There are still many areas where women and girls need skill development, opportunity, and encouragement to succeed. Coaching is one such area that continues to evolve for women, and officiating is another. The Coaching Association of Canada and its Women in Coaching program is an excellent example of how mentoring programs, specific training, and consistent dedicated attention are enabling women to achieve their goals in the coaching field.

Looking ahead, the vision for CAAWS is to see a sport and physical activity system in which girls and women are actively engaged as participants and leaders.

— KARIN LOFSTROM, EXECUTIVE DIRECTOR,
CANADIAN ASSOCIATION FOR THE ADVANCEMENT
OF WOMEN AND SPORT AND PHYSICAL ACTIVITY

PREFACE

Sheila Robertson
on behalf of the editorial board of the *Canadian Journal for Women in Coaching*

Our Beginning

IN RECENT YEARS, as the participation of girls and women in sport in Canada has skyrocketed, barriers have tumbled and opportunities have proliferated. Women are now found in every aspect of sport, from the playing fields to the boardrooms, as administrators and officials, at the grassroots level through to high performance.

While coaching, too, has been affected by this explosion, women who choose to coach continue to face serious challenges, generally as a result of programs that, when designed, do not consider their unique needs. Other barriers include a lack of mentoring, the failure of sport organizations to spotlight female role models, miscommunication, and a lack of access to information that is critical to professional success.

To address these challenges, in September 2000, the Women in Coaching program of the Coaching Association of Canada introduced the *Canadian Journal for Women in Coaching*. The premise of the *Journal* was that timely, accurate, targeted information goes a long way towards creating a healthier and more positive environment for female coaches, in Canada and around the world. During the research phase, a worldwide search turned up little information specific to female coaches. Anecdotally, we did know that dominant concerns include balancing family life, negotiating equitable compensation and satisfactory contracts, breaking into the high performance echelon, establishing personal behaviour guidelines, and understanding employee and employer rights.

As well as tackling and verifying these pertinent issues, the *Journal* went one step further and provided practical, hands-on, and proactive suggestions and solutions that inform coaches, sport organizations, their employers, the parents of their athletes, their clubs and association, and government decision makers. Above all, the *Journal* was designed to make sure that readers develop an understanding of the unique challenges female coaches face. We believed that if, through the *Journal,* those challenges were "put on the table" and workable solutions emerged, an important step would have been taken towards breaching the formidable barriers to getting ahead.

Our Book

AFTER TEN YEARS, thirty-nine articles, growing readership, and critical acclaim, the editorial board of the *Journal* believed that a celebration was in order. It was agreed that publishing a book that featured a cross-section of the wide-ranging subject matter covered in the *Journal* would be an exciting, challenging, and valuable exercise. Timely, too, since publication coincides with the 2010 Olympic and Paralympic Winter Games in Vancouver and Whistler, BC. Each article was reviewed and a decision reached on which would be updated and revised for inclusion in this book. Substantial work has been done to ensure that *Taking the Lead: Strategies and Solutions from Female Coaches* is much more than a collection of articles; it does, in fact, represent the current views of each author nicely tied together.

Much as we hope the reader will hang on every word, we recognize that some will be drawn to certain chapters before others. Please note that each chapter is self-contained and that reading in sequence is not required.

Our Objectives

SINCE ITS INCEPTION, the *Journal* has explored the situations of female coaches from almost every angle. We've reported on the value women bring to the coaching profession, female athletes wanting equal success in coaching, and female coaches juggling career aspirations and motherhood. We've addressed the silence that cloaks the very real problems of homophobia, harassment, and bullying. We've put Canada's female coaches under the microscope in an effort to draw influential attention to their situations, to stimulate debate, and to effect change that will lead to a more equitable environment.

We hope that the readers of this book will be inspired by the personal stories, disturbed by the realities, encouraged by the recommendations, and challenged to join in addressing and correcting the issues.

Specifically, we hope that the book
- provides an eloquent overview of the challenges and issues female coaches face
- provides practical, hands-on, and proactive suggestions and solutions to the challenges and issues
- provides accurate and targeted information that will help to create a more positive environment for female coaches in Canada and around the world
- encourages more young women and women in general to become coaches

Our Approach

AS DRU MARSHALL explains in her Introduction to this book, for change to be effected, it is essential that we look at sport and coaching differently, ask some hard questions, and then fundamentally alter the models of our sporting world.

Keeping the questions Dru poses in mind will, we suggest, help readers to join the debate, find their own answers, and contribute to the solution. Success must be the work of all, not a few.

Our Thanks

WE THANK THE COACHING Association of Canada for providing the *Journal* with support, both financial and moral, since its inception.

We thank the University of Alberta Press for believing in our project, for providing substantial guidance, and for ensuring that the book became reality.

We thank our authors for the value of their contributions and for their support of the *Journal*.

We thank the expert readers of the manuscript for their positive comments and excellent suggestions for helping to improve the content.

> *Sheilagh Croxon*
> *Guylaine Demers*
> *Gretchen Kerr*
> *Dru Marshall*
> *Rose Mercier*
> *Sheila Robertson*
> *Penny Werthner*

INTRODUCTION

Dru Marshall

THE AUTHORS WHO HAVE been involved in the planning and writing of *Taking the Lead: Strategies and Solutions from Female Coaches* have been excited to engage in this venture. All of us, as we examine our sporting, business, or academic careers, have seen an increase in female participation in our fields of expertise. However, with rare exception, we have seen little or no change in the numbers of women who make it to the top: as national team coaches, chief executive officers of corporations, presidents of universities, or chairs of boards. Despite the odds, some women do make it—and in many cases, in those organizations, we see transformational leadership. Why, despite increased participation of women in various fields and numerous studies that demonstrate the importance of diversity in leadership teams for success, are women so under-represented at senior leadership levels?

Statistical Picture—Business

IS THERE TRULY A DEARTH of female leaders? Is there evidence on which to base a discussion? The answer is clearly yes, particularly if we examine the business, academic, and sport literature.

About thirty years ago, large numbers of women entered the labour market, and now almost half the work force is female. Recent studies in Canada (Jenner & Ferguson, 2009) demonstrate that women hold

- approximately 40% of the managerial positions
- less than 17% of corporate officer roles
- about 11% of senior leadership line roles, those positions often necessary to occupy before being promoted to the highest leadership ranks in a company
- less than 6% of CEO positions

This data is evidence of a clear gender gap; while close to half the labour force is female, less than 20% of the top jobs are held by women. There is also a gender gap in salary in Canada, with women earning about 65% of what men make in the same position, using median salary (Statistics Canada, 2008). Unfortunately, this data is not unique to Canada. In the United States, less than 3% (n=15) of Fortune 500 companies are run by female CEOs (Catalyst Short Report, 2008).

Statistical Picture—Academics

AN EXAMINATION OF THE post-secondary sector reveals a similar gender gap to business. That is, while greater than 50% of the student population in most post-secondary institutions in Canada is female, women

- make up approximately 32% of the faculty
- hold approximately 28% of tenured positions, 40% of tenure track positions, and about 45% of non-tenured track positions (Drakich & Stewart, 2007)

Female faculty are not appointed to the rank of full professor at the same speed or rate as male faculty, and they tend to be paid less. Women, both students and faculty, tend to be attracted to particular disciplines, for example, education, fine and applied arts and humanities, health professions, and social sciences.

In terms of leadership, women are under-represented in senior university and college administrative positions. Between 25 to 30% of the decanal positions, one of the more senior administrative positions in a post-secondary institution, are held by women (Grant, 2005). As of August 2008, of the ninety-four member institutions that comprise the Association of Universities and Colleges of Canada (AUCC), only fifteen were headed by women (approximately 16%). Thus, while there are a growing number of women on campuses, there remains a large gender gap in leadership in most institutions.

Statistical Picture—Sport

FEMALE ATHLETE PARTICIPATION rates have increased at all levels of the sport continuum in Canada. Not only do we have more female athletes competing, we have female athletes competing successfully, as evidenced by the proportion of medals won for Canada at the Olympic Games in Athens, Torino, and Beijing. However, when we examine leadership in sport, particularly in the coaching domain, we note a gender gap. National Coaching Certification Program (NCCP) statistics collected prior to the transition to a competency-based model demonstrated that approximately 30% of coaches at Levels 1 to 3 were female, while only 21% and 11% of the coaches at Levels 4 and 5, respectively, were female (Demers, 2009). Levels 4 and 5 represent levels of certification expected for national team coaching. It is not surprising to note, then, that over the last three Olympic Games, female head coaches have comprised between 7% (Athens) and 9% (Beijing) of the Canadian coaching staff.

Kerr, Marshall, Sharp, and Stirling (2006) examined the gender balance in the coaching ranks of eight sports (athletics, basketball, volleyball, ice hockey, rugby, soccer, swimming, and wrestling) that competed from club to national team levels. The sample included 1,564 head and assistant coaches, only 511 (33%) of whom were female. In the post-secondary sector across the eight sports studied, women held

- 14% of head coach positions in the Canadian Colleges Athletic Association (CCAA)
- 20% of head coach positions in Canadian Interuniversity Sport (CIS)
- 31% of head coach positions of female sport teams in CIS

In comparison, 42.8% of coaches of female athletes in the National Collegiate Athletic Association (NCAA) in the United States are women (Acosta & Carpenter, 2008). The larger proportion of female coaches in the United States has been attributed to Title IX, legislation passed in 1972 that mandated equal pay and resources to men's and women's athletic programs. Ironically, Title IX made coaching women's sports a viable alternative for male coaches, and there are fewer female head coaches of female sports in the NCAA now than there were before the legislation was passed.

The Issues

THUS, THERE IS CLEAR evidence from three different fields—business, academics, and sport—of a gender gap in leadership. A number of symbols have been used to describe the issues of women's leadership, two of which are the glass ceiling and the leadership labyrinth.

The glass ceiling was a phrase first used in 1986 by two reporters from the *Wall Street Journal*, Carol Hymowitz and Timothy Schellhardt, to describe the invisible barrier that women encountered when they had a senior executive job within sight. Some have suggested that corporate models, which have historically been designed by men, form the pillars on which the glass ceiling is supported (Desvaux, Devillard-Hoellinger, & Baumgarten, 2007). The concept of the glass ceiling is still used today, as evidenced by Hillary Clinton's comment in her concession speech about there being 18 million cracks in the ceiling (representing the approximate 18 million votes she received) after her loss to Barack Obama in the 2008 Democratic leadership campaign in the United States. However, Eagly and Carli (2007) suggest the glass ceiling concept now appears to be more wrong than right. Their critique highlights three main problems with the concept. First, the glass ceiling describes an absolute barrier at a high level in organizations. We know, though, that women have become CEOs of companies, presidents of universities, board chairs, presidents and prime ministers of various countries, and head coaches of Olympic teams. The barrier is therefore at least permeable, since some women have made it to the top. The second issue relates to women being misled about opportunities available. The transparency of a glass ceiling implies that obstructions can be seen, but some are not so subtle. Third, there is a suggestion that the concept of the glass ceiling as a single, unvarying obstacle at the penultimate stage of a career is too simplistic. That is, it fails to incorporate the challenges many women have that cause them to drop out at a much earlier stage on the way to the executive suite.

Eagly and Carli (2007) suggest a labyrinth as a symbol for the journey that many women take on the way to the top positions in a field. There is a clear goal to navigating a labyrinth, and while routes exist, they are not simple or direct. Typically, persistence is required, as is awareness of progress, and analysis of what lies ahead. Most importantly, the goal of navigating the labyrinth is attainable.

Why the Lack?

SO—WE HAVE EVIDENCE to indicate a significant gender gap in leadership, and there are symbols used to describe the issue of women's leadership. However, why is there a lack of women leaders? A number of reasons follow.

Some have suggested that discrimination against women in the work force prevents them from moving into leadership positions in organizations. Recent studies do suggest a significant gender gap in wages, after controlling for variables like education and work experience that is consistent with the presence of wage discrimination. Desvaux et al. (2007) found that more women (27%) than men (7%) felt discriminated against during their professional careers. In general, promotions come more slowly for women than men with equivalent qualifications, and males tend to receive more favourable evaluations than women leaders in similar positions of power, particularly in roles usually occupied by men. Further, the business literature suggests that men are biased against promoting women inside companies. Taken together, there is evidence to suggest systemic prejudice or discrimination against women. Further, this general bias seems to operate at all levels of the work force, not just at the top. It appears that in sport, and in coaching in particular, the same gender issues are evident (Cook, 1998; Spriggs, 2005; Sport Canada, 1999).

Why would there be a general bias against female leaders? Some have suggested this bias relates to a stereotyping of and resistance to female leadership in general. Studies of successful leaders show that regardless of gender, specific leadership traits are valuable. Examples include skills such as the ability to communicate, see alternate points of few, make decisions, solve conflicts, and manage time. Other research demonstrates that male and female leadership can be associated with gender-specific traits (Eagly & Carli, 2007). These studies suggest that female leaders are generally affectionate, friendly, helpful, kind, and sympathetic, while males are assertive, aggressive, ambitious, dominant, self-confident, self-reliant, and individualistic. While women tend to focus on process and need to understand why things are done in a particular way, men tend to focus on results and want to know how to get there. We could agree that these research findings are fairly general; we likely all know men who exhibit the female characteristics listed above, and women who exhibit the male traits. However, several researchers have demonstrated that men seem to have more freedom in leadership styles. That is, men can communicate in a warm or dominant manner, with seemingly no penalty either way. Women, on the other hand, are in a "double bind." If they are warm and affectionate, they are criticized for not being tough enough; if they are assertive and controlling, they are criticized for lacking warmth (Eagly & Carli, 2007). Either way, they may leave the impression that they don't have the "right stuff" or "leadership jelly." Unfortunately, stereotyping of female leadership in this way means that women are at risk of being evaluated unfairly and are less likely to be awarded prime assignments (Jenner & Ferguson, 2009).

Another reason for the lack of female leaders is exclusion from social networks or an under-investment in social capital. It is hard to engage and benefit from social networking if you are in the minority, particularly when activities may be designed to exclude you. In business, examples of activities that typically exclude women include "jock talk," late night boozing, and trips to strip clubs. These activities make it hard for women to break into male networks. However, socializing with colleagues, which appears to be the non-essential part of work, is one way to build social capital (Eagly & Carli, 2007). Family or work obligations for some women leave little time for socializing and building social networks.

The lack of female role models and mentors is also problematic (Jenner & Ferguson, 2009). There are currently too few women in top jobs to show that it is possible to achieve the highest positions. Role models are important at every step of the continuum—if people don't see others like them in positions, they may not recognize the possibilities available. At the 2009 Academy of Country Music Awards, Jennifer Nettles, the lead singer of Sugarland, was only the second woman to be nominated as a songwriter in the "Song of the Year" category since 1972. In accepting the award, she said, "I've always dreamed of writing and singing songs since I was a little girl...that thought isn't really important and doesn't really matter unless you are a daughter, sister, girlfriend, or mother." In other words, over 50% of songwriters could be women, and those aspiring young songwriters need role models, and aspiring young coaches and administrators do, too.

Corporate downsizing has resulted in "flattening" of corporate structures. As layers of management have been removed, promotion steps are far steeper than they used to be. Thus, fewer opportunities exist to re-enter the workplace at higher levels. This makes it difficult for some women who leave jobs to have a family or take care of an aging parent. When they re-enter the work force, they often have difficulty moving up the corporate ladder.

The dominant model in the business world today equates leadership with unfailing availability and total geographic mobility. In other words, leaders must be available anytime, anywhere (Desvaux et al., 2007). This model is difficult for women with family obligations. Women in the work force traditionally have had a "double burden"—work and domestic responsibilities. Family obligations, including having children and looking after elderly parents, generally result in women having fewer years of job experience and hours of employment per year, which tends to slow career progress and reduces earnings. Researchers have shown that more women than men have career interruptions (Hewlett, Buck Luce, & Schiller, 2005). For women, these career interruptions tend to take place at crucial times; in the case of having children, at a time when they are most pressured to prove themselves at work, and in the case of caring for elderly parents, at a time when they are at the cusp of moving into the upper echelons. Hewlett (2002) demonstrated that, in general, the higher up the corporate ladder women climb, the fewer children they have, whereas the reverse is true for men:

- 49% of the "best paid" women (> $100,000 per year) in the 41- to 55-year age range were childless compared to 19% of men
- 33% of "well paid" women ($55,000–$65,000, depending on age) were childless compared to 25% for men

It seems that the choice between professional success and work/life balance has more consequences for women, who may have to pay a higher price for success.

Finally, we see fewer women at the top of corporate companies because many women who have become disenchanted with the corporate world are "opting out" (Hewlett et al., 2005) and becoming self-employed consultants and entrepreneurs. These roles allow them greater freedom and autonomy, and allow them to feel valued for the contributions that they make.

Clearly, there are many reasons for the lack of female leaders in business, education, and sport. A critical question would be: Should we be trying to increase the numbers of female leaders? Research indicates a resounding "yes" to this question!

Why should we attempt to increase the number of female leaders? Some may argue that it is the moral and ethical thing to do; since women make up slightly more than 50% of the population, it is only right and fair that they be given equal opportunity. I believe a stronger argument, however, is the business case for diversity. Catalyst research on Fortune 500 companies shows that companies with the greatest gender diversity in executive ranks do financially better (Jenner & Ferguson, 2009). Diverse groups contain people who come from different perspectives, and this breadth of thought enhances opportunity for creativity and problem solving. Research suggests a threshold effect for women on executive teams. That is, performance of companies increases significantly once a certain critical mass is attained. In business, this critical mass seems to be at least three women on management committees that have an average of ten people (Desvaux et al., 2007). When there is a critical mass of women, their identities as women become less important and they are more likely to be seen for their competencies (Eagly & Carli, 2007).

Women remain an untapped leadership resource (Jenner & Ferguson, 2009). There is a predicted worldwide shortage of highly qualified workers. In Europe, for example, if the employment rate for women remains constant, they can expect a shortfall of 24 million people in the active work force by 2040; alternatively, if the employment rate for women can be raised to the same level as for men, the projected shortfall drops to 3 million (Desvaux et al., 2007). Given the above, it is clear that there is an under-leveraged business opportunity in the current lack of gender diversity.

Some Suggestions

THERE ARE A NUMBER of ways we can increase this untapped leadership resource.

First, it is important for women to establish networks. As stated earlier, work-related social activity should be considered an essential part of the job. Often social activity is the first thing to go when time is tight, but women need to ruthlessly and consciously shore up their social capital. Women gain from strong and supportive mentors and from connections with powerful networks (Eagly & Carli, 2007). Activities that result in increased connectivity and motivation are excellent retention tools and help to expand the female talent pool (Desvaux et al., 2007).

A second strategy relates to the development of a pipeline of qualified women. We should ensure that all women have access to developmental activities, not just the high potential employees. Important developmental activities include informal mentoring, networking, and visible role models (Jenner & Ferguson, 2009). Evidence indicates that some of this training should be for women only, as in these environments females feel comfortable, safe, and have no fear of looking incompetent in front of men. Women are also motivated by different things than men; for example, connection to colleagues, recognition from bosses, giving back to the community, flexibility versus compensation, so it makes sense that if training is to be optimized, it would be customized to the women involved (Hewlett, 2007). Women must also participate in developmental job experiences (Eagly & Carli, 2007). For aspiring national team coaches, this may mean actual coaching assignments with national teams, rather than managerial or video analysis tasks, including specific assignments like attacking set plays, technical skill development, and program planning. In order to ensure that the "pipeline" is full, current female leaders should recruit future female leaders. Leaders can come from a variety of places, and we should not hesitate to re-engage those talented women who have stepped off the career fast track for a period of time, or those who have retired from other leadership positions (Hewlett, 2007).

Role models are critical in the development of individuals. Unfortunately, a lack of female role models is often seen as a barrier to success (Catalyst Conference Board, 2002). Female role models are important for what they stand for—the possibility of success (Mason,

2009). The subliminal message of these role models? "If she can do it, so can I" (Hewlett, 2007). It is important for women to share their stories and "secrets" so that awareness can be raised about how to manage careers in androcentric environments. Coaching, mentoring, and networking can all help to raise navigational awareness and enable and empower women to make appropriate choices (Desvaux et al., 2007).

Employers should be encouraged to develop a new way of doing business by changing policies. For example, the establishment of family-friendly human resource practices allows women to stay in jobs they might leave otherwise. What would these practices look like? They would include the potential for flexible working hours, incorporated through initiatives such as flex-time, remote working or telecommuting, and job sharing (Desvaux et al., 2007). In sport, policies that allow travel with family enable coaches to stay in positions. Women who have decided to raise children, and those who have had career interruptions for other reasons, should be allowed more time, perhaps a year or two, to prove themselves worthy of advancement, particularly in workplaces that have an "up or out" career progression mentality (Eagly & Carli, 2007; Hewlett, 2007). This type of practice allows a workplace to capitalize on the investment they have made in the individual. Collectively, these types of policies and practices allow women to remain in the work force during the most demanding years of parental responsibilities, helping them to build social capital, maintain currency in their fields, and eventually compete for higher level positions (Eagly & Carli, 2007).

Another strategy for encouraging and developing female leadership is to change the actual work environment. Social environments need to be supportive of working women if they are to move into leadership positions. Support practices include childcare options and employee-sponsored on-site childcare, family support, and elder care (Eagly & Carli, 2007). Further, gender equality needs to be promoted in the workplace, including equal pay for equal work (Desvaux et al., 2007). Physical environments should also be supportive and welcoming for women. Mason (2009) shares the following story of a distinguished female professor of mechanical engineering who finally convinced her department to remove several dozen photos of male professors that were prominently displayed: "I fought for fifteen years to take down the photographs of fifty men that were on the walls of the department," she says. "I did not make a stink the first year, but those photos really did get to me."

Symbolic gestures such as changing the physical environment to welcome women make a difference.

Part of ensuring a welcoming environment is developing a critical mass of females on staff. As suggested earlier, a threshold of three women on management committees for an average membership of ten people seems to enhance organizational effectiveness (Desvaux et al., 2007). One woman can be easily ignored, whereas contributions from a critical mass are seen for what they are.

Should we be legislating changes? Quotas are generally not regarded as appropriate, as the secondary effects that result are viewed as being unsuccessful (Desvaux et al., 2007). Token women, for example, put into positions as a result of diversity policies tend to be ignored or marginalized (Eagly & Carli, 2007). Title IX was brought into effect in the United States in 1972 to help address discrimination in education and sport. From a positive perspective, Title IX has helped to increase opportunity for women in sport—fewer than 32,000 women participated in college sports before Title IX, and now over 150,000 women participate. However, athletic programs are still not equitable; while 53% of the National Collegiate Athletic Association Division 1 students are female, women's athletics receives only 36% of the operating budgets and 43% of the scholarships. Importantly, from a leadership standpoint, there were fewer female coaches and administrators in 2006 compared to 1972 (Catalyst Short Report, 2007).

In Canada, comparative national legislation to Title IX does not exist. However, we have seen attempts at policy that move towards equity in coach hiring practices such as the federal government's 1986 Policy on Women in Sport, which called for an increase in the proportion of female coaches; the Canada Games requirement to have at least one woman on the coaching staff for each female team (Kerr, Marshall, Sharp, & Stirling, 2006); or gender equity hiring practices typically found in university settings (Spriggs, 2005). As noted in earlier statistics, these policies have generally not been effective in Canada.

It should be noted that on August 29, 2009, Sport Canada released its long-awaited new sport policy for women and girls entitled "Actively Engaged: A Policy on Sport for Women and Girls." The new policy "places an emphasis on the active participation of women and girls and on improving their access to quality sport experiences and equitable support."

In some cases, quotas seem to have helped, as in Norway, which in 2006 passed legislation that all companies must have a minimum of two female directors on their boards. Norway already leads in the world in percentage of board seats held by women, at 44% (Catalyst Short Report, 2008a). In comparison, the same survey found that less that 10% of seats on boards were held by women in eleven of seventeen European countries. If quotas are set, it is important to develop strategies to support and evaluate movement towards successfully attaining goals; otherwise, initiatives are doomed to fail.

If women are to be truly successful, employers need to redefine leadership. Rather than focus on typically male or female leadership attributes, they should focus on desired leadership qualities to avoid stereotypic bias (Jenner & Ferguson, 2009). Gender stereotyping of leadership styles is likely to result in women being treated unfairly in job assignment, evaluation, and career advancement, and is also likely to hinder business performance (Warren, 2009). Employers should identify leadership qualities and competencies critical for success, regardless of gender, and should enhance transparency to ensure that all employees are aware of what is required to succeed (Jenner & Ferguson, 2009). What are desired leadership attributes? There are many leadership theories, but some common characteristics of successful leaders include being visionary and having the ability to get people to buy into that vision, social and emotional intelligence, creativity, flexibility, sound contextual knowledge, and integrity.

The chapters in this book will further describe issues women face as they navigate their way to the top, and will provide advice on how to navigate the obstacles.

REFERENCES

Acosta, R., & Carpenter, L. (2008). Women in intercollegiate sport: A longitudinal study—Thirty-one year update 1977–2008. Retrieved August 26, 2009, from http://webpages.charter.net/womeninsport/2008/Summary/Final.pdf

Catalyst Conference Board. (2002). Women in leadership: A European business imperative.

Catalyst Short Report. (2008). Expanding opportunities for women and business: Women CEOs of the Fortune 1000.

Catalyst Short Report. (2008a). Expanding opportunities for women and business: Women on boards in Europe.

Catalyst Short Report. (2007). Expanding opportunities for women and business: Women in sports.

Cook, S. (1998). More women playing college sports, but fewer role models. *Women in High Education, 7*(9).

Demers, G. (2009). "We are coaches": Program tackles the under-representation of female coaches. *Canadian Journal for Women in Coaching, 9*(2).

Desvaux, G., Devillard-Hoellinger, S., & Baumgarten, P. (2007). *Women matter. Gender diversity, a corporate performance driver.* McKinsey and Company.

Drakich, J., & Stewart, P. (2007). Forty years later, how are university women doing? *Academic Matters,* 6–9.

Eagly, A., & Carli, L. (2007). Women and the labyrinth of leadership. *Harvard Business Review,* September, 62–71.

Grant, K. (2005). Women in senior university administration in Canada in 2005: Where do we stand? *Senior Women Academic Administrators of Canada E-News.* Retrieved March 31, 2009, from http://www.aucc.ca/_pdf/english/aboutaucc/swaac_cmorris_sept_05_e.pdf

Hewlett, S. (2007). *Off-ramps and on-ramps. Keeping talented women on the road to success.* Boston: Harvard Business School Press.

Hewlett, S. (2002). Executive women and the myth of having it all. *Harvard Business Review,* April, 66–73.

Hewlett, S., Buck Luce, C., & Schiller, P. (2005). The hidden brain drain—Off ramps and on ramps in women's career. *HBR Report, Harvard Business Review, 83,* 31–57.

Jenner, L., & Ferguson, R. (2009). *2008 Catalyst census of women corporate officers and top earners of the FP500.* Catalyst.

Kerr, G., Marshall, D., Sharp, D.-M., & Stirling, A. (2006). *Women in coaching: A descriptive study.* Ottawa: Coaching Association of Canada.

Mason, M. (2009). Balancing act. Role models and mentors. *The Chronicle of Higher Education.* Retrieved March 31, 2009, from http://chronicle.com/jobs/news/2009/03/2009032501c.htm

Sport Canada. (2009). *Actively engaged: A policy on sport for women and girls.* Retrieved August 29, 2009, from http://www.pch.gc.ca/pgm/sc/pol/fewom/101-eng.cfm

Sport Canada. (1999). Sport gender snap shot (1997/1998): Survey results report. (May 1999). *Canadian Heritage.* Retrieved October 1, 2005, from http://www.pch.gc.ca/ progs/sc/pubs/sexe-gender/index_e.efm

Spriggs, K. (2005). Equity practices questionnaire. Responses of the membership final report. *Canadian Interuniversity Sport.* Retrieved May 9, 2009, from http://www.cisport.ca/e/research/documents/cis-Equity-Report-Executive-Summary.pdf

Statistics Canada. (2008). Average earnings by sex and work pattern, August 2008.

Warren, A. (2009). *Cascading gender biases, compounding effects: An assessment of talent management systems.* Catalyst.

Natascha Wesch coached Canada's women's sevens rugby team to a sixth-place finish at the Rugby World Cup Sevens 2009.

PHOTO: COURTESY OF NATASCHA WESCH

PART ONE

Issues

Rowing coach Laryssa Biesenthal, here with first-born daughter Avery Biesenthal Brambell, combines coaching and motherhood with equal success.

PHOTO: CARLA SARIS

THE PERILS AND PLEASURES
OF COACHING AND MOTHERHOOD

Sheila Robertson

ONE

Introduction

That the coaching profession is demanding is a hard fact of life.
The strains and stresses are well documented—odd hours, working
weekends, frequent travel, lengthy away-from-home training camps,
parental interference, under-funded programs, demanding boards of
directors. The list goes on. Balancing these demands are the rewards—
guiding athletes to achieve physical and social skills, building their
self-esteem and positive self-images, enabling them to achieve and
even exceed their potential, making a positive difference in their lives.

When asked what drives them, most coaches cite passion for
their profession as *the* powerful motivator. It's an emotion that can
conflict, often irreconcilably, with the equally passion-inspiring state
of motherhood. This conflict drives many female coaches from the
profession, some forever, and others for extended periods.

This chapter features five coaches who were profiled in the spring
of 2007. These coaches could be called successful by most measuring
sticks. One was a well-established and successful coach who was
"on sabbatical." The other four represented the next generation,
young mothers who were breaking into the upper levels of coaching.

For each coach, I "fast forward" to 2009 to revisit them and see what, if any, differences have occurred in their circumstances. In all but one case, the changes are substantial, and not necessarily positive.

As always, when trying to make sense of a female coach's life, there are more questions than answers. Their stories illustrate the complexities and challenges of combining coaching and motherhood to the detriment of neither.

Staying in the Profession

IN APRIL 2007, in a matter-of-fact tone, Sheilagh Croxon talked about her decision not to renew her contract as head coach of Canada's synchronized swimming team. Fresh from coaching her athletes to the team bronze medal at the 2000 Olympic Games, and two world championship medals in 2001, she asked Synchro Canada for a seven-month maternity leave when she became pregnant with her third child.

The organization agreed, but when Croxon requested some compensation, she was turned down flat. After a period of reflection, she decided to move in new directions. "I felt I had no choice. My position was based on a yearly contract and provided no benefits. Nor was I eligible for unemployment insurance. Marley was born on February 6, 2002, one week after I stepped off the pool deck. I would have preferred to have stopped coaching earlier, but I wasn't going to get paid."

Croxon, whose older children are Nicolas and Natalie, had stated her case in writing to the Synchro Canada board. She felt herself to be in a strong position. The Olympic medal (one of Canada's fourteen won at Sydney) and the world championship medals indicated a national team on the upswing after several down years. Implicit in her argument was her belief that refusing her leave with compensation would send a negative message to the organization's coaches, all of whom are women. "I wasn't looking for anything huge, just some sign of good faith, something to show that they valued me, that they understood, but they said no." No reason was given other than the board would stick to her contract as written. End of discussion.

Although Croxon fulfilled the balance of her contract after taking the seven months off without pay, her decision to resign was firm. "I would have stayed had the environment been more supportive. Since it wasn't, I realized I had to look out for myself and get into a better working arrangement, one that allowed some family consideration. It was painful, a real slap in the face, almost humiliating. I thought they would understand, and when they didn't, I took it as a sign that it was time to move on."

Croxon had fared better with her first two pregnancies, both of which occurred when she was a club consultant, even though she took only eight weeks off with each child. "I made the case for some support, and my club board paid someone else to coach for me and paid my salary as well. It may have been because a board of parents knows you better than a national board does. Maybe my personal interaction with that board made my situation more human for them."

Croxon's supportive husband, Jean Constantin, took paternity leave for each child. When Nicolas was born, he also took a leave-of-absence so that the family could relocate to Edmonton for nine months when the team centralized there before the 1996 Olympic Games. "The move was possible because Jean said he would come, and that shows what an open-minded man he is. Some people are not that supportive, because it goes against the norm."

Once her decision to leave was made, Croxon put her disappointment behind her and moved on to work that not only was good for her but was improving conditions for other female coaches. She is the Coaching Association of Canada's consultant responsible for its Women in Coaching program, a national campaign to increase the number of coaching opportunities for women at all levels of sport. In demand as an international consultant, she works with Olympic and national teams from around the world. Within Canada, she is a regular presenter of clinics, camps, and consultations, and is a mentor to several National Coaching Certification Program Level 4 candidates. In

2005, she established the Toronto-based International Centre of Excellence, where athletes and coaches flock to work with her. She served on the executive of the Canadian Professional Coaches Association (now Coaches of Canada) and is the chair of the Coaches Association of Ontario.

Croxon was heartened by the fact that Biz Price, her immediate successor, was made a Synchro Canada employee, and although Price's was also a one-year contact, she received benefits equivalent to those of the national office staff. Unfortunately, the structure around the national coach position was not strong enough to provide adequate support to Price. The learnings following disappointing results at the 2003 world championships were lost when Price was dismissed. Canada's loss was Spain's gain, as she played an integral role as assistant coach with the Spanish national team through 2004 and 2005. Since 2006, Price has been National Performance Director for synchronized swimming with British Swimming, a position she will hold through 2013.

Price's successor, Isabelle Taillon, was given a long-term contract. Said Croxon, "I felt that by leaving, I could do some good for the coaches who followed. My decision woke up a few people and made a difference, because now the coaches have acceptable working conditions. I've always been a ground breaker. I've had to fight for everything in my coaching career, but there is some satisfaction in knowing that you have made a difference for those who follow."

These days, one-year coaching contracts are generally frowned upon because they do not build stability or show long-term vision. Nor do they acknowledge that, in sport, it takes more than one year to produce success. Croxon said, "It's people like me, people who come up short, who spark change for the next generation. That's often the way it is."

Croxon is committed to encouraging sport organizations to understand the importance of creating conditions that work for the woman coach. "They need to realize that good people are everything, and that intellectual capital is not easily replaced. Key to that is identifying champions for women within Canada's sport system—men and women who really understand what being a mother is all about and what the demands are on the coach."

Fast Forward

In 2009, Sheilagh Croxon remains the Women in Coaching consultant, and the International Centre of Excellence continues to thrive, with athletes from Britain and Argentina seeking her coaching expertise. She took two New Zealand athletes—the duet team of Nina and Lisa Daniels—to the 2008 Olympic Games. Their goal during the three-and-a-half years they trained with her was to qualify for Beijing and when they succeeded, it marked New Zealand's first qualification in synchronized swimming in 24 years.

However, Croxon has made one crucial lifestyle change. In August 2007, she returned to full-time coaching, not to high performance but as head coach of a grassroots program, albeit at the Granite Club, one of Toronto's most prestigious sport venues.

Scepticism was her initial reaction to the unexpected job offer. She firmly believed she had left grassroots coaching behind twenty years earlier. After several discussions, however, she realized she was being offered the professional working conditions for which she has long advocated, including full-time employment and excellent benefits. Instead of a parent volunteer board—the bane of so many coaches—she reports to the director of athletics and has been able to hire qualified coaches, either full- or part-time, as needed. "This is a more professional situation than I ever had as a national coach. At first it was very challenging because you forget how tough it is to build a program from the base. But it forced me to become a better coach because I had to get in there and roll up my sleeves. It's reconnected me with what coaching is all about and I'm more in touch with the challenges coaches face."

Two years into the job, Croxon reports some impressive milestones. Offering both recreational and competitive programs, she notes that the competencies of the athletes have risen dramatically. Enrollment has increased by 21% to over 80 swimmers. "Now that we are having success, people are knocking at the door. This may be grassroots, but you can turn something around pretty quickly with a high performance mindset. People are starting to see what can be done when good coaching is available."

Included in the arrangement Croxon struck with the Granite Club was being able to train her international athletes in their pool. She coached Jennifer Knobbs, who won the national solo title in 2008 and, with Erin Wilson, also took the senior duet championship. Both are now at the sport's national training centre in Montreal. "Athletes like these have helped to build the club because they are role models for the younger kids and that has really, really helped the growth."

The Granite Club arrangement offers Croxon the best of both worlds. "I love coaching; I don't see it as a job, but I never thought that I would find such good working conditions at this level. A club! You're kidding!"

Stand Your Ground

IN 2007, NATASCHA WESCH was an upwardly mobile rugby coach. She had coached Rugby Canada's U-19 women's team and the Ontario U-17, U-19, and U-23 teams, and she was the head coach of the women's varsity team at the University of Western Ontario, where she was working on a doctorate in sport psychology. She spent five years as the Ontario Rugby Union's director of women's rugby. In December 2006, she became head coach of the National Women's Sevens Team. And oh, yes, on December 5, 2005, she gave birth to her daughter Machaila.

Wesch greeted the news of her pregnancy with delight and, like so many first-time mothers, assumed that her life wouldn't change. "To be honest, and I think it's the same for everybody, I had no idea what to expect, and I didn't believe it when people told me I was crazy to expect to carry on as usual."

Throughout the pregnancy, she coached non-stop, even flying with her university team to the national championship in her eighth month. And she informed Rugby Canada that she would coach after the birth and spelled out how she intended it to happen.

Wesch was frank about her needs. "I told them that it was my personal choice to nurse my daughter for one year, meaning three training camps were involved. I said that if you want me to coach this team, she is coming with me, and I need somebody to take care of her, and I expect the costs of a flight and a room for a babysitter to be incorporated into the budget. When it was suggested that I bottle-feed her and leave her at home with her dad, I said, 'Then I'm going to tell you that you've just lost your head coach!' It was black and white. As long as I wasn't paid a salary but was coaching as a volunteer, this was how it was going to be."

The wrinkle, said Eva Havaris, who as manager of rugby development was responsible for Wesch's budget, was that Rugby Canada lacked policies to cover Wesch's situation. Havaris contacted several organizations, including Sheilagh Croxon at the Coaching Association of Canada, and the Canadian Centre for Ethics in Sport, looking for a policy that would protect the interests of both parties. "Of course there weren't any, and there should be if we want more women involved in sport without creating barriers for them. A maternity leave policy is a matter of a best practice. I wanted Rugby Canada to take a stand, to be the first sport organization to do it, and be seen as a supporter of female coaches."

Wesch supported Havaris contacting Croxon to ask if she was asking too much and what Rugby Canada was allowed to do. "Sheilagh told them that if they wanted to keep me, they should accommodate me as much as possible. They could have said, 'Too bad, we're finding someone else,' but they knew the value I bring to the sport and the association and said, 'OK, that's the way it is.' Keep in mind, though, that I wasn't asking for a lot."

In the end, Rugby Canada agreed to factor Wesch's expenses into the budget. Ultimately, the decision was Havaris's. "I really believe in what Natascha does. She bends over backwards, and everybody in the coaching community in Canada knows about that and her accomplishments. This is someone who is going to continue to contribute. It's not as though she has hit the pinnacle of her career. In some ways, at the national level, she was just starting."

The lesson, says Wesch, is to know what you want and to stand your ground, which admittedly is not always easy. "I know my value. I was the only highly certified female rugby coach, and they want to keep people like me involved, so I knew I had leverage."

At the university, Wesch's situation was different. Coaching the varsity team was part of her workload, and the season, which ran from the end of August to mid-November, was over by the time Machaila was born. When the 2006 season rolled around, she was nine months old and ready for afternoon daycare. Wesch was with her until 11:00 a.m., and her husband, Chad Dawson, whose work permitted a flexibility that other spouses might not have, picked Machaila up at 4:30 p.m., leaving Wesch free to coach until 6:00 p.m. "We made the decision that it was going to be equal. We had 50/50 input into making her, so we were going to be 50/50 in caring for her. It was all about flexibility and having a spouse who is extremely supportive."

Wesch stresses the importance of establishing priorities. "Is it having your child with you? Is it being a mom? Is it being a mom and a coach? Whatever it is, stick to your guns and know what you want. Know clearly ahead of time what you want to accomplish and how you want to involve your child. I knew I wanted time to be my own person and have my individual life back, so to speak, but I also wanted to raise my daughter and not have her in daycare all day long."

Despite having a clear picture of how she would do her mothering, Wesch found it wasn't cut and dry. Unable to "carry on as usual," she faced some hard choices. "For the first three months I tried, unsuccessfully, to keep doing what I was doing before, and I was just getting frustrated. I went through a very difficult time with postpartum depression. It hit me like a rock and flattened me for seven months.

"What hit me the most was my inability to get things done. My PHD was on hold. My coaching career, which absolutely matters to me, was on hold. I was questioning everything, which is totally unlike me. I couldn't get out of the house, and I couldn't exercise. Although I love my daughter, it was like I had a ball and chain attached to me, limiting where I could go, and when it was really bad, I wanted to quit everything."

Realizing that something had to give, Wesch made some decisions. She didn't run again as an Ontario Rugby director, and she stopped coaching the Ontario and national U-19 teams so that she could focus on the university team and the women's sevens. She resumed her exercise routine and put Machaila in part-time daycare. "Although I felt really guilty, things started to feel so much better because I was able to be me for half a day."

Fast Forward

On the surface, Wesch has forged ahead. She completed her doctorate in September 2008 and is doing post-doctoral work at McMaster University, examining health psychology in the spinal cord injury population. She took the women's sevens from "inexperienced nobodies" to victors over the veteran American team at the World Cup qualifier in November 2008, securing a world ranking of third going into the Rugby World Cup Sevens in Dubai in March 2009. "This positioned us to possibly become the only national team ever to win a medal for Rugby Canada."

Wesch frankly admits that in 2006 she knew little about sevens; in fact, she adds, no one in Canada knew much from a women's perspective. Perhaps it is this lack of knowledge that has come back to haunt her.

As is typical of her, she poured considerable energy into learning everything she could about sevens. "I was frank with the athletes and told them we were going to learn together. I'm going to do my research, I'm going to do my best, and I expect you to do the same." Working for only an honorarium, she was somewhat surprised to find, when she did the math, that she was spending an average of thirty-five hours a week on getting the team ready for the World Cup. That on top of finishing her doctorate, working full-time at the University of Western Ontario, and being a committed wife and mother. One reward was the willingness of the athletes to do the work, buy into her vision, and accept her path to achieving their common goal. The other reward was building a world-class team.

Until the team's success at the World Cup qualifier, Wesch felt she was working in isolation. Rugby Canada seemed to expect a lot, but was unable or unwilling to provide adequate funding for growth and development opportunities. "I didn't feel valued or supported or even trusted. I made an effort to discuss my concerns, but didn't get anywhere. There was little or no communication and no leadership. I think people were fighting to stay alive and forgot that other people need support, too. On the other hand, I got used to them not caring as much about the women's program as the men's. And that did mean less pressure."

Wesch wondered why, given her limited sevens experience, Rugby Canada didn't enable her to tap into professional development opportunities. "Looking back, it seems like I was put into a situation to see if I would fail. Instead of helping me to get the knowledge I needed, providing me with the proper tools, it was a self-taught thing. There was no, 'What do you need from us to be the best team you can be?'"

Things changed with the qualification. Suddenly and unexpectedly, Wesch's team were contenders, and the focus shifted to outcomes. Consequently, some money became available and the athletes no longer had to foot the bill for their expenses. "Up to that point, the athletes paid for everything. Some forked over as much as twenty grand to play for their country over the previous two years. I was fighting tooth and nail to get money, and finally some became available in early February, just weeks before the big event, and that did take a lot of pressure off the athletes and coaches."

With the money came strings. "The message was, 'We're paying the bills now, so you have to perform.' I get that, but everyone who knows about winning teams knows you don't change things at the last minute."

Although the result was disappointing by some standards—Team Canada finished sixth out of sixteen teams—Wesch was pleased with how her players performed because, as she points out, outcomes are not always controllable. "As the tournament unfolded, not one team was unbeaten. We were the only team to put points on New Zealand and were within a couple of tries of winning the quarter-final match. That put us into the Plate, the second tier semi-final, against England, the team that was supposed to win it all."

Wesch left the tournament feeling proud of what the team had accomplished and expected that Rugby Canada would feel the same. To her dismay, it was a week before she heard a word from the organization and then it was, "'Thanks for your time. I'm sorry you didn't get the result you wanted. Please fill in the World Cup evaluation form.' There were no thanks from anyone and so I was left feeling disappointed. I told myself to be the sport psychologist I am and started helping myself."

It's not that Wesch regrets the time and energy she poured into the sevens. On the contrary, the learnings were tremendous. "I now know what it takes to build a team. I learned by watching other teams and by seeing how our team reacted. Now I feel that if I am thrown in with the big fish, okay, I can swim, so give me another shot at it."

To let Rugby Canada know how she wanted to move forward, Wesch contacted high performance director Geraint John, to request the opportunity to present her findings to the High Performance Committee, covering what she had done, the process she developed, the lessons she learned, what was needed to move forward, and the support necessary to take the team to the next World Cup. "They weren't asking, so I was going to tell them. My approach has always been to not wait for them to give me something, but to ask for it. Before, I just wanted the opportunity. Now, more was at stake because I loved the program, loved coaching the sevens, loved working with the athletes. I had a passion for it and knew I could do an even better job next time. I wanted that chance."

As it turned out, the only thing Wesch had a chance to do was meet John for an hour or so during a coaching clinic to provide a quick verbal overview of her written document. "I never got the opportunity to go before the High Performance Committee. All I could do was hand in my report and wait for the review process to unfold."

In a subsequent conversation with John, Wesch expressed her interest in staying involved with the national program in a coaching role. But she went one step further and explained that she was open to other opportunities that would provide learning experiences in order to develop her coaching skills further. She indicated her willingness to help with the other national teams as an assistant or mentor coach or manager. "I was clear that this wasn't the direction I wished to go, but I acknowledged that these roles might be opportunities to learn from others and stay involved."

Taking the initiative left Wesch feeling that her approach was both positive and effective. "I felt good in my own mind because I was pro-active and positive and I was sure this would be viewed positively."

Wesch's optimism was short-lived. Eventually she and John met again, this time to go over the summary report from the athletes' feedback. It was a disappointing meeting, to say the least. "The format of the review allowed only a few select quotes taken from the athletes. These were put into the document with subjective comments from whoever put the report together. Some of the feedback was constructive; some were personal attacks. Many of the 'facts' were inaccurate. I don't feel the way the report was put together was fair because it did not include all of the athletes' comments, making it impossible to get a true sense of the overall picture."

The outcome? John told Wesch that the women's national team programs were being restructured and that she was being moved out of her role as sevens coach. In fact, she was being moved out of all of Rugby Canada's coaching roles. Any future involvement would be as an apprentice coach within the national programs. "This meant that I could be involved only as an observing coach with no coaching role whatsoever.

"Obviously I was disappointed with the process and the outcome. What was most hurtful was that I was asked to take the lead and develop a team, but was given no support to learn the sevens or develop the required technical skills. Although I learned by observing others and by research, built the sevens program from scratch, developed a competition schedule, coached and managed the team to

compete on the World Cup stage, essentially doing what I was asked
to do, Rugby Canada viewed me as a failure and pushed me aside. This
experience made me question my abilities, but more so, it made me
wonder why."

Wesch has now put the experience behind her. "Life happens, and
I have learned a great deal from this. Now I move in a new direction
with my own sport psych consulting business. It's very rewarding,
and I'm putting my experiences and knowledge to good use!"

Ask For What You Need

WHEN ISABELLE TAILLON was the head coach of Synchro Canada's
national A team, she was the mother of three-year-old Matis and eight-
een-month-old Evans, and seemed to be a beneficiary of the changes
that arose directly out of Sheilagh Croxon's experience. She was also
fortunate to live in the Province of Quebec, where maternity leave is
guaranteed.

Hooked on coaching while a nineteen-year-old student at the Uni-
versité du Québec à Montréal, Taillon landed her first position in 1992
with the Dollard Synchro Club's junior program. Her progress was
aided by seasoned coach Diane Lachapelle. Taillon said, "She gave me
great athletes to work with, to prove I could make the most of them
and get results on the national scene. I was gaining confidence and
learning and was able to show what I could do." Invaluable international exposure came when she landed a consulting contract with
Hungary before the 2000 Olympic Games.

Taillon's relationship with Synchro Canada dates back to 1997,
when she was offered the position of national junior team assistant
coach. Except for a brief stint as head coach of the national B team, she
remained with the junior team until 2003.

Thirty-six weeks pregnant at the May 2003 national championships, Taillon returned home, delivered Matis in June, and began her
maternity leave. "I wasn't planning to do anything with the national
team that summer, but I was really torn because it is difficult for a

coach to take a leave. You wonder what's going to happen when you come back. Will you have the same relationship with your athletes, or will they do better with your replacement? Or will I still work with them when I come back? I was also wondering if I, as a new mom, would be able to continue my coaching career. You never know until it happens what's involved in being a mom."

That September, Taillon's life was turned upside down when Synchro Canada asked her to become head coach of the 2004 Olympic team. The lure proved irresistible, new baby or not. "I wanted so badly to be part of the Olympic adventure. Sometimes an opportunity comes and you just have to go for the challenge. I made the decision quite quickly and was supported by everyone around me. I had a lot of encouragement and solution-oriented suggestions on how to manage this with a newborn."

As head coach, Taillon was expected to relocate to the national training centre in Toronto, a move that was delayed for several months while the pool underwent repairs. In the interim, the team trained in Montreal, giving her welcome breathing space. By January, however, the move could no longer be postponed, and Taillon moved to Toronto, leaving her husband, Frédéric Bessette, and Matis behind, a circumstance she still has difficulty discussing.

She asked for, and was granted by Synchro Canada, a scheduling adjustment that freed her from coaching on the weekends and enabled her to leave for Montreal by train on Friday afternoon, returning in time for Monday morning practice. She paid her train fare and, later, her plane fare when train travel proved to be too tiring. She also paid her daycare costs. Faced with a 20-day training camp, Taillon asked Synchro Canada to cover her babysitter's room and board. Having her request granted was "amazing."

Asked why she didn't seek more financial support from Synchro Canada, Taillon points to her lack of experience. "I was too young to ask for much, and so I didn't negotiate anything in particular to help me through this. As a result, I wasn't comfortable in asking the federation to pay for unplanned fees during my mandate. I relied on my family support system. What should I have asked for? For trips exceeding two weeks, that Synchro Canada pay for my babysitter and my children to come with me. For Synchro Canada to top up the provincial government maternity leave payments. For a small bonus for daycare."

Daycare was a trigger, especially when Evans (born in August 2005, just after the World Aquatic Championships) joined the family. "My babysitter was my mom, but I paid her, and if Fred wasn't available and I was away, she put in far more than the usual hours. A regular daycare system or babysitter wasn't possible because of a coach's hours and travel." Taillon didn't consider a nanny because that is not the norm in Quebec. "Only the really wealthy seem to have a nanny. I don't know anyone who does."

Taillon, who signed a four-year contract after Athens, says that Synchro Canada was open to her situation. "I know they realized it was a challenge, and when I did ask for little things, they always did what's possible, but I found it difficult to ask because I assumed I had to figure it out."

Months away from the 2008 Olympic Games, Taillon described her efforts to be national coach and mother as "a work in progress. The main reason I can do it is my husband, who always says we'll figure things out, and my strong family network." It also helped that for the quadrennial, the team was centralized in Montreal, so no more commuting to Toronto.

Her passion for coaching is why Taillon's life was a juggling act. "Was it totally fair to my children? Was it totally working? I don't know. I am sure women in other professions do a lot of innovative thinking to make everything work, but the travel and the weird training and competition schedules make coaching even more difficult. Was it worth it? Yes, because I had two families, my biological family and the team family. That's the reason I did it—for the athletes I coached, for the people I worked with, and for the Olympic adventure. That and the passion for coaching that consumed me."

Fast Forward

Taillon's coaching world collapsed only days after she led her athletes to silver medals in duet and team, a mere 4/100ths behind the United States, at the 2007 Pan American Games. Eleven months before the 2008 Olympic Games, a newly-hired chief technical director, with no formal background in the sport, cancelled the contracts of Taillon and her assistants, Denise Sauvé and Karine Doré, and re-opened the hiring process.

The move shocked Taillon, who had returned from the Pan American Games pleased with the performances. "We were so close to gold medals (and a lot of people thought we should have won) so I was not expecting this. My contract didn't protect me from this kind of action. We were told the organization wanted a new opportunity to make sure the best people were in place to take the team to Beijing."

It should be noted that the Pan American Games were a qualification event for Beijing, with only the winners assured of a berth. In some quarters, having to compete at a later qualifier was considered a failure, but this reaction ignores dramatic changes to the sport internationally. "Canadian synchro has been so successful in the past, with a winning Olympic tradition, that Synchro Canada expected it to continue. There was a kind of impatience, and I guess, doubt about my qualifications and my leadership."

Determined not to abandon her team, Taillon decided to fight back. She applied to be re-hired and insisted on a face-to-face interview. Feeling it had gone well, she was taken aback when told that she would not get the job because the athletes did not want her. "When I heard that, I immediately withdrew my application and left the room. I learned much later that the team was split, that some didn't want us back while others were very sad to lose their coaches and their support team."

Taillon refused an offer to be a part-time second assistant coach. "I no longer shared the vision of the organization, and I couldn't accept after the way things were being done."

For several weeks after that interview, Taillon threw herself into a frenzy of activity. "I had never cooked, and I was making everything—muffins, cakes, pancakes—cleaning the house, throwing things away. It was like I was purging synchronized swimming. I was like a mad woman, but it felt good."

These days, Taillon is happily working close to home as director of Le Complexe Multisport Saint-Eustache. As well as various sports, the complex has a martial arts dojo, a multi-disciplinary gymnasium, an indoor soccer field, and reception rooms. She is charged with developing the business and draws on her coaching background for programming, scheduling, and client servicing. "My experience as a national coach and my coaching skills are directly applicable to this job, and it is far less stressful." She drives Matis to school every morning, cooks "like a pro," and enjoys her home life. "When I first stopped coaching, it was like dropping in on my family; I was so engaged in my work that at first I felt a bit like a stranger to their world."

While Taillon misses the passion she had for coaching, she has no desire ever to return. "Between the ages of eighteen and thirty-five, all I did was coach. It was dominating my life totally, and I don't want myself to be controlled that way again. I don't regret it, because living in that extreme zone is something that very few can experience, but now I want a more relaxed lifestyle and more time with my kids." She does, however, occasionally accept international contracts, including one with Biz Price in the summer of 2008. "There we were, two coaches who Synchro Canada let go eleven months before two Olympic Games, working together for England."

Supported by the Workplace and by a Different Tradition

LIKE ALL OF THE OLYMPIC Oval's speed skating coaches, Xiuli Wang is an employee of that facility and, as such, comes under the employment policies of the University of Calgary. A portion of her salary is paid by Speed Skating Canada (ssc), although the organization does not directly provide benefits to coaches, nor does it have an official policy covering female coaches and maternity leave. "However, we have been very understanding in such instances in the past and have on occasion paid for a new mother's husband to come to meetings and competitions to assist with care for their baby," said manager of communications, Mylène Croteau.

Wang informed the Oval management of her pregnancy early in 2003 to allow plenty of time for her replacement to be selected. An arrangement was subsequently worked out with coach Arno Hoogveld, with whom she had worked since arriving in Calgary in 1997. "The Oval was totally supportive and so was ssc. We discussed which coach was best suited to fill my spot. It was very important to me to have a strong partner coach because I didn't want anything to go wrong. I totally trust Arno and had no problem with him coaching my athletes. I believed he could do a good job, and he did. I really appreciated him."

After the twenty-eighth week of her pregnancy, when air travel was no longer covered by insurance, Hoogveld took the skaters on the road and Wang coached those who stayed behind. According to Moira Marshall, at that time the Oval's director of sport, this was a fairly standard arrangement at the Oval. "We often have coaches pair up and co-coach so that one can travel to World Cups and one can stay home with the skaters who did not qualify." As well as covering situations such as maternity leave, Marshall said that this approach also gave the coaches a break from having to travel extensively for many years in a row.

On December 29, 2003, Wang and her husband, Zonghang Zhao, welcomed their son, Yan Kun, and Wang went on a two-and-a-half-month maternity leave, during which time the university contributed funding to the Oval to cover her replacement. Wang continued to write the skaters' programs at home, with Hoogveld implementing them and covering travel. Although she could have taken one year of maternity leave, she chose the shorter period in order to be involved in the high performance decision-making meetings that take place in Ottawa every spring. "I didn't want anybody to make a decision for me that I didn't know about."

Also in the mix was coach Kevin Crockett, who was hired to work with Marshall during her own maternity leave, which overlapped

Wang's. He then moved over to assist with Wang's non-travelling skaters. "In my opinion, the Oval went above and beyond what is expected in these situations to ensure that the athletes were looked after properly," said Marshall.

Then-Olympic Oval director Mark Greenwald said that although the Oval may not have specific policies for maternity or paternity leaves, it did have a strong record of supporting individuals and working them back into the system if they desire to return. "Given the extreme amount of commitment to developing these individuals and the experience they eventually possess, we would be remiss to not be supportive during these times," he said. "Coaches need at least the opportunity to attempt to lead balanced lives, and coaching should not be a limiting factor or detriment to having a family. I certainly struggled with the logistics of balancing a coaching team when one coach is on such a leave, and there were times when the timing wasn't great, but we always made it work."

Wang, who has won seven Petro-Canada Coaching Excellence Awards and four ssc Female Coach of the Year awards, as well as the 2006 Jack Donohue Coach of the Year award, noted that the timing of Yan Kun's birth could not have been better. "I tried to plan for the baby to come and not affect the job too much. After December, the really major training is pretty much done and the skaters go to competitions, and that was during the time I was off. I never thought about not going back. My skaters were the best in Canada in the distance disciplines, and I believed it was my responsibility to get them to the podium in Torino in 2006."[1]

Even though Wang's employment situation could be considered enviable, she believes it would have been difficult to fulfill her coaching responsibilities had it not been for strong family support. Her parents, who were visiting when she learned she was pregnant, stayed on until Yan Kun was two years old. He was then cared for by his paternal grandparents. "I cannot imagine doing this job without family support. Without the grandparents, that is a big question mark. In Chinese culture, we have really close family relationships. We don't send our parents to a nursing home when they get older, unless they are very sick. It's our job to take care of our parents, and our parents have no problem taking care of the grandchild."

Fast Forward

In February 2009, the Olympic Oval was hit by staff cuts that included Greenwald and Marshall, and an increase in athletes' fees resulting from a $1 million funding shortfall. WinSport Canada, formerly the Calgary Olympic Development Corporation, which funds two-thirds of the facility, had to slash its spending because of big stock market losses; the remaining one-third comes from the University of Calgary. "We subsidized sport for the last twenty years based on the economic climate," said Kam Kiland, who replaced Greenwald as Oval director. "We had some money and we could do that. Now our number one goal is to have the lights on and the ice in, and support athletes by giving them the best training centre in the world."

Wang was unperturbed by the situation. She couldn't afford to be, with the 2010 Olympic Winter Games so close at hand. All her attention and energy were focused on preparing her skaters for electrifying performances. That she was able to concentrate was due largely to Own the Podium, the "national sport technical initiative designed to help Canada's winter athletes to win the most medals at the Games" (Own the Podium, 2009). Own the Podium ensures that the necessary support staff is in place, and as a national team coach, Wang is secure, at least for the foreseeable future.

"Regarding the changes at the Olympic Oval, the coaches who are part of the facility have not been affected by the funding cuts," said Catriona Le May Doan, the former speed skating star who is now the Oval associate director. "They are still employed by the University of Calgary, and that policy has not been changed."

Wang now uses daycare, conveniently located in her Calgary neighbourhood, to provide out-of-school care for Yan Kun. Daycare staff drive him to and from school when Wang is unavailable. "When I'm travelling, my husband does it all," said Wang, who is taking a wait-and-see approach to her future after the 2010 Olympic Games.

In May 2009, Own the Podium, WinSport Canada, and the University of Calgary announced a solution to the funding shortfall. WinSport increased its contribution by an additional $700,000 from other sources for a total of $1.4 million. The university's one-third contribution of $700,000 was raised to $933,000. Own the Podium provided $300,000 to fill the funding gap. These contributions ensured that ice was available for the speed skaters from July 2009 until the Olympic Games began in mid-February 2010.

So Far, So Good

AVERY BIESENTHAL BRAMBELL was born on December 2, 2006 to Lauryeca Biesenthal, at that time Rowing Canada Aviron's (RCA) lightweight women's coach, and Iain Brambell, a veteran of the men's lightweight four. Her arrival was timely, as the sport's downtime is in December and January, and there is a traditional Christmas break. "I was thinking, okay, she's coming on December 6, so I can coach right up to that point. I did a dryland week just days before she was born, because I thought it would be easier to get to hospital being on land than on the water."

Biesenthal, a double Olympic bronze medallist and six-time world championship medallist, began her coaching career in 1996, working with high school teams. In 2002, Rowing Canada hired her as a technical administrative assistant for the London (Ontario) High Performance Training Centre, and she coached at the 2002 Universiade and Commonwealth championships. In 2003, she coached at the U-23 world championships and the Pan American Games. In 2004, RCA selected her to coach its Olympic lightweight women's double, and contracted her for the next quadrennial.

Determined to take only six weeks off after Avery's birth, even though she was entitled to a year, Biesenthal said the short time frame was necessary with the Olympic Games opening on August 8, 2008, and her crew still needing to qualify.

A planner by nature, Biesenthal first consulted RCA's high performance director at the time, Alan Roaf, and then spoke to her rowers,
letting them know what she thought would work for everybody. "This
was athlete driven. They said that rather than having a new coach
for six weeks, they would buy into my suggestion of a cross-training
camp for the time I would be off. My idea was to build more power by
training on ergometers [dryland rowing machines] to get tougher,
which we needed to be to compete better internationally. I wanted to
get them off the water and try different activities, so I arranged a week
of speed skating in Calgary and another of skiing to complement the
cross-training. I would stay in touch by phone and through
the Internet."

Biesenthal next met with executive director Ian Moss and national
team co-ordinator Adam Parfitt. Moss reminded her that she could
take a year off if she felt she needed to, but Biesenthal explained that
while she wanted a family, she also wanted to coach and thought that
as long as she structured it right, she should be able to balance both.
"Of course, as a first-time mom, you don't really know what it's going
to be like. Everyone said six weeks was a short leave, and I said, fine,
she'll just fit into our lifestyle, no problem, and so far she has."

Rowing Canada doesn't have a written maternity policy, but deals
with each situation as it arises. In Biesenthal's case, the organization
wanted to give her the options she needed to balance new motherhood
with her intentions to continue to drive her program. "We let her tell
us how she needed to design things," said Moss. "We didn't place any
work pressure on her, and told her repeatedly to monitor the situation
monthly in terms of her needs. Baby and mother come first obviously,
and Rowing Canada was fully prepared to create whatever scenario was
required to give her the time on her own with her family, which she, of
course, had every right to, and not worry about the program itself."

A priority was hiring a nanny, and Biesenthal's atypical schedule
proved a stumbling block. "I coached for three hours in the morning,
came home for about four hours, and then coached for another
three hours. I wanted that time in the middle of the day to myself
with Avery." The solution was to hire a student who was both an

experienced nanny and a rower for the University of Victoria. "She totally got my schedule, and it worked out perfectly. She was fantastic. She rowed with her team in the morning, and when she finished, we basically handed Avery over and I went to practice."

Biesenthal, who was thrilled to be back on the water, found the break was good for her athletes. "The women were as enthusiastic as I was; they were really pumped. And it was real life for them to see me having a child plus coaching, and it seemed to keep every-body motivated."

Once she was back at work, Biesenthal and Moss worked out how Rowing Canada would provide support. Although the arrangement was a flexible work in progress, the focus was on three key areas. "The intent was to make sure that Laryssa had support to cover the baby's needs at home while she was coaching, if family support wasn't available or if she wasn't able to bring the baby with her to practice," said Moss. Support also covered a travelling nanny for training camps and international competitions as required, and an interim coach if necessary. "Rowing Canada had to set the best working environment for Laryssa and her athletes to continue their focus on Olympic qualification preparation," said Moss. "This was a critical year and a critical time within that year. The right set-up was for her to determine and for us to accommodate. Ultimately, we both knew that we were doing this for all the right reasons, and that is what we focused on. The details would sort themselves out."

The first test came in January 2008 when Biesenthal flew to Hamilton to attend Rowing Canada's annual coaches' conference, baby in tow and Brambell along to provide childcare. Said Biesenthal, "A supportive spouse is essential. Iain was fantastic at the conference. Two other babies were there, and Iain was totally comfortable walking the mall with the two mothers. We called him 'Super Nanny.'"

The experience convinced Biesenthal to try to travel a day ahead of the team. "The more I could make it smooth, the more we weren't in the spotlight, not holding anything up, the more I could do beforehand so it was seamless, that was the best way to make everything work."

Moss added, "Rowing Canada was very protective of Laryssa and her position. She had proven her capability of coaching at the world-class level, and we certainly knew that she was fully committed to the future. If anything, we had to remind her that her personal life had changed and that she needed to take that into account. So we let Laryssa drive the plan, and we were always prepared to step in with Plan B if she ever needed it."

Fast Forward

Laryssa Biesenthal has departed the country, and Australia is the beneficiary of her proven coaching talents.

Always on the lookout for opportunities to improve her coaching, as a matter of course, Biesenthal monitored opportunities, particularly those abroad. A drastic change wasn't likely in November 2008, with her about to give birth to a second child. Still, when an ad posted by Rowing Australia for a senior women's coach appeared on the web page of the Fédération Internationale des Sociétés d'Aviron, she threw her name into the mix. It was an exciting opportunity made all the more attractive by the post-2008 Olympic decision to create a National Rowing Centre of Excellence as a joint venture between Rowing Australia and the Australian Institute of Sport (AIS), based in Canberra. The venture would incorporate Rowing Australia's High Performance Program with the institute's Residential Scholarship and National Camp Programs. "I had decided to take a break from coaching once the second baby arrived, but I thought it worth exploring this opportunity. I have always been interested in doing a stint in another country, after being an athlete and a coach in the Canadian system, because I wanted to grow and become a better coach. I knew I needed to seek different challenges. A rowing stroke is a rowing stroke, but every country has its own artistic flair. Working within a rowing power-house like Australia would, I knew, be a fantastic opportunity."

Ryley, born on November 17, 2008, was a mere two weeks old when her mother was interviewed for the position. Brambell had to be on the job as executive director of BC Athlete Voice, so his father was pressed into caring for his newest granddaughter while almost-two-year-old

Avery napped. Biesenthal did the seventy-minute interview in her laundry room, surely a first for a high performance coaching job.

On the other end of the line was a five-person interview panel consisting of national high performance director Andrew Matheson; Lyall McCarthy and Noel Donaldson, head coaches of the women's and men's programs respectively; sport medicine co-ordinator Ivan Hooper; and operations manager Matt Draper. "It was challenging to prepare, and it was a tough interview. They had given me questions a couple of days before, and I did a lot of soul-searching about how I ran my program in Canada."

It didn't take long for Matheson to leave a telephone message inviting Biesenthal to Canberra for a second interview. Nor did it take her long to accept the offer. Arrangements were made for Avery to stay with her grandparents, and on December 14, Biesenthal, Brambell, and four-week-old Ryley set out.

The week-long visit was a whirlwind. Early on, Biesenthal was informed that the job was hers. A visit to the human resource department settled details like salary—"very decent"—a four-year contract, due to expire in December 2012, superannuation guarantee contributions on top of the salary, facility access, swim and fitness classes, corporate clothing, and, of special interest to Biesenthal, childcare. "I was dealt with really professionally, signed the contract, and we flew home on December 21."

The Caretaker's Cottage Childcare Centre at AIS was a huge factor in the family's decision to make the move. It provides employees with childcare for babies to five year olds. "When we saw the centre, and all the other things available through the institute, we were blown away. The centre has little rooms for the different ages, home-cooked meals, and beautiful surroundings. It was all too attractive to turn down."

Biesenthal, who made the move at the end of February 2009, is in Australia on an e457 visa, which is available to "lawfully operating Australian businesses sponsoring temporary overseas employees." Clearly relishing the experience to date, she notes that in Canada, when she tried to put together a high performance team of physiologist, strength trainer, nutritionist, doctor, and physiotherapist, she was told that she was utilizing too many outside sources and should "keep it simple. Now I'm in Australia, and they have all of this and then some. The AIS provides so much assistance for athletes and coaches, and it dovetails with what I was trying to do in Canada."

At the moment, Biesenthal is working with development athletes, who have been brought to the Centre of Excellence for the first couple of years of the quadrennial. However, in May 2009, she was named as the Senior A Sweep Coach for the national team, which meant attending the world championships in charge of the women's heavy-weight pair and four. She says that working conditions are "great," and adds that she has a "great office mate" in the AIS senior men's coach, Rhett Ayliffe, who coached the men's double to the gold medal in Beijing. The other coaches, all of whom have had plenty of inter-national success, are a ready source of information. It is, she says, a very dynamic team.

Brambell's situation is of some concern. The 2008 Olympic bronze medallist in lightweight fours willingly left his position in Canada to share his wife's adventure. He is also a committed parent who is making the most of caring for his daughters. "How many other dads get time like this with their children?" asks Biesenthal. "We have been able to give the girls a long time to settle in, but Iain wants to start job hunting. Another example of how great the institute is—he's a teacher and when we first arrived, they put him in touch with a teaching job that had a rowing element to it. He didn't accept, because he's not sure if he wants to return to teaching, but it was a very nice offer."

In the meantime, Avery has settled into preschool at the childcare centre, not at all worried about leaving her parents. "She goes right in and makes herself at home," reports her mother, who adds: "I am LOVING my role down here!"

Travelling to competitions with her children remains to be settled, but Biesenthal is sure something positive will be worked out. "Ours is a new situation for the institute, but Andrew is very supportive. They said there would be money to assist us going to the world cham-pionships (which was fantastic), and Lyall stresses the importance of making things work for me and my family. As well, the entire office has young children under five so it is very family friendly. Being a mother and a high performance coach is not considered odd."

Conclusion

AS THE 2007 INTERVIEWS revealed, there were few guidelines, let alone policies, for sport organizations to follow when a coach wanted to combine her career with motherhood.

Although some organizations do not see it as their responsibility, others are open to supporting the coach—"just tell us how." This leaves it squarely up to the coach to negotiate a suitable arrangement for and by herself.

Like the other national sport organizations in the 2007 interviews, Synchro Canada did not have a formal maternity or parental leave policy. It appeared to have a culture of support, arising directly out of the Croxon situation. Marian Stuffco, the organization's interim CEO in 2007, pointed to good negotiating skills as essential. For coaches who may need help, she recommended tapping into the skills of a third-party advocate. "Such a female coach may have come through a process that benefited her—or not—and may be able to inform the sport organization of the merits of retaining a female coach through her maternity experience and her parenting because of the value that brings to the organization as a whole. The mentoring could take the form of helping the coach to phrase the script or participating in the face-to-face or phone call that outlines the situation."

Stuffco added that supporting female coaches builds strong families. "There should be complete facilitation by the national sport organization to support families who request it. If we are going to say that sport is the answer to social justice, to family unity, to health care, then we had better ensure that in the internal paradigm, we are building strong family support."

It would be helpful, she said, if sport organizations, led by Sport Canada and the Coaching Association of Canada, worked together to formulate one policy that could be widely adopted. However, funding its implementation could be a stumbling block. "Where is the money to come from?" she asked. "Sport Canada? The Coaching Association of Canada? Would the money come out of a national sport organization's Sport Canada contribution, which in most cases is already stretched beyond the limit? Or might Sport Canada consider establishing a separate pot to be used only for parental leave? This is a discussion worth having because, if the sport community values the contribution of women who are committed to the profession of coaching and who also chose motherhood, we must ensure that they are given the support they deserve so that their athletes continue to reap the benefits of their coaching skills."

Although agreeing that obstacles remain, Croxon is encouraged by the progress made since her resignation. "We are seeing signs that for women and men alike, coaches' working conditions are more professional, there are better jobs, more money is being put into coaching, and there's starting to be greater recognition of the role of the coach in an athlete's results. A core of women is making coaching and motherhood work, and they will become the role models for the next generation. We must continue to highlight these women who are making it work, as this is inextricably linked to increasing the number of female coaches in the Canadian sport system.

"So, yes, change is coming, but it is going to be slow."

Dismayed by the challenges encountered by Taillon and Wesch, Croxon attributes each situation to a lack of support by national sport organizations, and not to them being mothers. "It points to organizations having knee-jerk reactions to a disappointing performance result."

It also reveals, she says, a lack of understanding of the dynamics of coaching a team of female athletes. "Every difficult time, when things may not go according to plan, is an investment in the future goal, whether the Olympic Games, a world championship, or a World Cup. That's how a coach learns, how her team becomes stronger and improves."

The real challenge is ensuring that decision makers understand several key points: that support has to be given equally to coaches and

Angela Martin (far left, back row), was the assistant coach of the victorious Team Ontario's women's hockey team at the 2007 Canada Winter Games.

PHOTO: JOHN SIMS, TEAM ONTARIO

athletes, that there are two sides to every story, that there needs to be sufficient time to debrief post-event, and that the appropriate people must be involved in that process. "Too often people making decisions panic and react prematurely, and fail to understand what it is like to coach a team. And too often these people listen to the disgruntled athlete who points a finger at the coach rather than taking responsibility for her own performance, or lack of it. What you learn going through the quadrennial is so instrumental in what happens that final year. When a coach is changed eleven months out, as in Isabelle's case, a lot of learning is lost. Unless a coach is incompetent, such an action reveals a failure to understand the importance of learning from challenges."

Croxon recommends that national sport organizations develop a longer-term vision of the pathway of a team, one that reflects an understanding of the process of forming a team, that they practice due diligence, and that they consider options to firing a coach, such as assignment to another role. "Treating coaches poorly sets an example for people coming up the ranks and makes them wonder if they really want to enter the environment. Organizations need to be totally aware of the repercussions, which are much more far-reaching than just letting a coach go. You're losing someone valuable, someone who has dedicated her entire life to the profession, and you're causing athletes who might be considering a coaching career to reconsider, and what a loss that will be."

Next Steps

PLENTY OF THINKING HAS gone into ways to change the scenarios described in this chapter. For a comprehensive strategy, refer to Appendix 1: A Five-Point Collaborative Strategy for Change, developed for the Coaching Association of Canada to illustrate how to improve opportunities for women to succeed in the coaching profession.

As well, "They Never Give Up: Once a Coach, Always a Coach," *Canadian Journal for Women in Coaching*, Volume 8, Number 2, April 2008, provides a straightforward list of recommendations for female coaches and for Canada's sport organizations.

Recommendations for Female Coaches

HERE ARE RECOMMENDATIONS for eight simple steps that female coaches can take to educate themselves about their rights.

- Find out what your province or territory's policies are for maternity leave.
- Tell your sport organization about your specific needs.
- Establish your priorities.
- Consider a co-coach relationship.
- Develop a support network.
- Learn how to advocate effectively on your own behalf.
- Find an advocate within your organization.
- Get to know your board of directors so that they can relate to you on a more human level.

Recommendations for Sport Organizations

HERE ARE RECOMMENDATIONS for twenty-five steps that sport organizations, with the financial support of Sport Canada and the provincial/territorial governments, must take to develop and support female coaches.

Mentoring

ESTABLISH a mentorship program that helps female coaches to see the path they need to follow in order to get club, provincial, and high performance positions.

PAIR young coaches with senior counterparts to discuss career issues.

Childcare

PROVIDE coaching staff with childcare.

ENSURE that female coaches maintain contact and remain involved with their sport organization during maternity leave.

PERMIT "ramping down" to shorter hours, with flexibility to tend to family matters.

PROVIDE babysitting services during major competitions and training camps.

SUPPORT babies accompanying their coach mothers to practices, competitions, and training camps, with appropriate childcare provided.

Recruiting

ENCOURAGE young female athletes to consider coaching, support them with mentorship, and be up front about the issues they will face, in particular childcare.

PROVIDE financial incentives to make a coaching career feasible.

CREATE and promote opportunities for female coaches.

FIND better avenues to bring more young women into coaching.

PROMOTE the benefits that high performance sport offers the greater community.

END the divisive mentality that pits government against government, be it federal, provincial/territorial, or municipal.

Work Conditions

OFFER flexible arrival and departure times.

LIMIT active coaching time to twenty hours a week so that coaches can work on the National Coaching Certification Program and handle their administrative responsibilities.

CHANGE the traditional structure and hold midday practices.

GUARANTEE that coaches are qualified, well organized, and paid commensurate with their skill level.

SUPPORT organizations that support their coaches.

PROVIDE coaches with travel credits.

Education

RUN coaching clinics with female course conductors.

INTRODUCE business training to the National Coaching Certification Program.

PUBLICIZE the Coaching Association of Canada's Women in Coaching program to a much greater extent, in particular the grants and scholarships that are available.

DEVELOP and market a seminar that addresses the emotional and practical issues faced by female coaches who return to work.

TELL the stories of female coaches to show that it is acceptable to have children *and* coach.

PROVIDE coaches with the opportunity to interact with other coaches at symposiums and clinics.

NOTE

1. Wang succeeded admirably in 2006. Clara Hughes won the 5000m race and shared the women's team pursuit silver medal with Kristina Groves, who also won the 1500m silver medal. Two other Wang skaters, Arne Dankers and Steven Elm, were silver medallists in men's team pursuit.

REFERENCE

Own the Podium Website. (2009). Retrieved from http://www.ownthepodium2010.com

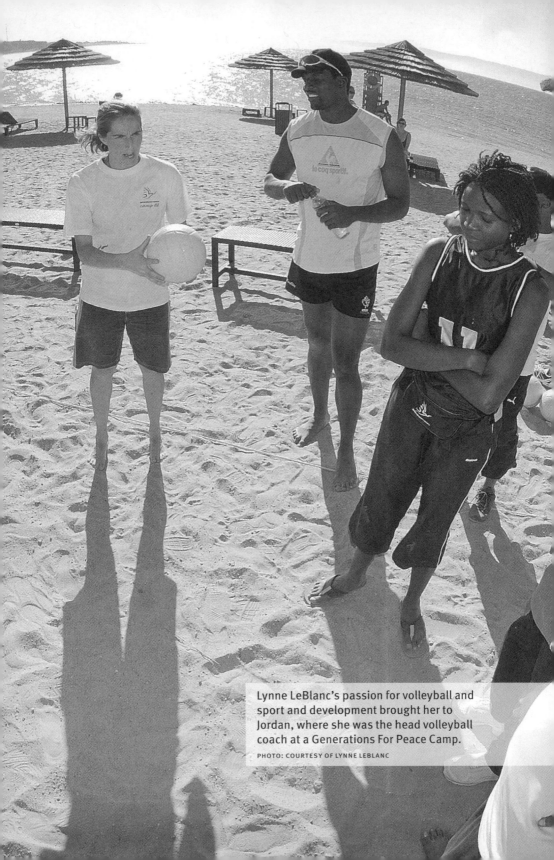

Lynne LeBlanc's passion for volleyball and sport and development brought her to Jordan, where she was the head volleyball coach at a Generations For Peace Camp.

PHOTO: COURTESY OF LYNNE LEBLANC

CHANGING THE ANDROCENTRIC WORLD OF SPORT—IS IT POSSIBLE?

Penny Werthner, Diane Culver, and Rose Mercier

Introduction

Why, when the sporting world is frequently a negative place for girls and women, do we continue trying and wanting to be part of it? What must change to ensure a healthier, more caring environment?
Penny Werthner, Diane Culver, and Rose Mercier demonstrate that it is possible for sport to evolve from an androcentric environment—preoccupied with men and the activities of men to the exclusion of women—to one that is inclusive and satisfying.

Consider the realities they describe.

- The "one size fits all" concept, which the market-driven sporting goods industry is abandoning through necessity, survives and thrives in other aspects of sport.
- The number of female coaches at the national level is incredibly low, and will remain so unless there are widespread organizational and institutional changes.
- Male professional sport, and increasingly sex and drugs, dominate the North American sport scene, making sport a difficult, even undesirable, option for girls and women.

- Fitting women into the existing male model of coaching leads to isolation, limits opportunities, and results in a high drop-out rate.

This chapter is provocative. The authors are intent upon charting a course that could lead to sport—that "wonderful and important form of personal expression"—occurring in an environment that is "welcoming, respectful, and enjoyable" for girls and women. All that is required is the will on the part of all of us who value sport.

MOST READERS OF THIS BOOK are individuals who are involved in sport in several different ways—playing, participating, coaching at various levels, enjoying aspects of sport at a recreational and fitness level, and perhaps ensuring that your child has ample opportunity to partici-pate. Your numbers, as young girls and women, are growing in terms of participation, but are still relatively small in other aspects. What is it about the sporting world that continues to severely hinder more women from participating and enjoying those experiences, and from becoming coaches and leaders? Why is the sporting world frequently a negative place for girls and women? In this chapter, we explore those two questions by (a) looking at the context of the world of sport as it presently exists, (b) critically reflecting on some of the policies and pro-grams in place that encourage girls and women to be part of this world, (c) presenting research and thinking that has tried to examine and explain the issues and context for women and for women in sport, and finally (d) suggesting possible ways to begin to create a new sporting world that is inclusive for all.

Personal Experiences and the Context of the World of Sport

AS WOMEN ATTEMPTING to understand, and then moving on to ques-tioning the world around us and ultimately bringing a deeper analysis to this world of sport, we can begin by looking no further than our own personal experiences. Take a moment to think of your own experience in sport, perhaps as a coach or participant, or as someone who dropped out of this world. Ask yourself what has hindered you from greater development or more joy in participation, in being physically active, or having an opportunity to compete or coach.

One of the authors, Penny Werthner, is a former competitor in athletics and experienced first-hand the discrepancies between what young women and young men are allowed to do in her sport of athletics. Early in her career as a high performance athlete, it became clear that there were limitations in her sport based on her gender. Men, not women, could compete at the Olympic Games in 1500m, 5000m, 10,000m, and the marathon. The 1500m for women became an Olympic race only in 1972, and the marathon for women was only introduced in the 1984 Olympic Games in Los Angeles.

Another author, Diane Culver, once a National Alpine Ski Team member and a national team coach in both Canada and New Zealand prior to becoming an academic, feels she experienced no overt discrimination. However, she remembers that, as a coach and as the first woman to represent Canada on the Canadian Demonstration Ski Team, she was often referred to as "the girl." When she had children, she was sometimes questioned about her level of commitment to the profession. Not an unfamiliar story for many female coaches. She eventually moved out of coaching at the national level, but continues to coach Masters and instruct skiing.

While these personal examples are historical, similar stories abound in many sporting disciplines. In the sport of canoe/kayak, at the Olympic level, women are only allowed to compete in 500m races, while the men compete in both 500m and 1000m. Caroline Brunet, one of Canada's most successful female athletes, and a two-time Olympic silver medallist in 500m kayak, has said: "Women should have the right to race the same distances as men...it is time to grow up. Women should have the same rights as men." Brunet's comment was made in 1997. Nothing has changed in that sport, although in 2009, there have been discussions within the International Canoe Federation about adding an event for women.

Prior to the 2010 Olympic Winter Games, a group of young Canadian women fought a legal battle to compete in the sport of ski jumping. The International Olympic Committee refused to grant them that privilege and the British Columbia Supreme Court ruled that, although barring female ski jumpers from competing constitutes discrimination, the court did not have the authority to force their inclusion.

It's not just at the Olympic level that the male norm has made it less than inviting for women and girls to engage in sport. Ask any female hockey player about the difficulty of finding correctly fitting equipment. Many sports have needed female trailblazers to challenge the assumptions about equipment. One of those trailblazers, Georgena Terry, a mechanical engineer in the United States, pioneered many of the changes to the construction of bicycles when she began to build bicycles in 1985 that were designed to fit the female anatomy. If you have ever ridden a bicycle that had a top tube that was too long for your upper body, even after making all the possible adjustments, you will appreciate the many advances that have been made. One has only to go on the Internet and Google women's sport to see the multitude of websites devoted to women's sport clothing and equipment, testimony to the immense changes in the last twenty years. In fact, probably more progress has been made in adapting equipment and clothing to women's sporting needs than adapting sport and sporting professions to women's lives. The "one size fits all" concept, which the sporting goods industry has firmly moved away from, survives and thrives in other aspects of sport.

Critical Reflection on Current Policies and Programs

IF WE LOOK AT SPORT from the coach's perspective, we still find, in 2009, a low percentage of female coaches at all levels of sport. In a study on coaches at the university, college, provincial, Canada Games,

Coach Tanya Dubnicoff, a former world champion, talks tactics with track cyclist Monique Sullivan.

PHOTO: DENISE KELLY

and national level of sport in Canada, funded by the Coaching Association of Canada, entitled *A Report on the Status of Coaches in Canada* (Reade et al., 2009), only 26% of the coaches who responded were female. Only 20% of the coaches of carded athletes (athletes who are competing at the national level of sport and are funded by the Government of Canada) were female. At the national level of sport, only a handful of national sport organizations are employing women as provincial or national coaches. There have been programs designed to increase the number of female coaches at national levels, and several sports have introduced their own initiatives. But the statistics have told the same story for years now. Most programs have been short term, usually lasting a fiscal year.

One strategy for increasing the impact of such programs is to ensure they are of sufficient duration. The Coaching Association of Canada's Women in Coaching program has been showing the way by funding multi-year initiatives designed to facilitate the movement of female coaches into provincial and national coaching positions. The program has been an important innovation, and a number of female coaches who have participated have found coaching positions in sport. Such programs, however, will achieve optimal results only when combined with organizational and institutional changes.

Over the years, a variety of explanations have been offered for the differences between men's experiences and women's experiences in competition or in a career in sport. Among the arguments still heard are the following:

"Women don't really want to coach at the national level. They don't have the expertise or the motivation."

"Women will eventually get pregnant and leave, so why should we bother?"

"We want the best person for the job."

"We can't have her bringing her baby to the Olympic Games."

"There just aren't as many women competitors."

"There are already too many events at the Olympics."

So, what is the starting point for change when such arguments are reverberating in our heads?

Androcentrism

WE SUGGEST BEGINNING with the word "androcentric," which comes from the Greek aner/andros meaning "male human being." *Merriam-Webster's Online Dictionary* defines androcentric as "dominated by or emphasizing masculine interests or a masculine point of view." Elizabeth Johnson (1992) defines androcentrism as "the name commonly given to the personal pattern of thinking and acting that takes the characteristics of ruling men to be the normative for all humanity... women, children, and those men who do not fit this standard are considered not fully human but secondarily so, in a way derivative from and dependent upon the normative man. In its language and theoretical framework, the androcentric worldview self-affirms the ruling male as normal and standard, and alienates the female and non-ruling male as deficient, auxiliary 'other'" (p. 23, 24). If we examine the nature of definitions, we have a starting point. We have a framework for thinking about a sport world that has as its basis many norms that come from men's characteristics, lives, and experiences. Sport is not alone in having such a framework.

If we look beyond the boundaries of sport, we begin to see the prevalence of androcentrism in other domains. In *Thinking Critically About Research on Sex and Gender*, Paula and Jeremy Caplan (1994) provide numerous examples of how androcentric research has historically dominated many fields of research. This research has subsequently significantly influenced the ways in which we view our world, and the ways in which we act and behave. One of the more powerful examples of androcentrism they noted is the influential work of Lawrence Kohlberg on the stages of moral development (Kohlberg, 1981). One of his conclusions was that not everyone reaches the higher stages of moral development and that, in general, females' moral reasoning tends to be halted at a lower stage than that of males. Carol Gilligan, in her book *In a Different Voice* (1982), noted a serious flaw in Kohlberg's conclusions: the participants in his study, upon which his conclusions are based, were all twelve-year-old males! What is even more tragic and, at the same time profoundly telling, is that Kohlberg's research findings are still extensively cited to this day. Many fields, including medicine, economics, science, and education, yield their own examples of the profound impact of an androcentric perspective on women's lives. For example, the medical research that led many North Americans to ingest an Aspirin a day was founded on research done on an entirely male population. As we have learned more recently, women and men have different patterns of susceptibility to heart disease and present symptoms differently.

Numerous authors have written on the androcentric nature of sport. Cook (2007) notes that sport has historically been cited as a patriarchal institution and male domain where women are seen as trespassers. Hall (2002) states that female athleticism and the traditional definition of femininity are thought to be "mutually exclusive" (p. 147). Women who are athletically successful, aggressive, and capable of leadership strongly defy the conventional definition of femininity and, as a result, often face painful social consequences (Krane, 2001). Griffin (1998) argues that sport has traditionally been considered a domain where boys were taught to be masculine and become men. Women's participation in sport as athletes and coaches is challenging and "diluting the importance and exclusivity of sport as a training ground for learning and accepting traditional male gender roles" (Griffin, p. 17). Wellman and Blinde (1997) suggest that the reason for such a hostile climate for women in sport is that "sport has traditionally been defined as a male activity, and women who enter the competitive sport context are assumed to violate gender norms established for women" (p. 64).

Really, we need only look as far as our local and national newspapers to see what androcentrism in the sporting world looks like. In most newspapers in North America, there are usually six to seven pages of sport news—mostly all professional and, for the most part, male and American—covering the National Basketball Association, the National Hockey League, hockey's Memorial Cup, the Indianapolis 500, the men's professional golf tour, and so on. If there is coverage of women's sport and "amateur" and local sport competitions and individuals, it is more often than not buried in small print on the back pages of the newspaper. Only for the two weeks of each Olympic Games does non-professional sport receive exposure, and we wonder why so many young girls and women of all ages do not want to have any part of the competitive sporting world. Seeing and reading about their own sport experiences would have a powerful impact on the possibilities in sport that girls and women can imagine for themselves.

The media is but one example, albeit a pervasive and powerful one, of the inherent nature of the world of sport in North America—a world dominated by male professional sport at best, and sex and drugs at worst. While we are seeing more and more women participating, playing, and competing in more sporting activities, they are still doing so within a sporting world that is created and dominated by a male perspective. Is it any wonder that we lose girls from sport and that we lose, or in fact rarely have, women in leadership and head coaching positions at the national level? More often than not, it is a world that, over the long term, does not fit for many women.

Research on the Issues

IN 1990, SPORT CANADA published "The Gender Structure of National Sport Organizations." In this report, Hall, Cullen, and Slack (1990) discuss two points of view in research about making changes to the under-representation of women in leadership roles. The first of these, "the person-centred or individualistic approach, attributes women's limited representation...to factors that are perceived to be internal to women themselves" (p. 29). In other words, women are assumed to lack the proper training, motivation, and/or skills to succeed. The focus is on describing these stereotypes and the implications, and then either demonstrating that women and men do not, in fact, differ in their abilities, or showing women how to acquire the necessary attitudes, skills, and motivation to succeed. The primary focus is on how women must change to fit the organization with little question of the organization's role. "The organization is a given into which everyone— both men and women—must fit. Men, because of their socialization, fit better than women do. Women, if they want to participate, must change to fit the system" (p. 29).

If you apply this person-centred perspective to coaching, you would have to conclude that we are currently doing all that can be done to increase the number of women in provincial-, national-, and international-level coaching positions. We look hard for every opportunity to prove that men and women do not differ in their abilities to coach if they are in similar roles. We identify the types of knowledge, skills, and attitudes that it takes to become a successful national and international coach. We provide programs that accelerate the learning process. And yet...there has been no appreciable difference in the numbers of women coaching at that level over several years of focused effort. Some women succeed, so it is said that there's nothing wrong with the system.

Is the only conclusion then that most women must not really want to coach at that level? Or is the answer more profound?

Hall, Cullen, and Slack (1990) go on to state: "The second perspective, the organization-centred perspective, focuses on changing the organization itself, rather than the women (or men) in it. This perspective...argues that people's behaviour is shaped by the organizational structures and systems in which they find themselves...Differences in men's and women's behaviour can be attributed to the fact that women are more likely to be found in positions of low opportunity and low power, and are likely to be proportionately under-represented, or tokens, in decision-making" (p. 30). In this perspective, the focus of change is the organization itself. The authors go on to say, "Behavioural change in both women and men will then follow from the changes made within the organization" (p. 30).

The report goes on to provide sport leaders' analysis of the lack of women in leadership roles. The explanations are depressingly familiar:

Men, on the other hand, saw the lack of qualified women with the right experience as the key factor in women's under-representation. (p. 31)

An alternative way of describing women's understanding of how to achieve responsible positions in sport organizations is that it is a matter of being the "right" person (i.e., the person with the "right" personality traits, in the "right" place, at the "right" time). (p. 31, 32)

While these perceptions may reflect individual experience, the authors state that "this orientation can also lead to a passive and dysfunctional approach to correcting the problem" (p. 32).

From a more recent and broader research perspective, Susan Pinker's *The Sexual Paradox* (2008) meticulously examines the science of sex differences, and concludes that a more nuanced understanding of gender differences is required. She states that the feminist movement "created the expectation that all differences between men and women were created by unjust practices and therefore could be erased by changing some" (p. 9). She argues, however, with support from a great deal of research, that sex differences do indeed exist and ignoring this fact has "the unintended effect of devaluing women's cognitive strengths and preferences" (p. 261).

Pinker also presents intriguing perspectives and research on the nature of the differences between women and men. For example, in examining the research around competition, she states that while individual women can easily be more competitive than individual men, on average, "girls' and women's style of competing looks different" (p. 199). In citing research with preschool girls and boys, it was found that boys used competition and physical tactics fifty times more than girls, and girls used talking and turn-taking twenty times more often than boys. Certainly Pinker would argue that this is one of the many differences that need to be considered in exploring how we, as women, can shape our careers over a lifetime.

An underlying question that runs throughout Pinker's book is: Is a system that was designed for men really the right thing for women? In examining the research on women's career choices, and the seemingly increasing numbers of women opting out of high pressure jobs in order to do more meaningful work, or work fewer hours, Pinker suggests that indeed many women are choosing not to work the full-time, sixty-hour work week for forty years. As an example, she cites the current research on the increasing numbers of women entering medicine. She calls it a good-news, bad-news scenario. She references a study by Hrdy (1999) that states the good news is female physicians are more likely to be patient-centred, to offer more psychological support, and to work with the disadvantaged in the community. The bad news is that female physicians are working fewer hours than men, and taking time off to have children. Of course, this is causing some chaos in the system and is not considered the "norm." Clearly our "system" may have to change as the number of female physicians grows. We could perhaps use this example to help us think about how to create a new system of coaching, one that would be more enticing for female coaches.

In thinking of changing the "system" of how we work to make it more viable for women in many different careers, Pinker argues that we must do so, because women will always be the primary care-givers. She states that "swaths of data" show more women than men make adjustments to their careers to care for family members. She acknowledges that men help their relatives more than ever before, but it is still women who interrupt their careers to do so. The author does ask whether women are "strong-armed" into helping, and goes on to suggest that empathy for others can trump an exclusive focus on status and money, at least for some women. She supports her argument with numerous studies, but one that stands out is the recent work of Sloan Wilson and Csikszentmihalyi (2007), who researched how altruism and caring for others informed teenagers' life decisions. The research followed 1,000 teenagers for over five years. When asked questions such as how often do you volunteer or perform community service outside of school, female students scored higher than male students in helping attitudes.

All of the research that Pinker has gathered to support her argument of recognizing that sex differences do exist certainly gives us food for thought. To a degree, the notion of differences does speak to many of our personal experiences, can help explain why we have significantly small numbers of women in leadership roles, and can help us see the very nature of the androcentric world we live in. But, as Pinker says in her conclusion, we cannot let statistical differences speak for individuals, or justify unfair practices. What we must do is recognize what exists and work to shape a new environment.

If we turn back to the world of sport, if there is ever to be a real change in the number and involvement of women in coaching, we need to move beyond thinking that women are the problem or that men are the problem. We need to understand that the structure of an organization is not neutral, that organizations are structured through an invisible gender-biased view of reality, and that individual solutions will not result in sustainable changes for women in coaching and leadership roles in sport. If we ignore or deny the need for organizational structures that co-ordinate work and family in such a way that males and females could easily participate in both, and if we assume that the ideals we have set up are gender neutral, then we cannot fashion real solutions. We must be willing to examine the deepest assumptions we hold when thinking about the sport world, and when we describe the process and skills of coaching.

Author Penny Werthner worked with a group of female coaches to examine the reasons for the lack of women coaching at the national level. The women worked very hard to question the roots of this continuing problem, and identify the factors that reinforce and perpetuate the status quo. (Interestingly, one of the main factors identified was an androcentric coaching model.) At the end of the weekend, the coaches were evaluating the work they had done, and one noted that the best aspect of the session was hearing the voices of other female coaches—voices that she noted were a silent minority when they gathered at her sport organization meetings.

If women's voices are not heard, and their experience not factored into decisions, how can sport reflect a more inclusive perspective?

It is interesting to reflect that gender was not considered a factor of any note in the study of leadership until the 1970s. The leadership theories that emerged at that time were based solely on the study of male executives. It is these leadership theories on which North America and Western Europe founded work and organizational structures. There is a shift occurring in our society's ideas about leadership that can have important ramifications for our current coaching model. The traditional view of leadership was founded on male-oriented values of rationality, competition, and independence. The assumptions that everything must be based on reason, that only the strong survive, and that it is every man for himself are so deeply embedded in our political and social institutions that they are invisible. They have shaped the culture of our organizations, and sport is no exception. The organizational view that assumes the male model to be the norm does not work well for women. Some of the most basic tenets, which we take for granted, come from these assumptions. When we simply try to fit women into this existing model, they often, and yet not surprisingly, are isolated, receive little support, have limited opportunities, and do not stay around, thereby perpetuating the prevailing thinking that women cannot "take the pressure."

As noted in the Introduction of this book, Eagly and Carli (2007) explored the problem of the continuing lack of women in leadership roles, particularly in the world of business, and argued that the metaphor of the "glass ceiling," coined in 1986, was now more wrong than right. The metaphor, according to the authors, implies that women and men have equal access to entry and mid-level positions and that the problem for women arises only at the highest levels, such as chairman, president, chief executive officer. Eagly and Carli suggest, however, that women face problems at every phase of their working lives. So, the authors created a new metaphor, the labyrinth, to illustrate what confronts women. "Passage through a labyrinth is not simple or direct, but requires persistence, awareness of one's progress, and a careful analysis of the puzzles that lie ahead" (p. 64).

Eagly and Carli (2007) cite a large number of research studies to support the issues and prejudices women face, such as resistance to the style of women's leadership, the difficult balancing act between work and family life, and the continuing wage discrepancies. These authors also discuss a number of issues that are often subtle in nature, but have a profoundly negative impact on women's careers. One is the age-old dilemma of the double bind for women who aspire to be leaders in any field; when women speak up and assert themselves, they are often vilified. "They were labelled 'control freaks': men acting the same way were called 'passionate'" (p. 66). Another is the many indirect consequences of having a family and aspiring to be successful. One way they discuss this is in terms of social capital—working women with families have little time to network outside of office hours, let alone play four hours of golf on a weekend. A third but subtle issue is the assumption by decision makers that women with children will not be able to take on more demanding positions because of childcare responsibilities; therefore, they are often not even considered for promotions.

In concluding, Eagly and Carli list a number of management interventions that are not unlike what has been suggested before—increase people's awareness of the prejudices against female leaders and work to dispel those perceptions; change the long-hours norm of the workplace; reduce the subjectivity of performance evaluations; establish family-friendly human resources practices; and ensure a critical mass of women in executive positions. Clearly, their metaphor of the labyrinth is a useful one to think about a woman's lifelong career development, and the many obstacles she may face along the way.

We need to look at sport and coaching closely. We need to ask some hard questions.

- Why do we, almost without exception, continue to have only one head coach of many of our national and provincial teams?
- Why do we continue to resist new models of team coaching or co-coaching?
- Why are so many coaches reluctant to share their knowledge with others they perceive not to be their equals? Are they afraid that someone will sweep by them in the race that goes only to the swift?
- Why do we continue to perpetuate the thinking and behaviours that say emotion and intense feelings are to be avoided in the coaching process, and confine ourselves to the tangible quantitative measures and scientific research?

- Why do we continue to hire coaches on the sole basis of technical expertise, while almost universally ignoring the importance of effective interpersonal skills? Such skills are crucial in enabling young children to enjoy their sport experience, helping to keep athletes at all levels involved throughout their lifetime, and creating the kind of environment that allows young adults to excel in competitive sport and high performance athletes to achieve international success.

And then, we suggest, we need to alter the models of our sporting world fundamentally.

What Values Underlie Such Thinking?

As WE CONTINUE to rethink leadership, values, and the profession of coaching, the attributes and characteristics of the traditional masculine model of leadership most certainly need to be re-evaluated and altered. The emerging form of leadership will be characterized by empowering oneself; enabling other coaches, colleagues, and one's athletes; fostering self-confidence; and developing an organizational vision that embodies the goals, needs, and values of both leaders and followers, of both girls and boys, women and men. This will require, without a doubt, organizations to adopt new values and act in new ways.

A wonderfully informative example of one woman's quest for freedom through sport is that of Hassiba Boulmerka, the extraordinary Algerian middle distance runner who won the gold medal in the women's 1,500m at the 1992 Olympic Games. William Morgan wrote about her in a chapter in Genevieve Rail's *Sport and Postmodern Times* (1998). Boulmerka claimed that her international athletic experience provided her with a powerful chance to express herself and, by speaking out, she could not only extol the values inherent in excelling in sport, but could use her visibility to attempt to create and promote the more secular and democratic Muslim culture that, for a time, allowed her to excel as a female athlete and as a Muslim woman. She spoke out about the possibilities for women in her country and within the sporting world. Difficulties arose for Boulmerka when a more fundamentalist form of Muslim culture rose to power and she became a target of great criticism, illustrating for us the difficulty in trying to make change solely as an individual. Just as one woman's words and breakthrough achievements cannot reframe the profound religious and political worldview in Algeria, androcentrism in sport cannot be remedied solely through individual solutions. It will take visionary organizations and individuals within those organizations to rethink how coaching can equally fit the life patterns and needs of both women and men.

Suggestions for Creating an Inclusive World of Sport

How can we go about challenging the models that presently exist in sport and begin to create a better sport environment that is inclusive of young female participants and athletes, older women, and female coaches at all levels of play and competition?

Here are a few starting points, based on our experiences and the work of Pinker (2008), Eagly and Carli (2007), and Hall et al. (1990).

- Develop coaching models that equally value female and male lives and offer alternatives to both women and men.
- Create performance review models that go beyond androcentric definitions of coaching competencies.
- Involve women in leadership in significant enough numbers that their voices are heard and their experiences and perspective are reflected in decisions made in sport organizations.
- On an individual basis, continuously challenge those aspects of coaching that are anchored in androcentric values or models.
- Provide opportunities for female coaches to speak at conferences and workshops.
- Ask female coaches to write articles for the sport organization's newsletter or magazine.

- Propose that there be female and male co-chairs for workshops, conferences, and committees.
- Ensure balanced visual evidence of female and male coaches in newsletters and media guides, and on web pages.

You might wonder if it is really possible to change anything... in your lifetime anyway! And you may well be asking by now, if the sporting world is such a negative place for girls and women, why continue trying and wanting to be a part of it? Why not just opt out, as so many other girls and women have? The simple answer is that sport can be a wonderful and important form of personal expression. Being physically active is instrumental in each individual's well-being. A strong sense of fitness leads naturally to the desire to begin to compete, to challenge oneself in a new way. There are too many powerful positives that are available through sport. We need to create an environment in the world of sport where that environment is welcoming, respectful, and enjoyable for women.

In *Women, Men, and Power*, Hilary Lips (1991) writes: "It will take ferocious creativity to do the restructuring so as to arrive at a society where both female-male equality and important communal values are protected, where the economic structure is designed with consideration for the needs of female and male employees and their families. Nothing is more certain than that such a goal will never be reached if women are the only ones who change" (p. 200).

REFERENCES

Androcentric, *adj.* (2009). *Merriam-Webster's online dictionary.* Retrieved June 25, 2009, from http://www.merriam-webster.com/dictionary/androcentric

Caplan, P.J., & Caplan, J.B. (1994). *Thinking critically about research on sex and gender.* New York: HarperCollins College Publishers.

Cook, S.G. (2007). How to address homophobia in women's athletics. *Women in Higher Education, 16*(5).

Eagly, A., & Carli, L. (2007). Women and the labyrinth of leadership. *Harvard Business Review*, September, 62–71.

Gilligan, C. (1982). *In a different voice: Psychological theory and women's development.* Cambridge, MA: Harvard University Press.

Griffin, P. (1998). *Strong women, deep closets: Lesbians and homophobia in sport*. Champaign, IL: Human Kinetics.

Hall, M.A. (2002). *The girl and the game: A history of women's sports in Canada*. Peterborough: Broadview Press Ltd.

Hall, M.A., Cullen, D., & Slack, T. (1990). The gender structure of national sport organizations. *Sport Canada Occasional Papers, 2*(1).

Hrdy, S.B. (1999). *Mother nature: Maternal instincts and how they shape the human species*. New York: Random House.

Johnson, E.A. (1992). *She who is: The mystery of God in feminist theological discourse.* New York: The Crossroad Publishing Company.

Kohlberg, L. (1981). *The philosophy of moral development*. New York: Harper & Row.

Krane, V. (2001). We can be athletic and feminine, but do we want to? Challenging hegemonic femininity in women's sport. *Quest, 53*(1).

Lips, H. (1991). *Women, men, and power*. Mountain View, CA: Mayfield Publishing.

Morgan, W.J. (1998). Hassiba Boulmerka and Islamic green: International sports, cultural differences, and their postmodern interpretation. In Rail, G. (Ed.). *Sport and postmodern times*. Albany: State University of New York Press.

Pinker, S. (2008). *The sexual paradox: Extreme men, gifted women and the real gender gap*. Toronto: Random House Canada.

Reade, I. et al. (2009). *A report on the status of coaches in Canada*. Ottawa: Coaching Association of Canada.

Sloan Wilson, D., & Csikszentmihalyi, M. (2007). Health and the ecology of altruism. In Post, S.G. (Ed.). *Altruism and health: Perspectives from empirical research.* New York: Oxford University Press.

Wellman, S., & Blinde, E. (1997). Women coaches regarding coaching careers and recruitment of athletes. *Women in Sport and Physical Activity Journal, 6*(2).

Linda Marquis is the head coach of the Rouge et Or women's basketball team at Laval University.

FEMALE COACHES' EXPERIENCE OF HARASSMENT AND BULLYING

Gretchen Kerr

Introduction

The touchy subject of harassment and bullying is one of the sordid underbellies of the sport culture. As Gretchen Kerr points out, although much has been recorded about female athletes' experiences of harassment and bullying, her study is the first to explore female coaches' experiences of the dual transgressions. Kerr notes that difficulties in attracting and retaining female coaches have been attributed to such factors as domestic responsibilities, the lack of recruitment and mentoring programs, and an absence of role models. Could harassment and bullying also be contributing causes? It appears so.

The author builds a strong case for dealing openly with this contentious but muzzled issue. As the study's participants reveal with candour, they have generally perceived their choices to be speaking out and risk losing their hard-fought-for positions, or staying silent. Not very palatable options.

Kerr acknowledges that her sample was small. Nevertheless, the participants' responses are a powerful indictment of a persistent and ugly culture. She prescribes further research in order to "better understand and enhance women's experiences in the coaching profession." Let us hope that publishing this material will encourage decision makers at all levels to, at least, support further investigation and, even better, initiate strong actions to end the harassment and bullying of female coaches.

ALTHOUGH NUMEROUS RESEARCHERS have investigated female athletes' experiences of harassment and bullying, with findings of disturbing rates of occurrence (Brackenridge, 2001; Fasting, Brackenridge, & Sungot-Borgen, 2004; Hinkle, 2005; Holman, 1995; Kirby & Greaves, 1996; McGlone, 2005; Volkewein, 1996), surprisingly little is known about these experiences among female coaches. Researchers report that in general workplace settings, 10 to 50% of female employees experience harassment each year (Konik & Cortina, 2008; Rayner, Hoel, & Cooper, 2002; Zapf, Einarsen, Hoel, & Vartia, 2003). Given the prevalence of sexual harassment of women in other workplace settings, it seems reasonable to expect that female coaches are not immune to these experiences.

Further, one is left to ponder whether experiences of harassment and bullying account, in part, for the existing difficulties in recruiting and retaining female coaches. In spite of the increasing participation rates of girls and women in sport, from grassroots community-based programs to international competition, and the successful performance outcomes of female athletes, the number of women in coaching positions has not increased proportionally, if at all (Coaching Association of Canada, 2002; LeDrew & Zimmerman, 1994). There are substantially fewer female than male coaches at virtually all levels of sport, but particularly at the elite level. Recent Canadian data indicate that approximately 30% of head and assistant coach positions are held by women (Kerr, Marshall, Sharp, & Stirling, 2006). Moreover, the literature indicates that females tend to drop out of the profession within the first five years of coaching. The difficulties in attracting and retaining female coaches have been attributed to conflicts with domestic responsibilities, harassment, and the lack of recruitment programs, mentoring programs, and role models (Demers, 2004; Hall,

1996; Hanson & Kraus, 1999; Marshall, 2001; McKay, 1999; Mercier & Werthner, 2001).

In the general workplace literature, harassment and bullying have been linked with attrition, absenteeism, decreased productivity, and negative health outcomes (Hoel & Salin, 2003; Keashly & Jagatic, 2003). Although some research has explored the effects of recruitment and mentoring programs in attracting and retaining female coaches, no previous literature has explored female coaches' experiences of harassment and bullying.

The purpose of the study from which this chapter is drawn, therefore, was to examine whether female coaches experienced harassment and bullying as they moved from entry-level positions to more senior positions within the coaching ranks.

Before proceeding, it is important to clarify the meaning of the terms "harassment" and "bullying," particularly in light of the fact that these terms are defined in different ways in the literature.

Harassment refers to unwanted or coerced behaviours that are in violation of an individual's human rights. They represent an abuse of power, authority, and trust (International Olympic Committee, 2007). The Canadian Association for the Advancement of Women and Sport and Physical Activity (1994) defined harassment as any "comment, conduct, or gesture directed toward an individual or a group of individuals which is insulting, intimidating, humiliating, malicious, degrading or offensive." Harassment occurs when a person in a position of authority, power, or trust engages in these behaviours. Within the sport context, harassment can occur between a coach and an athlete, an athletic director and a coach, or a head coach and an assistant coach, as some examples. Harassment may take many forms, including but not limited to sexual, ethnic, physical, emotional, gender, religious, socioeconomic, racial, and homophobic harassment.

Bullying refers to repeated physical, verbal, or psychological attacks or intimidations that are intended to cause fear, distress, or harm to the victim (Ferrington, 1993). In the workplace, bullying has been defined as repeated and persistent negative acts toward one or more individuals which involve a perceived power imbalance and create a hostile work environment (Hoel & Cooper, 2001; Zapf et al., 2003). Similar to harassment, bullying is based on an imbalance of power. The bully holds power through gender, social status within a group, physical size, or certain personality traits (Salin, 2003). In bullying, the perpetrator is a peer; in harassment, the perpetrator is in a position of power or authority. Bullying behaviour in sport may include repeated incidents of a coach spreading rumours about, name-calling, or humiliating a fellow coach. Another example is when an athlete repeatedly isolates a fellow athlete or prevents him or her from participating in social or team-related events. Sexual bullying may occur if a peer repeatedly engages in conduct of a sexual nature or makes comments that are viewed as offensive or degrading by the target.

For the purposes of this chapter, the distinction between harassment and bullying made by Stirling (2008) will be used; namely, harassment and bullying differ because of the nature of the relationship in which the behaviour occurs. Although both harassment and bullying occur within relationships with power differentials, harassment occurs when instigated by someone in an ascribed position of power or authority over the victim, and bullying occurs when the instigator is a peer.

Methods

Participants

The participants in the study included eight Canadian female coaches between the ages of forty-two and fifty-six. Each had worked at the national level of sport for a minimum of ten years and currently held head coach positions for female teams. One of the inclusion criteria was to be a coach within a traditionally male-coach-dominated sport. As a result, coaches from sports such as rhythmic gymnastics and synchronized swimming were excluded, and coaches from sports such as basketball, volleyball, hockey, swimming, and athletics were included.

Measures

A semi-structured interview was designed. The first question was, "Please tell me about the process by which you entered coaching and came to hold a head coach position." This was followed, if needed, by such probes as, "What were your experiences with the head coach when you were an assistant?" and "What challenges did you encounter en route to becoming a head coach?"

Procedures

A snowball sampling method was used to recruit participants. Each coach was contacted personally by phone or email and told about the purpose of the study and the study requirements. The potential participant was told that this study would seek to explore experiences of harassment and bullying as female coaches moved through the coaching ranks. If the coach indicated interest, a mutually convenient time and place to meet for the interview was established. Before data collection began, the participant was given a letter of information about the study and a consent form to sign and was assured of confidentiality, anonymity, and the right to withdraw from the study at any time without penalty. Once consent was obtained, the participant chose a pseudonym and the interview began.

Each interview lasted between one and two hours. The data were transcribed verbatim and analyzed inductively, from the identification of meaning units to the classification of the units into themes. The interview transcripts and findings were sent back to the participants for review and comment. No changes were made based upon the participants' feedback.

Results

SEVEN OF THE EIGHT PARTICIPANTS experienced harassment or bullying to one degree or another. Some of these experiences were described as minor; others were serious and pervasive.

Experiences of Harassment and Bullying

The participants described coaching environments as, at times, being characterized by offensive, sexual comments. For example, sexist jokes were common occurrences. Two of the women were present when male coaches, both in comparable positions and in positions of authority, discussed the physical appearance of female athletes on their teams. These discussions involved body disparagement and comments of a sexual nature. For example, one participant offered the following: "We were all standing around watching warm-ups—four guys and me. They began commenting on the athleticism and athletic builds of some of the female athletes...but then this conversation turned to comments about who was 'hottest.' Before I could figure out what to say, they were rating the athletes on a one-to-ten scale according to how 'hot' the athletes were. I was horrified. Some of these guys have daughters the age of the athletes. I was also horrified by my lack of ability to stop their comments." Thus, although the participants were not the targets of the sexist comments or jokes, they were personally offended by their colleagues' comments.

Two participants recalled that, in their early days of coaching competitively, the male head coaches at the time had sexual relations with some of the female assistant coaches. According to these participants, the assistant coaches who responded positively to these advances were subsequently chosen for select teams or team trips. Although the sport organizations were aware of certain indiscretions, no interventions occurred. As one participant recalled, "The head coach at the time would routinely sleep with his female assistant coaches. It wouldn't have been so bad to see two adults having a consensual relationship, but when the particular assistant coach was then selected for important competitions or trips, the rest of us couldn't help but suspect that the fact they were having sex had something to do with the decision. And when the head coach developed a new interest in someone else, the former lover was dropped like a 'hot potato.' It was really hard to watch the damage done to these young, aspiring coaches, and it wreaked havoc with the team dynamics."

Almost all of the participants described repeatedly being socially excluded from activities with their male peers and superiors while they were assistant coaches. Until they became head coaches, they were not informed of coaches' meetings on several occasions and were not invited to socialize with their male colleagues while travelling. Whether the group of coaches went out for a social drink or played a round of golf, these female coaches were not included. One of the participants recalled a recent travel experience when the male coaches went out to a strip club after the competition, leaving the female coach to ensure that the athletes met their curfew.

Some of the participants reportedly declined to reveal their homosexuality to their male peers and superiors while they were assistant coaches. They felt a clear expectation of heterosexuality, and sexist comments and homophobic jokes reinforced this expectation. These coaches were concerned, as minority females, about further marginalizing themselves by disclosing their sexuality. As one participant recalled, "It was tough enough being the only female. Trying to be accepted and included by the males who had much more coaching experience than I was tough. And there were all kinds of messages about heterosexuality, from what the group of them talked about to the jokes they told. There was no way I was going to marginalize myself by letting them know I was a lesbian...not a chance."

Once these women became head coaches, they disclosed their sexuality.

The only participant who did not report experiences of harassment and bullying coached in an environment that differed from that of the others. Specifically, this coach had primarily worked with other female coaches, and there had been a longer history in this particular sport of having women on the coaching staff.

Effects of Harassment and Bullying

Most of the participants initiated a dialogue about the effects of harassment and bullying, eagerly disclosing feelings of isolation, frustration, and anger. As one participant disclosed, "I felt very alone in my days as an assistant coach. I didn't have other coaches to turn to, or to vent to, or to get some sort of support." In spite of the recognition that the conduct they were exposed to was demeaning and unfair, they felt a need to remain silent and refrain from expressing objections. They perceived a need to fit in and not "rock the boat" in order to move ahead through the coaching ranks. As one participant said, "I knew what was going on was wrong, but I didn't think I should make waves or I'd be out of a job. This was really hard for me, because I've never been one to keep my mouth shut."

For the coaches who believed they could not disclose their sexuality, the perceived need to pretend to be someone they were not was extremely distressing and energy-draining. "Watching what I said and did in front of these guys was exhausting."

Upon reflection, several participants expressed anger at the system. As they moved up the coaching ranks, they perceived a need to accept inappropriate conduct in order to advance, but retrospectively they were angry that a culture of harassment and bullying was accepted. These women alleged that the sport organizations knew of the female-unfriendly environments, but did not intervene, and through their lack of action these organizations were complicit in the harassment and bullying.

Although experiences of harassment and bullying lessened as the coaches moved into head coach positions, they still faced sexist and homophobic environments. At this point in their careers, however, they were more likely to intervene, as recalled by one of the participants: "Once I felt more secure in the head coach position, I felt it was my responsibility to educate others about how to create a sport environment that is friendly for females—both athletes and coaches. So I started to call people on their sexist and homophobic jokes and the disparaging comments made about bodies. I think unless you've been a young woman, you can't fully appreciate the impact of negative comments about your body. I needed to tell my male peers this."

Survival Tips

When asked why she continued coaching in the face of harassment and bullying, one participant said, "I was competitive as an athlete, and this stayed with me as a coach...I wasn't going to let them get the best of me." All of the coaches referred to an element of competitiveness; they wanted head coaching positions and, to get there, they had to "put up with" some maltreatment and keep silent about it.

Many of the participants referred to their desire to make sport a better place for girls and women, for the athletes and young coaches who were following behind them. As one participant remarked, "I was convinced that more female coaches were needed, that with the growing numbers of girls and young women participating in sport, we needed more female coaches as role models and leaders. I wanted to make sport a better place for other women, and I just kept my focus on doing that.

"There were many times I thought of giving it all up. But I loved working with the athletes and I kept thinking that if I could just hang in there long enough to become a head coach, things would improve, things would get better. And I was determined to make things better for other women coming up through the system as coaches."

Discussion

THE RESULTS INDICATE THAT within this small sample, harassment and bullying are experienced by some women in the coaching profession. All but one of these women reportedly experienced being harassed or bullied by their male counterparts who either were in more senior positions or had longer tenures as highly competitive coaches than they did. The power imbalance based upon sex and experience on the job that characterizes harassment has been well-supported in the general workplace literature (Acker, 1990; Welsh, 1999).

The most common types of harassment and bullying reportedly experienced by the participants were gender- and sexuality-based harassment and bullying, as well as social bullying. Gender harassment refers to disparaging conduct—verbal, physical, or symbolic behaviours that convey offensive attitudes about women but are not intended to elicit sexual co-operation (Konik & Cortina, 2008). This finding supports those of others (McKay, 1999) who report that virtually all women in coaching and sport administration positions have experienced or witnessed sexual harassment in the workplace. Additionally, a plethora of existing literature highlights the homophobic nature of the sport culture and incidents of harassment based upon sexual orientation (Demers, 2004; Pronger, 2005). In the general workplace, 25 to 66% of sexual minorities have encountered workplace discrimination because of their sexual orientation (Konik & Cortina, 2008). The study highlighted the experience of social bullying or exclusion faced by these women, an experience not previously reported in the sport literature.

Previous literature consistently indicates that females who work in traditional male work environments often experience more harassment and bullying than those who work in female-dominated environments (Gutek, Cohen, & Konrad, 1990). Coaching has traditionally been, and continues to be, dominated by males. As several authors have noted (Berdahl, 2007; Chamberlain, Crowley, Tope, & Hodson, 2008; Welsh, 1999), females in such contexts may be perceived as threats to men's sense of masculinity, solidarity, and pride. In fact, harassing behaviours based on either gender or sexual orientation have common roots in maintaining traditional patriarchal gender roles (Berdahl, 2007).

Furthermore, the general workplace literature suggests that minority employees may be more vulnerable to harassment because these employees already face a certain degree of social isolation and exclusion (Salin, 2003; Tsui & Gutek, 1999). The coaches in the study were in minority positions as females and expressed isolation and a lack of social support; these feelings were particularly profound for lesbian coaches. Interestingly, the one coach who did not report experiences of bullying or harassment had female colleagues in the coaching environment as she progressed through the ranks. Together, these findings suggest that perceived social isolation is a risk factor for the experience of harassment and bullying.

Previous literature suggests that "powerlessness and low relative status are core determinants" of insults to one's dignity at work (Jacoby, 2004). One of the most important causes of powerlessness in the workplace is job insecurity, possibly because employees are fighting against others to keep their positions (Hearn & Parkin, 2001). In competitive sport, particularly at the assistant coach level, positions are often tenuous. In many instances, assistant coaches are hired on part-time, term contracts; moreover, there are often several assistant coaches vying for power and full-time positions. Even for full-time head coaches, employment can be affected by the performance of the team and, therefore, these coaches are not necessarily in secure positions.

Heide and Miner (1992) report that when an expectation for future employment exists, there is also potential for future rewards and sanctions, thus contributing to greater co-operation among employees. On the other hand, the limited associations that people have in insecure or temporary positions, with little chance of future rewards and sanctions, may lead to more experiences of harassment and bullying. Related to job insecurity, previous literature indicates that individuals who lack financial security report more experiences with sexual harassment (Uggen & Blackstone, 2004). Coaching positions do not typically provide much in the way of job or financial security, thus potentially contributing to an environment ripe for harassment and bullying. Future research may advance our understanding of the relationship between job security, harassment, and bullying by comparing contexts in which both head and assistant coaches are employed on a full-time, long-term basis to contexts where they are not.

The general harassment and bullying literature recognizes the crucial role that third parties (Skarlicki & Kulik, 2005) or bystanders play in preventing or intervening in such behaviours. Within the workplace, co-workers in similar positions have the potential to provide "guardianship" against harassment and bullying. Working closely together over time may accentuate the interpersonal costs of harassment and bullying (Chamberlain et al., 2008). In the case of all but one of the coaches in the study, similar third parties, namely female coaches at the same rank, were virtually absent.

Existing literature indicates that harassment is more common in work environments that involve physically demanding work or that emphasize physical prowess and the body (Lopez, Hodson, & Roscigno, 2009; Ragins & Scandura, 1995). Although the work of coaches is not necessarily physically demanding in the sense of hard physical labour, it does exist in a culture that focuses on the body and physicality. The nature of coaching involves a focus on the body, how it works, how it appears, and how well it functions to produce athletic performance. Coaches are constantly surrounded by finely tuned, young, athletic bodies. One wonders whether this focus on the body makes the profession of coaching more vulnerable to experiences of sexual harassment and sexual bullying in particular.

As Chamberlain and colleagues (2008) and others have emphasized, the organizational context is a crucial determinant of the occurrence of harassment as well as the specific forms it takes. Within sport, Brackenridge (2001) highlights the importance of viewing victims and perpetrators within domain-specific contexts, as the legitimacy and acceptance of behaviours such as harassment and bullying are influenced by the social environment. Sport has a long tradition of being characterized by an ideology of masculinity, specifically an idealized form of masculinity that is associated with toughness, power, aggressiveness, competitiveness, and domination over others (Coakley & Donnelly, 2003). Furthermore, sport has been characterized by a "heterosexual imperative," the need for and expectation of heterosexuality in order to participate and excel in sport (Shogan, 1999). This ideology is narrow, monolithic, and resistant to the progress of many groups.

Conclusion

TAKEN TOGETHER, the findings of the study suggest that the unique aspects of the coaching profession make it susceptible to abuses of power. More specifically, job and financial insecurity, minority status, social isolation, a focus on the body and physicality, and a culture of masculinity may make female coaches particularly vulnerable to experiences of harassment and bullying. The most commonly reported abuses of power experienced by these women were gender abuses, homophobia, and social harassment and bullying.

The study is limited by the small number of female participants and the retrospective nature of the data. Future research would benefit from exploring the experiences of harassment and bullying of other traditionally marginalized groups in coaching. Ideally, the data would be collected prospectively as coaches move into and through the coaching ranks. Future studies should attempt to elucidate the different forms of harassment and bullying experienced as well as the intersection of these experiences. It is unclear whether sexual harassment, homophobia, and social exclusion are similar or fundamentally different forms of oppression. Furthermore, these data were obtained from coaches who "endured" the system to become head coaches. The results of this study beg the question of whether experiences of harassment and bullying contribute to attrition of women from coaching or their reluctance to enter the profession entirely. There is significant work yet to be undertaken to better understand and enhance women's experiences in the coaching profession.

It should be acknowledged that the snowball sampling used to recruit participants in this study may have led to a biased sample as each participant was asked to suggest other coaches who may be able to speak to experiences of harassment and bullying. The findings should therefore be interpreted as indicating that such experiences exist for female coaches, but should not be generalized to suggest prevalence rates.

REFERENCES

Acker, J. (1990). Hierarchies, jobs, bodies: A theory of gendered organizations. *Gender and Society, 4*(2), 139–158.

Berdahl, J. (2007). Harassment based on sex: Protecting social status in the context of gender hierarchy. *Academy of Management Review, 32*(2), 641–658.

Brackenridge, C. (2001). *Spoilsports: Understanding and preventing sexual exploitation in sport.* London: Routledge.

Canadian Association for the Advancement of Women and Sport and Physical Activity. (1994). *Harassment in sport.* Ottawa: Rachel Corbett.

Chamberlain, L., Crowley, M., Tope, D., & Hodson, R. (2008). Sexual harassment in organizational context. *Work and Occupations, 35*(3), 262–295.

Coaching Association of Canada. (2002). Facts and stats. Retrieved from http://www.coach.ca/eng/WOMEN/stats/faqs.cfm#3

Coakley, J., & Donnelly, P. (2003). *Sports in society.* Toronto: McGraw Hill.

Demers, G. (2004). Why female athletes decide to become coaches—or not. *Canadian Journal for Women in Coaching, 4*(5). Retrieved from http://www.coach.ca/e/journal/july2004/index.htm

Fasting, K., Brackenridge, C., & Sungot-Borgen, J. (2004). Prevalence of sexual harassment among Norwegian female elite athletes in relation to sport type. *International Review for the Sociology of Sport, 39,* 373–386.

Ferrington, D. (1993). Understanding and preventing bullying. In Tonry, M. (Ed.). *Crime and justice: A review of research, 17,* 381–458. Chicago: University of Chicago Press.

Gutek, B., Cohen, A., & Konrad, A. (1990). Predicting social-sexual behavior at work: A contact hypothesis. *Academy of Management Journal, 33*(3), 560–577.

Hall, A.M. (1996). *Feminism and sporting bodies: Essays on theory and practice.* Champaign, IL: Human Kinetics.

Hanson, S.L., & Kraus, R.S. (1999). Women in male domains: Sport and science. *Sociology of Sport Journal, 16*(2), 92–110.

Hearn, J., & Parkin, W. (2001). *Gender, sexuality and violence in organizations: The unspoken forces of organizational violations.* London: Sage.

Heide, J., & Miner, A. (1992). The shadow of the future: Effects of anticipated interaction and frequency of contact on buyer-seller cooperation. *Academy of Management Journal, 35,* 265–291.

Hinkle, S. (2005). *Cognitive dissonance in athletic hazing: The roles of commitment and athletic identity.* Unpublished dissertation. University of Northern Colorado. Greeley, Colorado.

Hoel, H., & Cooper, C. (2001). Origins of bullying: Theoretical frameworks for explaining workplace bullying. In Tehrani, N. (Ed.). *Building a culture of respect: Managing bullying at work.* London: Taylor and Francis.

Hoel, H., & Salin, D. (2003). Organisational antecedents of workplace bullying. In Einarsen, S. et al. (Eds.). *Bullying and emotional abuse in the workplace: International perspectives in research and practice.* London: Taylor and Francis.

Holman, M. (1995). *Female and male athletes' accounts and meanings of sexual harassment in Canadian interuniversity athletics.* Unpublished doctoral thesis. University of Windsor. Ontario.

International Olympic Committee. (2007). Adoption of consensus statement on sexual harassment and abuse in sport. Lausanne, Switzerland.

Jacoby, S. (2004). *Employing bureaucracy: Managers, unions and the transformation of work in the twentieth century.* Mahwah, NJ: Lawrence-Erlbaum.

Keashly, L., & Jagatic, K. (2003). By any other name: American perspectives on workplace bullying. In Einarsen, S. et al. (Eds.). *Bullying and emotional abuse in the workplace: International perspectives in research and practice.* London: Taylor and Francis.

Kerr, G., Marshall, D., Sharp, D.-M., & Stirling, A. (2006). *Women in coaching: A descriptive study.* Ottawa: Coaching Association of Canada.

Kirby, S., & Greaves, L. (1996). Foul play: Sexual harassment in sport. Paper presented at the Pre-Olympic Scientific Congress. Dallas, Texas, July 11-15.

Konik, J., & Cortina, L. (2008). Policing gender at work: Intersections of harassment based on sex and sexuality. *Social Justice Research, 21,* 313-337.

LeDrew, J., & Zimmerman, C. (1994). Moving towards an acceptance of females in coaching. *Physical Educator, 51*(1), 6-13.

Lopez, S., Hodson, R., & Roscigno, V. (2009). Power, status and abuse at work: General and sexual harassment compared. *Sociological Quarterly, 50*(1), 3-27.

Marshall, D. (2001). Developing the next generation of women coaches. *Canadian Journal for Women in Coaching, 1*(4). Retrieved from http://www.coach.ca/e/journal/mar2001/index.htm

McGlone, C. (2005). *Hazing in N.C.A.A. Division 1 women's athletics: An exploratory analysis.* Unpublished dissertation. University of New Mexico. Albuquerque, New Mexico.

McKay, J. (1999). Gender and organizational power in Canadian sport. In White, P., & Young, K. (Eds.). *Sport and gender in Canada.* Don Mills: Oxford University Press.

Mercier, R., & Werthner, P. (2001). Changing the androcentric world of sports. *Canadian Journal for Women in Coaching, 1*(6). Retrieved from http://www.coach.ca/e/journal/july2001/index.htm

Pronger, B. (2005). Sport and masculinity: The estrangement of gay men. In Eitzen, D.S. (Ed.). *Sport in contemporary society.* London: Boulder.

Ragins, B., & Scandura, T. (1995). Antecedents and work-related correlates of reported sexual harassment: An empirical investigation of competing hypotheses. *Sex Roles, 32*(7-8), 429-455.

Rayner, C., Hoel, H., & Cooper, C. (2002). *Workplace bullying.* London: Taylor and Francis.

Salin, D. (2003). Ways of explaining workplace bullying: A review of enabling, motivating and precipitating structures and processes in the work environment. *Human Relations, 56*(10), 1213–1232.

Shogan, D. (1999). *The making of high performance athletes: Discipline, diversity and ethics.* Toronto: University of Toronto Press.

Skarlicki, D., & Kulik, C. (2005). Third-party reactions to employee (mis)treatment: A justice perspective. *Research in Organizational Behavior, 26,* 183–226.

Stirling, A. (2008). Definition and constituents of maltreatment in sport: Establishing a conceptual framework for research practitioners. *British Journal of Sports Medicine,* November 21.

Tsui, A., & Gutek, B. (1999). *Demographic differences in organizations: Current research and future directions.* New York: Lexington.

Uggen, C., & Blackstone, A. (2004). Sexual harassment as a gendered expression of power. *American Sociological Review, 69,* 64–92.

Volkwein, K. (1996). Sexual harassment in sport: Perceptions and experiences of female student-athletes. Paper presented at the Pre-Olympic Scientific Congress. Dallas, Texas, July 11–15.

Welsh, S. (1999). Gender and sexual harassment. *Annual Review of Sociology, 25,* 169–190.

Zapf, D., Einarsen, S., Hoel, H., & Vartia, M. (2003). Empirical findings on bullying in the workplace. In Einarsen, S. et al. (Eds.). *Bullying and emotional abuse in the workplace: International perspectives in research and practice.* London: Taylor and Francis.

HOMOPHOBIA IN SPORT—
FACT OF LIFE, TABOO SUBJECT

Guylaine Demers

FOUR

Introduction

Much is whispered; little is said outright. Behind the silence are many stories of sadness, shame, secrecy, and stigma. Frank and factual, this chapter is a long-overdue assessment of a situation that should and must be discussed if our sport world is ever to become an environment that welcomes everyone, regardless of race, colour, creed, or sexual orientation. Pulling no punches, Guylaine Demers writes of the reality she calls "the wall of silence." She tells us what academic literature has to say on the subject, and then brings it to life with moving commentary by gay and lesbian athletes and coaches. Finally, she proposes common-sense, practical solutions that could erase homophobia from sport—not overnight, of course, but this discussion is an essential first step.

We are proud to be a forum for putting homophobia squarely where it belongs—out of the closet and into the open. It is our hope that this chapter achieves the author's goal of helping to create "welcoming sport environments for all homosexual athletes and coaches." It is far too important an issue to be ignored.

Preamble

To begin, we need to have a common understanding of what the word "homophobia" means. The *Canadian Oxford Dictionary* defines it as "a hatred or fear of homosexuals or homosexuality." Thus, the title of this chapter suggests that the sport world is not a particularly welcoming place for homosexuals. In my view, not only are they unwelcome, but people also ignore the facts, taking the easy way out by pretending that there are no homosexuals in sport. This is not the case.

Lesbian, gay, bisexual, transsexual, and two-spirited[1] (LGBTT) rights regularly make the news in Canada. In the world of sport, however, people seem to suffer from tunnel vision—they do not see the issue or recognize that diverse sexualities exist. The subject of homosexuality in sport is clearly taboo, and the deafening silence reflects prejudice against homosexuals, who stay "in the closet" out of fear of reprisals that can take many forms. The purpose is to break down the wall of silence and openly discuss the reality of homosexuals in sport, because it concerns all those involved in the sport community.

Most of my remarks focus on homosexual women, but I devote a section to gay men because some women may coach male athletes. A separate section is necessary because lesbian and gay experiences of sport differ in several respects.

When I agreed to write this chapter, I set myself three goals: review the literature on homophobia in sport to gain a clearer understanding of the issue; relate what I found in the literature to specific cases (experiences of female athletes and coaches); and suggest ways of moving beyond criticism and devising practical solutions. Ultimately, the challenge I have set for myself is to help create welcoming sport environments for all LGBTT athletes and coaches.

Background

Canada enjoys an international reputation as a country that respects human rights, and where every person is entitled to live in peace and security. Recently, Canada asserted its position as a world leader in this area by recognizing the legal rights of homosexuals, including the right to same-sex marriage. However, the openness of Canadian society in general has yet to be embraced by the world of sport. So far, this issue has not had the priority that has been accorded to other equality strands such as gender, disability, or ethnicity. Indeed, Canada has taken huge strides in making sport more inclusive, as shown by the fact that girls, people with a disability, and members of visible minorities are increasingly able to participate in sports. Yet homosexuality remains a taboo subject for the sport community, and lesbians and gays are not always welcome. In a review of sexual orientation in sport, Brackenridge et al. (2008) argue that the process to make the sport context free of discrimination and harassment for LGBTT people has been hampered by two factors: social attitudes and lack of information.

> *Social attitudes have meant that there has been a reluctance even to recognize that sports participation by those whose sexual orientation is anything other than heterosexual can be problematic. Discrimination can run deep: it may be implicit through "heteronormative" attitudes, which view heterosexuality as the "normal" sexual orientation, as well as explicit through homophobia, and does result in self-censorship by LGBTT people.*
>
> *Information gaps are substantial. Whilst non-inclusive attitudes, homophobia and self-censorship are well-documented, they remain anecdotal—we cannot quantify how prevalent they are. We cannot even do the simple analyses—as we can for women, older people, those with a disability or from a minority ethnic background—that would tell us to what extent LGBTT people undertake different levels of sports participation. Such information would underpin the more in-depth understanding that qualitative investigations can provide and also ensure that sexual orientation is given a more prominent place in the sports policy agenda. (p. 7)*

Reprinted with permission from Sportscotland, 2009

This chapter is intended to inform sport stakeholders about what is known about sexual orientation in sport and to draw out implications and practical recommendations. One of my first motivations was concern that sport organizations might not yet be properly equipped to manage issues of diversity in sexual orientation.

Why Be Concerned About Homophobia in Sport?[2]

HOMOPHOBIA AFFECTS EVERY man and every woman, whatever their sexual orientation. The fear of homosexuality is used to frighten both homosexual and heterosexual women away from sport. By implying that women who play sports are lesbian, women may avoid sports entirely thus denying themselves opportunities for positive and healthy experiences. The misunderstanding about sexual orientation can also lead to harassment, uneasiness, anxiety, isolation, and violence. Behaviour and feelings of these kinds create unsafe environments that impede learning, adversely affect friendships, and hurt teams, athletes, and coaches alike. For example, players' locker rooms have often been associated with sexist and homophobic behaviour; female athletes are often called lesbians in an attempt to cast doubts on the validity of their performances and discourage them from competing; lesbian, gay, and bisexual coaches and athletes are victims of harassment and discrimination. The goal in opposing homophobia is to create a sports world into which all women and men are welcomed with open arms, and in which they are protected against all forms of discrimination. A number of studies have shown that gays and lesbians who decide to come out reap such benefits as less stress and anxiety, more social support, and greater self-esteem as a gay or lesbian (Brackenridge et al., 2008; Caudwell, 2004; Griffin, 1998; Iannotta, 2003).

What Does the Literature Tell Us?

BRACKENRIDGE ET AL. (2008) found that the research literature is popu-
lated mainly by studies of lesbians and lesbianism in sport. They argue
that this is no surprise since it was feminism that first addressed
the practice of sexual diversity in sport. There is definitely a lack of
data and evidence. Most of the literature is weighted towards identity
and experience studies. We are missing research to assess the types,
extent, and impact of homophobia on LGBTT athletes, coaches, and
other support roles. This means that to this day it is impossible to get a
clear idea of the extent and scope of the problem.

That being said, there can be no doubt that the problem exists, that
it is found in all sports, that it is experienced by both male and female
athletes, and that it also affects coaches and sport administrators.
Most authors agree that the proportion of homosexuals in sport must
be at least as high as the proportion generally attributed to society as
a whole, which is one in every ten people. The vast majority of studies
on homophobia have been small scale, which is understandable when
you consider that it is a taboo subject. The results pertain to just one
team or a small number of athletes or coaches. However, if we look at
the studies as a whole, we soon realize that the experiences reported
in them have many similarities. Although we cannot quantify homophobia in Canadian sport, we can describe it in some detail, and use
the information as a springboard for devising some potential measures
to help eradicate the problem.

Themes Identified

MY REVIEW OF A NUMBER of books and articles on homophobia in
sport enabled me to identify a range of themes as explained in Figure 1.

First, the studies fall into two groups: those conducted in the education sector, and those conducted in an organized sport context. The
first group includes studies on homosexual teachers and students as
victims of homophobia, and on the role of leaders in the education

FIGURE 1

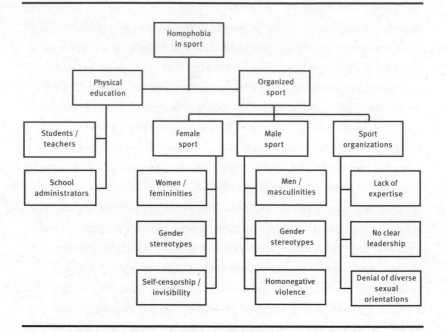

system in combatting homophobia. In the second group, there is a major difference between studies on female sport and studies on male sport, and most of them focus on athletes and teammates, with only a small proportion dealing with homosexual coaches. Finally, very few studies focus on the role of sport organizations in combatting homophobia.

Organized Sport for Women: The Athletes' Situation

IN WOMEN'S SPORTS, the words "female athlete" and "lesbian" are often uttered in the same breath (Peper, 1994). Researchers attribute this to the process of socialization of girls, which even today perpetuates the cult of female fragility and delicateness. It is not considered normal for a girl to exhibit athletic qualities, such as strength, at a high level. When a girl does exhibit such qualities, she is immediately labelled as not feminine, and suspicions arise about her sexual orientation. By definition, sport and sporting attributes are a male preserve. A number of studies have shown that the source of homophobia in women's sports is the desire to discredit performances by female athletes and discourage them from participating in sports.

This perspective on athleticism is one of the major differences between homophobia as experienced by women and homophobia as experienced by men. A female athlete exhibiting several athletic qualities, such as strong physical abilities, is often automatically labelled a lesbian. It follows that female athletes may feel that they have to prove they are not lesbians. As a result, many of them lend considerable importance to their physical appearance in asserting their femininity and, by extension, their heterosexuality by using make-up and wearing "feminine" clothing (Hargreaves, 2000). Many girls and young women drop sports because they do not want to be branded as lesbians.

Another difference between male and female homophobia is the greater openness of women toward lesbian team members. Lesbians who are open about their sexual orientation to other team members are well accepted most of the time. Some studies show that female athletes prefer everything to be out in the open and people to be clear about their sexual orientation. As a result, the new generation of heterosexual women on a team no longer fear that they will be labelled as lesbians for practising their sport. On that note, Brackenridge et al. (2008) states that young people "often express more enlightened attitudes to diversity than older generations." In their 2002 study, Forbes, Lathrop, and Stevens also found that female athletes competing in team sports self-reported a relatively high degree of personal comfort with lesbians as their teammates. Because of this spirit of openness, lesbians can talk about their partners just as their heterosexual teammates talk about theirs. These statements do have to be qualified, however. In fact, one explanation offered by researchers in the field of gay and lesbians studies points to "the phenomenon of external and internal homonegativism—namely, the years of socialization in which homonegativism is tolerated and homonegative practices are common and often not punished lead to desensitization and denial of the problem" (Lenskyj, 1999). There is some evidence that some changes are happening, but it is far too early to say that homophobia in women's sport is behind us. In fact, some studies reported that team members accept lesbians coming out as long as the information stays within the four walls of the locker room. They insist on this in order to protect the team's image and reputation (Griffin, 1998). Some researchers also report that teammates react in a variety of different ways when a lesbian comes out: some refuse to share a room with a lesbian on a road trip; others feel uncomfortable changing in the locker room (Fusco, 1998). Hargreaves (2000) reported the following examples of abusive remarks, from competitors and from spectators, to a predominantly lesbian soccer team in the United Kingdom: "You're disgusting; Perverted sluts; Weirdos; Fags; Black dyke, Black dyke, Black dyke; What's she like in bed, then?; Go on, tackle, get at her—that's what she wants" (p. 138). Clearly, homophobic and heterosexist attitudes are still prevalent in women's sport. More research is definitely needed in regard to the many different dimensions of sport. Attitudes might differ depending on team versus individual sports, or in elite versus recreational contexts.

The following are some common findings and conclusions of a number of authors.

- Many coaches, sport activity co-ordinators, and parents use their own fear of homosexuality and unfair stereotypes of female athletes to dissuade girls from participating in sports.

- Since the early 1980s, the media has more frequently discussed the association between lesbianism and sport. Every two or three years, another lesbian story briefly grabs public attention and then fades away—the case of tennis player Amélie Mauresmo is a good example. Many people, including journalists, made veiled references to her sexual orientation, so she decided to be proactive and stated publicly that she was a lesbian. At the same time, she made it clear that being a lesbian was part of her private life and had nothing to do with her status as a professional tennis player. She came out primarily to quash all the rumours.

- Sport organizations avoid talking about lesbian participation in their sport because it could affect public relations, sponsorships, recruitment, and the image of women in the sport.
- The old association between women's sports and lesbianism puts many women on the defensive about showing their athletic prowess. They put a great deal of energy into ensuring that they are perceived to be heterosexual. This sensitivity to "lesbian" as a negative label creates a climate of hostility, causing many lesbian athletes and coaches to hide their sexual orientation so that they can continue to participate in their sport.
- The most revealing picture of homophobia in women's sports was painted by Pat Griffin in her book, *Strong Women, Deep Closets* (1998). The very title highlights the contradiction between the fact that some women are strong, talented athletes, yet they feel they have to conceal details about their love life and personal life in order to stay in women's sports.
- The survival strategies used first and foremost by lesbian athletes and coaches are to "live with their secret" and to "be as invisible as possible." The need to protect themselves in this way is an integral part of the history of lesbians in sport.
- One of the most effective ways of controlling women's access to the world of sport is to question the femininity and heterosexuality of female athletes. This forces them to prove their heterosexuality constantly.

Organized Sport for Men: The Athletes' Situation

IN THE CASE OF MEN, the issue of homophobia in sport revolves around the social role assigned to men in North American society. It is considered perfectly normal and desirable for a boy to play several sports. In contrast, suspicions are raised when a boy shows no interest in sport. Playing sports is considered part of the normal process of development from boyhood to adulthood. In fact, boys are socialized to become male by avoiding all references to femaleness and homosexuality. Curry (2001) cogently explains the process: "The reasoning may be seen as follows: (a) "real men" are defined by what they are not (women and homosexual); (b) it is useful to maintain a separation from femaleness or gayness so as not to be identified as such; (c) expression of dislike for femaleness or homosexuality demonstrates to oneself and others that one is separate from it and therefore must be masculine" (p. 67).

Whereas a girl is labelled a "lesbian" if she shows fine athletic qualities, a boy will be considered "one of the guys" if he has all the attributes of an athlete and performs at a high level. A male athlete is automatically considered heterosexual because sport enables him to define himself as a man.

Furthermore, boys' participation in several sports is associated with the development of their manliness, competitive spirit, and strength of character; in short, with their masculinity. In such an environment, many gays with the requisite athletic abilities can belong to a sport team without giving away their sexual orientation.

Another distinguishing characteristic of male sport team locker rooms is the language used in them. A number of studies draw attention to the extremely homophobic and misogynistic statements made by male athletes and coaches (Curry, 1991; Lajeunesse, 2009). It is not surprising that, in such circumstances, gays try to remain invisible.

Male athletes are hostile to the presence of gay athletes among them, and gays who come out become the victims of considerable violence and rejection. Violence is another factor that sets the male sports context apart from the female sports context (Pronger, 2000).

Another common finding relates to "male bonding" on sports teams. Sport gives many men an opportunity to experiment with homoeroticism (Lajeunesse, 2009). Life in the locker room enables them to have physical contact with other men such as slaps on the buttocks, hugging, and kissing on the cheeks in a context where such behaviour is totally acceptable. The surprising fact is none of the men on the team associate the behaviour with homosexuality. At the same time, adopting the same behaviour outside the locker room would trigger the "gay" label immediately.

Here are some common findings and conclusions of a number of authors for men's sports.

- Gay athletes are terrified by the prospect of coming out of the closet because of the potential consequences—rejection by their coaches or negative reactions on the part of teammates. ("Will they think I'm going to try to seduce them?")
- In an attempt to deny their homosexuality completely, some gays will become extremely violent toward gays and lesbians, particularly during their teenage years.
- Homophobia is part and parcel of male sports, because to be "one of the guys" is, by definition, to be homophobic.
- Team sports give boys and adult men an opportunity to engage in homosexual behaviour without being perceived as gay.

Organized Sport for Women: The Coaches' Situation

AS WE HAVE SEEN, THE PRACTICE of labelling female athletes—especially those who demonstrate great athletic abilities—as butch, dykes, lesbians, freaks, or sickos still occurs in the Canadian sport context. Female coaches are not exempt, but unlike female athletes who are labelled lesbian because of their great athletic abilities, female coaches become suspect when they don't have a male partner. Indeed, the headline of this section could have been: Sexually suspect—a woman, a coach, and single. There is huge pressure on female coaches to conform to heterosexual norms and pass as heterosexuals. According to Griffin (cited by Hargreaves, 2000), "Much of the prejudice and discrimination against lesbians in sport arises from the fear that they are predators who will seduce and corrupt girls and young women which...taps into the deepest fears of parents and heterosexual athletes and coaches" (p. 138). So, if you are a coach, married, and, as a bonus, a mom, you are "safe;" safe for yourself, but most importantly, safe for your athletes.

On that note, I had a revealing experience recently. I was giving a lecture on homophobia in sport and had invited a female coach to talk about her supporting role with her lesbian athletes. The first thing she said to the group, before even saying her name, was: "I am not a lesbian." I was speechless and, at first, did not understand the statement. After the class, many students told me they all had thought she was a lesbian and were surprised to hear this was not the case. I asked them why they thought she was a lesbian, and they said it was because she is single and they had never seen her with a man/partner. I asked them: "What about that male coach (I gave them his name)? Do you think he is gay?" Without hesitation, they all said: "NO, he's straight." I asked: "Have you ever seen him with a woman/partner? Is he married?" At that moment, they realized that they were using different norms to judge a female coach's sexual orientation. I now knew why the speaker started her story talking about her sexual orientation. She was well aware that she was not judged on the same criteria as her male counterparts. It is very clear to me that female coaches are double jeopardized: as women, they are not competent in coaching unless proven competent (which is the opposite for male coaches), and if they are single, then they are lesbian without a doubt!

We have seen that as a woman and as a coach, pressure comes from everywhere. If you happen to be a lesbian coach, it is even worse. Lesbian coaches face different impacts on their coaching career. In fact, being a lesbian dramatically limits career options and adversely affects hiring opportunities at the assistant coach and head coach levels. Taking on a coach who has been labelled a lesbian is a major concern for an organization intent on protecting the image of its sport program. Here is a true story from the homophobia workshop developed by the Canadian Association for the Advancement of Women and Sport and Physical Activity (2007):

> A national female coach, who is out to her employer but not to the public, is provided with a male date by her sport organization to accompany her to "formal" functions so that people won't think she is a lesbian.

Another situation female coaches face—lesbian or not—is related to athlete recruitment. Often prospective athletes, their parents, and their current coaches try to find out whether there are any lesbians on the team or among the coaching staff. Insinuating that there are lesbians on opposing teams is a common recruitment tactic. Krane and Barber (2005) found that this practice, called negative recruiting, involves denigrating rival coaches and programs during the recruitment process. Whether true or not, some coaches will state that rival coaches are lesbian or that there are lesbian athletes on their teams. That has happened to me more then once. The other teams' coaches (all male) would approach my athletes in gymnasiums, in bars, anywhere, telling them that I was a lesbian, that they should not play for me, but should play for them. Because I was out to my athletes, they were able to defend themselves, but were traumatized by the experience. Those male coaches were using that "tactic" to undermine my credibility towards my athletes. I was the only female coach in the league, and I was winning. THAT was disturbing.

Homophobic discrimination can wreck sporting careers in concrete ways. Lesbian coaches can fail to secure promotion or get positions. As Hargreaves (2000) stated, "Lesbians who are professional sportswomen have the particular fear of losing their livelihood and their chosen way of life as a direct result of disclosure of their sexual orientation" (p. 139).

There is ample evidence that lesbian coaches have to survive in an inhospitable climate and function in a homonegative environment. Krane and Barber (2005) were able to uncover the complexity of the sport experience for these individuals:

> These coaches [participants in their study] were engaged in implicitly heterosexist and homonegative professional climates. Many unspoken assumptions conspired in this heterosexism and permeated the culture of women's sport, creating a climate of fear, silence, and hypervigilance. This social context...created a complex web that juxtaposed their social identity as "coach" and their social identity as "lesbian" against commanding social norms...The coaches used a number of strategies to remain productive in this setting, such as seeking protection, compartmentalizing their lives, and remaining silent. (p. 79)

No doubt there is a huge need to educate athletes, coaches, and sport administrators about the negative environment that has been created around female coaches, and especially around lesbian coaches.

Organized Sport: The Sport Organizations

WHILE THERE IS A BASIC AWARENESS among sport organizations that there are issues relating to LGBTT people that have to do with participation, discrimination, and homophobia in sport, there is a lack of expertise (and in some cases desire) to do what is required to address them (Brackenridge et al., 2008). The lack of data and evidence is striking, with the result that sport organizations can ignore the problem. As a result, it remains hidden. There is little literature on policy and the management implications of sexual orientation equality in sport. The few studies that have examined the role of sport organizations in combatting homophobia all conclude that it is the responsibility of sport administrators, coaches, and parents to create a safe sport environment for all athletes, whatever their sexual orientation. Still, there is no clear leadership on this issue, and even some in high-level management positions appear to be hesitant to take a stand on policy.

Most of the early initiatives on this issue emanated from the United States with strong leadership from the Women's Sports Foundation. Following that example, anti-homophobia initiatives took place in Canada, Norway, Australia, and more recently in Britain. I found no studies that reported on the evaluation of such initiatives. See the section called "Anti-Homophobia Programs" later in this chapter. It describes two programs (one American and one Australian) and a Canadian workshop that are designed to combat homophobia in sport while targeting stakeholders in the sport community.

Brackenridge et al. (2008) conducted seven interviews from a range of stakeholders within the British sport system. The resulting recommendations for sport policy development can be adapted elsewhere and include

- provision of lifestyle support expertise for talented and elite athletes, focused on coming out, working with LGBTT/heterosexual peers, managing sexual orientation in different cultures, and dealing with homophobia
- practical and policy guidance on assuring inclusive sport for LGBTT people, especially for clubs, governing bodies, and high performance sport organizations
- development and dissemination of advice and guidance materials and systems for sports people dealing with sexual orientation issues
- case studies to illustrate how processes and practices in different sports contexts can be adjusted to include LGBTT sports people, coaches, and other support roles
- development of leadership training about sexual orientation equality and impact assessment guidance, delivered to all sport body CEOs and key public officials working in sport

Real-Life Cases: Athletes' Experiences of Homophobia

IN RESEARCHING THIS CHAPTER, I had the good fortune to meet some lesbian athletes and coaches who were willing to share their stories with me. I am grateful for their openness, spirit of sharing, and the trust they placed in me. I was able to draw on their experiences to illustrate the findings and conclusions of the literature on homophobia in sport with concrete examples. Note that all the women were involved in team sports, and that all insisted on anonymity.

In this section, I tell their stories by focusing on the points they share. Homophobia has changed over the last thirty years or so. I met women who were high performance athletes in the 1980s, others who were performing at a very high level in the 1990s, and some who are currently top-flight university athletes.

The Coming Out of Female Athletes

The interviewees who were competing in the 1980s and 1990s never dared to come out publicly. Just as the findings of the literature show, they were extremely afraid of what their teammates would think of them. A number of times they referred to the fear of rejection, the fear of damaging—or being accused of damaging—team unity and spirit, and the fear of causing teammates to change their attitude toward them by becoming more distant, for example. None of the interviewees who had shared their secret with teammates whom they really trusted had suffered from this selective coming out. This fact confirms the conclusion drawn by researchers that athletes are quite receptive to team members who come out, as long as the information stays within the four walls of the locker room.

One particularly interesting fact that emerged during the interviews was that two athletes came out by confiding in their coaches, not their teammates. They told me that having a female coach was a major factor in their decision to share their secret with that person. They also referred to their coaches' values, and the fact they were centred on respect for the individual. They were, therefore, fairly confident that the coaches would react positively, and they were right in their assumption. The coaches reacted with total respect. Both athletes reiterated how significant and decisive a factor their coaches' reactions were at that moment in their lives. They were able to continue their season with one less weight on their shoulders.

Coming out selectively was a considerable relief for the athletes. They had at last found somebody who would lend an ear as they recounted the highs and lows of their love life. In contrast, staying in the closet is a heavy burden to bear, as the following anecdote illustrates. One of the interviewees told me that, one day, she came to the gymnasium sad and unmotivated—her heart had been broken for the first time. At one point during the training session, she broke down and started crying. She told the team and her coach that "Richard" had left her, when in fact it was Louise. The story speaks volumes about the heavy burden lesbian athletes have to bear when they stay silent about their sexual orientation.

Notwithstanding a few sad stories about women who never dared to come out, the situation facing lesbian athletes has changed. Some athletes who are competing today told me that all their teammates know they are lesbians even though they have never officially announced the fact. It was left unspoken and unsaid, and all members of the team seemed at ease with the situation. None of the interviewees reported any unpleasant or disturbing events in connection with their sexual orientation. Some even told me that teammates joked with them about it, and that their orientation was well accepted. For example, another player would say, "We know you're not interested in bar hopping with us and finding some good-looking guys!" The interviewees told me they did not feel the need to make an official announcement because the other players and the coach were aware of their sexual orientation. They have never broached the issue openly. They feel no pressure from their teammates and are very happy with their love life.

That being said, some lesbians do not dare come out, even though they know other lesbians on their team. I met two such athletes. They told me that they had not yet informed their parents, and they preferred to keep their secret until they felt ready to disclose their sexual orientation.

The Coming Out of Coaches

I met only one coach who is officially "out," and he coaches a male team. He came out at thirty-seven years of age. He had been coaching in the same place for ten years when he decided that he had had enough of all the pretence. Like most homosexual coaches, he had preferred to stay silent for all those years out of fear of his employer's reaction, of athletes refusing to play for him, and of being considered a sexual predator, especially when he was coaching at the youth level. His situation is fully consistent with what is reported in the literature. Coaches believe that coming out will cause more problems and pose more risks than concealing their sexual orientation.

Two female coaches I met have not yet come out to their athletes. One coaches a women's team sport, and the other a mixed individual sport. Both are in long-term relationships. They believe that the athletes harbour suspicions about their orientation, but that they are not at all uncomfortable with it. They have never broached the issue officially with the athletes, and do not feel the need to do so. However, after the interview, it became clearer to them that they might have to assume some responsibility for combatting homophobia in sport. It is my understanding that they are now considering coming out in order to help lesbian athletes feel that they can openly and safely confide in their coach or tell their teammates about their sexual orientation if they so wish.

So What Do We Do Now?

FROM THE OUTSET OF this endeavour, I was determined to propose potential solutions and outline ongoing projects that are achieving positive results. As coaches of athletes who may be gay or lesbian, you need to be aware of how important your role is in combatting homophobia. When an athlete confides in you, your reaction will be a decisive factor in that person's life. It is very difficult to come out if the person in whom the athlete confides reacts negatively, because the consequences may be disastrous. Remember: The suicide rate for homosexual teenagers is ten to twelve times higher than the rate for heterosexual teenagers. Suicide is the leading cause of death among homosexual males aged fourteen to twenty-nine years. So you must take action, and to help you, I have drawn up a short list of practical measures. I also outline two programs designed specifically to eliminate homophobia in sport.

Practical Measures
- Take the time to read and learn about homophobia and homosexuality in general.
- Do not tolerate disparaging remarks about gays and lesbians.
- Use inclusive language: Do not assume that all your athletes are heterosexual.

- Find out about neighbourhood homosexual support groups, peer help groups on campus, telephone help lines for homosexuals, and peer help groups for parents with homosexual children.
- Take your cue from programs such as the Women's Sports Foundation's *It Takes a Team!* (Griffin et al., 2002) to launch awareness-raising activities in your community.
- Make it clear to the people around you that you are open to diversity in all members of your team.
- If you have gay or lesbian friends, ask them how you can help to combat homophobia.

Anti-Homophobia Programs

"Harassment-Free Sport: Guidelines to Address Homophobia and Sexuality Discrimination in Sport" was developed by the Australian Sports Commission (2000). The guidelines include how to stop discrimination, hypothetical situations and solutions, and more.

It Takes a Team! (Griffin et al., 2002) is an exhaustive, well-thought-out program containing a host of ideas that can be put into practice quickly. In my view, it is the best sport-specific, anti-homophobia program. One of the authors is Pat Griffin, the leading expert on homophobia research. I highly recommend her book, *Strong Women, Deep Closets* (1998), which gives a clear and detailed picture of the situation facing lesbians in sport. She also has a website called *Lesbian and Gay Sports*.

The Canadian Association for the Advancement of Women and Sport and Physical Activity has developed a workshop designed especially for Canadian sport organizations called *Seeing the Invisible, Speaking About the Unspoken: Addressing Homophobia in Sport* (2007). The workshop's outcome is to increase awareness and understanding of homophobia so that participants can use their influence to help change the sport environment.

See also the list of Helpful Organizations at the end of this chapter.

Conclusion

IN THE SUMMER OF 2006, Montreal hosted the first World Outgames, an international sporting event for lesbians and gays. I competed in golf. It is hard to describe the emotion I experienced: I was part of something bigger than myself and I belonged...just to be able to take my partner's hand on the golf course without fear of being judged, excluded, or harassed was a totally new experience. For the first time in my life, I was in a prejudice-free space, something that mainstream sport has failed to offer me. That was quite an experience, and I won't forget it for years to come.

From that experience, I realized that I was part of the problem, and part of the solution as well. I totally share Hargreaves' (2000) point of view about our individual role to fight homophobia in sport: "Many lesbian sportswomen live constantly with the tension created between their gayness and their desire for integration, which could be eased if they were courageous enough to come out in mainstream sport in greater numbers, and if more heterosexual sportswomen were prepared to stand up and speak out against heterosexism and homophobia" (p. 173).

Homophobia is not a form of discrimination that will simply go away by virtue of silence. As Lenskyj (1999) observes, "The vicious cycle of invisibility and homophobia in women's sport needs to be interrupted in a number of levels, both individual and institutional, before social change can be affected" (p. 76). Following Lenskyj's thought, it is imperative that sport organizations adjust to new social and legal equalities discourses. As Brackenridge et al. (2008) wrote, "Unless sport is able to reinvent itself and to accommodate and celebrate diversity in sexual orientation, as it has already begun to do with race, (dis)ability and gender, then it will become increasingly irrelevant to many "outsiders" for whom a non-heterosexual sexual orientation is a significant and perhaps defining feature of their identity" (p. 21).

In order to move forward, we definitely need more research. Specifically, we need flexible measures of LGBTT identities and experiences in sport; data on LGBTT participation in all sports roles; qualitative and biographical data about LGBTT people in sport; LGBTT people's own priorities for policy and practice in sport; what counts as good practice for LGBTT people in sports organizations' policy, service delivery, and capacity building; and information on bisexuality in sport (Brackenridge et al., 2008).

So, my final word is straightforward: Everyone has to oppose homophobia and related discrimination in sport. There is no doubt that one of the most effective tools in counteracting homophobia is increased lesbian and gay visibility. Research indicates that, for most people, contact with "out" lesbian and gay people who embrace their sexual identities reduces prejudice (Griffin, 1998). We have to give LGBTT people the chance to come out safely without any fear. I hope you become advocates for gay and lesbian rights, whether you are LGBTT or not. The world of sport is still homophobic, and we need every possible ally to fight against it.

HELPFUL ORGANIZATIONS

Blackstripe
Provides information for and about lesbian, gay, bisexual, and transgendered people of African descent.

Canadian Association for the Advancement of Women and Sport and Physical Activity (CAAWS)
Provides resources and workshops about homophobia and how it affects sport organizations. http://www.caaws.ca

Center for the Study of Sport in Society
A Northeastern University program that offers educational programs to eliminate violence, sexism, racism, and homophobia in sport.

Deaf Queer Resource Center (DQRC)
Provides information and resources about the deaf LGBTT community.

Égale Action
The Quebec association for the advancement of women in sport and physical activity.

Federation of Gay Games
Organizers of an international quadrennial competition and cultural festival for gay athletes. http://www.gaygames.com

Gay and Lesbian Alliance Against Defamation (GLAAD)
Offers training and technical assistance on dealing with the media.
http://www.glaad.org

Gay and Lesbian Athletics Foundation (GLAF)
Promotes recognition, understanding, and respect among all members of the athletics community, regardless of sexual orientation; support and education for a fair and inclusive environment.

Gay and Lesbian International Sport Association (GLISA)
International association advocating for the rights of homosexuals in sport.
http://www.glisa.org

Gay, Lesbian, and Straight Education Network (GLSEN)
Provides education and advocacy that contribute to ending anti-gay bias in schools. http://www.glsen.org

It Takes a Team
Program designed to provide leaders in the sport community with the tools they need to create a safe, welcoming environment for homosexual athletes.
http://www.ittakesateam.org

Lesbian and Gay Sports
Website of Pat Griffin, author, professor, and activist on issues of social justice in sport and education. http://www.lesbianandgaysports.com

Ms. Foundation for Women
Provides various programs, grants, and resources for girls and women.
http://www.msfoundation.org

National Center for Lesbian Rights (NCLR)
The Homophobia in Sport Project provides advice, education, and legal support to coaches, athletes, and sport personnel who feel they are living a negative sport experience because of discrimination or harassment on the basis of sexual orientation. http://www.nclrights.org

National Collegiate Athletic Association (NCAA)
Provides various educational and outreach programs for student-athletes and institutional staff. http://www.ncaa.org

OutSports
A website for gay male sports fans and athletes. http://www.outsports.com

Parents, Families, and Friends of Lesbians and Gays (PFLAG)
Provides support, education, and advocacy for parents, siblings, and friends, and for LGBTT youth and adults. http://www.pflag.org

Positive Space Campaign
A campaign at Canadian universities and colleges designed to create campuses free of discrimination based on sexual orientation.

Safe Schools Coalition
A public/private partnership in support of lesbian, gay, bisexual, and transgender youth, with an outstanding collection of resources.

Safe Schools Program for Gay and Lesbian Students

A state-wide program of the Massachusetts Department of Education offering training and technical assistance to public schools.

Tucker Center for Research on Girls and Women in Sport

A University of Minnesota research centre that produces videos and educational resources. http://www.cehd.umn.edu/tuckercenter

Women's Sports Foundation

Grant programs and resources on topics and issues in women's sports, including homophobia. http://www.womenssportsfoundation.org

NOTES

1. The term "two-spirited" derives from a Native tradition and describes people who display characteristics of both genders. It is used today in reference to LGBTT persons of Native origin.

2. Based on the introduction to *It Takes a Team!* (Griffin et al., 2002), and on the Canadian Association for the Advancement of Women and Sport and Physical Activity's position paper on homophobia (2007).

REFERENCES

Australian Sports Commission. (2000). Harassment-free sport: Guidelines to address homophobia and sexuality discrimination in sport. Retrieved from http://www.ausport.gov.au/ethics/docs/homo_sexuality.pdf

Brackenridge, C., Alldred, P., Jarvis, A., Maddocks, K., & Rivers, I. (2008). *A review of sexual orientation in sport.* Edinburgh: Sportscotland.

Canadian Association for the Advancement of Women and Sport and Physical Activity. (2007). Seeing the invisible, speaking about the unspoken: Addressing homophobia in sport. Workshop for sport organizations. Retrieved from http://www.caaws.ca

Caudwell, J. (2004). Out on the field: Women's experiences of gender and sexuality in football. In Wagg, S. (Ed.). *British football and social exclusion.* London: Routledge.

Curry, T.J. (2001). Reply to "A conversation (re)analysis of fraternal bonding in the locker room." *Sociology of Sport Journal, 18*(3), 339–344.

Curry, T.J. (1991). Fraternal bonding in the locker room: Pro-feminist analysis of talk about competition and winning. *Sociology of Sport Journal,* (8), 119–135.

Forbes, S.L., Lathrop, A.H., & Stevens, D.E. (2002). A pervasive silence: Lesbophobia and team cohesion in sport. *Canadian Woman Studies, 21*(3), 32–39.

Fusco, C. (1998). Lesbians and locker rooms: The subjective experiences of lesbians in sport. In Rail, G. (Ed.). *Sport and postmodern times.* Albany: State University of New York Press.

Griffin, P., Perrotti, J., Priest, L., & Muska, M. (2002). *It takes a team! Making sports safe for lesbian, gay, bisexual, and transgender athletes and coaches.* An education kit for athletes, coaches, and athletic directors. New York: Women's Sports Foundation. Retrieved from http://www.ittakesateam.org

Griffin, P. (1998). *Strong women, deep closets: Lesbians and homophobia in sport.* Champaign, IL: Human Kinetics.

Hargreaves, J. (2000). *Heroines of sport: The politics of difference and identity.* London: Routledge.

Homophobia, *n.* (2004). *Canadian Oxford dictionary.* Toronto: Oxford University Press.

Iannotta, J.G. (2003). Sexuality and resistance: Identity, homophobia and social justice in women's athletics. Doctoral thesis, Michigan State University. UMI number: 3092749.

Krane, V., & Barber, H. (2005). Identity tensions in lesbian intercollegiate coaches. *Research Quarterly for Exercise and Sport, 76*(1), 67–81.

Lajeunesse, S.L. (2009). *L'épreuve de la masculinité: Sport, rituels et homophobie.* Le Triadou, France: H & O Éditions.

Lenskyj, H.J. (1999). Women, sport and sexualities: Breaking the silences. In White, P., & Young, K. (Eds.) *Sport and gender in Canada.* Toronto: Oxford University Press.

Peper, K. (1994). Female athlete = lesbian: A myth constructed from gender role expectations and lesbiphobia. In Ringer, R.J. (Ed.). *Queer words, queer images: Communication and construction of homosexuality.* New York: New York University Press.

Pronger, B. (2000). Homosexuality and sport: Who's winning? In McKay, J. et al. (Eds.). *Masculinities, gender relations and sport.* London: Sage.

Athletics coach Carla Nicholls works on the start technique of 400-metres hurdler Cassie Hawrysh at the University of Regina track.

PHOTO: JANZ STEIN

PART TWO

Skills

Basketball coach Sandy Chambers makes her point in no uncertain terms.

PHOTO: 2009 CANADA GAMES—F. SCOTT GRANT

COMMUNICATING WITH CLARITY: GUIDELINES TO HELP FEMALE COACHES SUCCEED

Penny Werthner and Shaunna Taylor

FIVE

Introduction

Because so many female coaches place a high value on communication, Penny Werthner and Shaunna Taylor describe their observations and recommendations for the connection between skillful communication and successful coaching. They spell out the specific skills of an effective communicator, and explain how these skills can be developed and applied.

Points covered include handling contentious issues; increasing your confidence, professionalism, and effectiveness; modelling the behaviours you want to see in your athletes and colleagues; developing good listening habits; speaking with clarity; giving and receiving criticism; and resolving conflicts effectively.

MANY LEADING COACHES SAY their ability to communicate skillfully is key to their success. They believe the quality and effectiveness of their communication is directly linked to building mutually respectful relationships with their athletes and their colleagues.

What are the specific skills that enable you to become an effective communicator? How do you go about using and sharing these skills with your athletes, and those you work alongside? Why is it crucial for you, as a coach, to be able to communicate well? Simply stated, skillful communication is crucial because so much of what you do involves providing information to your athletes, your head coach or assistant coaches, your club, and your provincial or national sport organization, as well as exchanging information with a variety of individuals or groups, such as sport scientists. Effective communication has been defined as those interactions between team members that result in enhanced team attributes and/or functioning. Further to this, if there is no communication, there is no team, simply a set of individuals (Sullivan & Feltz, 2003; Sullivan & Gee, 2007).

As the coach, you direct daily practices or training sessions with your athletes. You intervene during those practices to give feedback to your athletes in the form of corrections, encouragement, and changes in training direction. You listen to questions or comments from your athletes or your head or assistant coaches in order to make changes in a training session, or to the yearly training and competitive plan. You meet with your athletes to discuss issues and concerns and, by doing so, build a cohesive team. You work closely with your club executive and/or your sport association to clarify your job description and roles and responsibilities, and to make plans for the future. All of this, and much more that you do as a coach, involves communication.

Now that we understand why it is important and relevant to communicate effectively, we can begin to look at the specific skill sets you need to become an effective communicator, and how to develop and use those skills in working with athletes and colleagues.

Effective Communication Skills

- Be Assertive
- Communicate Non-Verbally
- Know How to Listen Well

- Speak Clearly and Concisely
- Give Constructive Feedback
- Be Able to Receive Criticism
- Choose the Right Words
- Resolve Conflict Effectively

Be Assertive

IN THINKING ABOUT GOOD communication, it is important to understand the differences between being assertive and being aggressive or passive. Skillful communication is about two individuals or groups who are engaged in a discussion, being able to remain assertive. The danger, particularly when something contentious or difficult is being discussed, is that one of the individuals—you or your athlete or colleague—falls into the trap of becoming either aggressive or passive.

Certain markers tend to be characteristic of female language patterns. Since the 1970s, communication researchers have looked at ways that women can learn to use powerful versus powerless verbal and non-verbal communication (Bradac & Street, 1990; Erickson et al., 1978; Lakoff, 1975). In other words, are you using your words and actions to be assertive rather than passive?

What does it mean to be assertive rather than aggressive or passive? According to *Merriam Webster's Online Dictionary*, to assert means to state positively, to affirm. The definition for aggression includes "a disposition to dominate," and "marked by combative readiness." Passive means "tending not to take an active or dominant part"; subjected to or affected by the action of another. Being assertive in communicating with your athletes means you value and care for each one of them as an individual. (Over the years, many athletes have said that they wish their coach had treated them as an individual, and not always as just a part of the team.) Being assertive means you treat your athletes, their parents, and your colleagues with respect, even when you are not in agreement.

Being assertive means that you take action and initiate meetings and discussions, rather than waiting for something to happen and reacting to it. It means speaking with confidence and conviction, which will, in turn, increase the likelihood of increased confidence in your athletes and staff (Sparks & Areni, 2002). Being assertive means you stand up for yourself and speak about your beliefs and vision for the team, yet are willing to listen to what your athletes have to say. After listening well, you are able, in a clear and direct manner, to explain how the team will be run, and on what your decisions will be based. You are able to do this without attacking or belittling an athlete or colleague who may question a decision. These are key practices for leaders of teams or groups who provide clear and effective leadership (Sparks et al., 1998).

These examples illustrate how to assert yourself, which, in turn, increases your confidence, your professionalism, and your ability to deal effectively with the many issues you face as a coach. Most importantly, you will be able to develop athletes and colleagues who are comfortable coming to talk with you about their suggestions, thoughts, and concerns. And with that information, you are able to make better decisions with an athlete or a colleague, and for your team as a whole.

Communicate Non-Verbally

YOU WANT YOUR ATHLETES to come to practice every day, ready to work and keen to be there. You can encourage this kind of behaviour by modelling it yourself, and often in a non-verbal way. How you present yourself in your coaching environment has great potential to influence your athletes and the coaches you work with (Timm & Schroeder, 2000). Look at each of your colleagues and athletes when you arrive for a training session. Smile. Ask a few questions about how they are. Wait for the answers. These are effective ways to set the tone for the daily practice. You will be effectively modelling the very behaviours you want your athletes to exhibit at every session—upbeat, ready to practice, and with complete concentration on the training. If you notice one of your athletes displaying poor non-verbal behaviour, such as rolling her eyes, not looking at you when you are addressing the team, or talking while you are talking, you will need to address it or it will become destructive to the team. Look at the examples in the section on speaking clearly and concisely to see how to do that well.

Know How to Listen Well

ONE OF THE MORE DIFFICULT and least understood skills of effective communication is the ability to listen well to what is being said by another individual or group. In fact, when you are listening well, you listen to understand what the other person is thinking or feeling, rather than focusing on your response. One of the most powerful ways to enhance understanding is to stop talking! And you have to remember that understanding what someone says does not necessarily mean agreement. To listen effectively, you need to permit yourself to listen to who is speaking—whether it is one of your athletes, a parent, your club president, or your head coach—to hear clearly what they are saying, before you respond or even begin to think about how to resolve a problem (Bruner, 2008; Elman, 2001).

To be an effective communicator means to give and receive information effectively and constructively. Effective listeners are active listeners, and they use empathy to their advantage: the more you try to understand where your communication partners are coming from, the better you can match and effectively address their messages with your own. The ultimate success of a team might depend on the quality of the conversation and the listening that everyone engages in (Gray & Robertson, 2005).

Why is it so important for a coach to use this skill of listening? First of all, so much conflict between individuals or groups results because of incorrect assumptions—and incorrect assumptions often happen because we are eager to respond and solve rather than listen first. "Oh, I thought the practice was at three o'clock." "I thought we were practicing this play." "I thought you meant..." "I thought my job was to..."

These are examples of what can happen when one does not listen well—whether it is you not listening to your athletes, or your athletes not listening to you. When you are able to listen first to what the head coach or an athlete is saying, and then clarify those thoughts, comments, or concerns with an appropriate question or two, there is a lot less misunderstanding and a great deal less conflict. Effective teaching involves effective understanding while minimizing conflict (Imhoff, 1998).

Second, and equally important, when you listen to your athletes, you are better able to understand what they are thinking and feeling, and you can then make specific and effective corrections to a training session or create a better plan for a future competition. You certainly cannot do this well if you are guessing what an athlete is thinking. Listening is one of the most important ways groups learn to relate to one another, and good listening can maintain and build productive relationships (Halone, 2001; Hughes, 2002).

Third, when you regularly allow your athletes to express their thoughts and concerns, they begin to take responsibility for their actions and think for themselves. Taking personal responsibility and becoming, to a degree, an independent thinker is what they need to be doing, and exactly what you need them to be capable of doing on the field or track or in the pool, in training, and particularly during competition. After all, it is the athletes who ultimately have to get out there and run the race or play the game.

Habits of Good Listening

- Remind yourself that you, your athletes, and the other coaches are all trying to accomplish the same goal: to perform well at the upcoming trials, the provincial, national, or world championships, or the Olympic Games.
- Look at who is speaking to you, and focus on what they are saying, really listening to what they are saying, not immediately coming up with a response. You will get to a solution; you need to make sure first that you are solving the right issue.
- Ask questions to ensure you understand the issue (and in the case of your athletes, to help them discover their own solutions).

- If an athlete or parent is emotional, listen first, then acknowledge her feelings, and then try to guide her in finding a solution. (If the emotions are directed toward you, in the form of an attack, you need to be assertive and set a time to talk when things are calmer.)
- Do your best to be empathetic and non-judgemental. You may not agree with what is being said. You simply need to ensure that you are clear on what the issues or problems are before making any decisions.

An important note: Allowing yourself to listen to your athletes does not mean you then allow them to make all the decisions. What it does mean is that when you are able to listen well, you are able to make an informed decision. You can decide if a change is warranted, and if it is not, then you can clearly explain your reasoning.

Speak Clearly and Concisely

TWO SIGNIFICANT ASPECTS of your job are giving direction and instruction to your athletes during training sessions and competition, and dealing with issues or conflicts as they arise. In both situations, you must speak clearly and concisely. However, it is more difficult to be clear and concise when there are problems.

For example, one of your athletes is late for training three days in a row, and you are beginning to feel angry. What is the best way to deal with such behaviour?

- Name the behaviour. "You have been late three days in a row."
- Name what you are feeling. "I'm quite upset."
- Say what you need. "I need to talk with you about this because we cannot get the practice done effectively when you are a half hour late."

Here's another example. Your club executive has not completed your job evaluation on the agreed-upon date.

- Name the subject. "I wanted to talk with you about my coaching evaluation."
- Name what you are feeling. "I'm feeling frustrated."
- Say what you need. "I would like us to sit down and talk about how and when this evaluation will be done."

"I" messages such as these are clear, concise, and come from what you feel and what you need. Name the issue in an even tone of voice, with no judgement or sarcasm attached. Name the emotion you are experiencing, but stop there. Do not go on with all the concurrent feelings you might be having. State what you need, because only you know what that is.

The guiding assumption here is that your goal is to resolve the issue or conflict effectively. To do that, the other person needs to listen to you, and they can do this only if you do not put them on the defensive. (When you are on the defensive, you are busy thinking up excuses for your behaviour, rather than listening to what is being said and trying to come up with a solution.) Speaking clearly and concisely with an "I" message allows you to choose precise, truthful, and powerful language over defensive and powerless language, for best results (Bradac & Street, 1990; Erickson et al., 1978; Lakoff, 1975).

Give Constructive Feedback

YOUR COACHING JOB, SIMPLY STATED, is to help each athlete to become increasingly better at executing the speed, skills, or game strategies of your sport. As a result, you are constantly feeding back information to your athletes. What is important to understand in terms of feedback is that almost every athlete needs a "healthy" balance of critique-to-praise ratio. What that healthy ratio is varies from athlete to athlete, and varies according to the proximity to a competition.

Giving critical feedback has been cited as one of the least favourite tasks by leaders in the business world, yet in the same breath it is also cited as being essential to success (Latting, 1992; Lizzio et al., 2008). The key is for coaches and leaders of all types of teams (in sport, business, and education) to ensure that their feedback is constructive.

It seems that what helps an athlete most is to state the problem clearly. If, for example, it is the execution of a specific skill, it helps to break the skill down into manageable chunks, both by using words and by executing the technique or tactic physically. If the athlete is experienced, ask her to think about what would work well. Certainly, such dialogue in the middle of a practice is not always possible, but when it is, it pays off immeasurably. You end up with a thoughtful, resourceful, and responsible athlete.

Generally speaking, the closer to the competition, the more you need to shift your feedback to what the athlete is doing well, and away from what is not going well. You do this, first of all, because at some point it is too late to fix something. You have to go with what you have until after the competition. Second, and perhaps most importantly, you do this because the level of confidence of most athletes is fragile, and the fragility increases as competition nears. Most athletes will begin to question their readiness, their skills, their ability. This is a natural reaction to stress. A significant part of your job as a coach is to alleviate that stress and reassure each of your athletes or your team that they are well prepared.

Another important note: Shifting your feedback ratio toward "what we are doing well" does not mean that you do not critique. It means you are doing less critiquing close to a competition. Shifting that ratio and being positive means intentionally observing what your athlete or team is doing well, and specifically feeding back that information to them.

Be Able to Receive Criticism

PART OF BECOMING AN EFFECTIVE coach is developing a good working relationship with your athletes and colleagues. Nurturing such relationships is helped immeasurably by a willingness on your part to listen to suggestions or criticism from an athlete, group of athletes, or from colleagues. The ability to receive criticism without getting defensive is a difficult skill to acquire.

One aspect of this skill is not to take the criticism too personally, to step back a bit from the comment (sometimes easier said than done), and to look at it from the perspective of how the information might help the team or help you in your coaching role. When you are being criticized, ask questions for clarification. If an athlete attacks you by saying, "You are always picking on me," or "You're not fair to everyone," ask for an example so that you can understand the actual behaviour you are being accused of exhibiting. You may have been unfair, but perhaps not. You need to ensure you actually did something poorly or unfairly before you take ownership and apologize. It may be appropriate to apologize, and it can be powerful in building your relationship with your athletes, but only if you are at fault.

Choose the Right Words

ACCORDING TO BANDURA (1986, 1997), verbal persuasion is one of the most important determinants of efficacy. The words we choose—using assertive, clear, and precise language—can have a huge impact on how effective our message will be. Communication that is largely task-oriented in high-achieving teams tends to fall into the following categories: orienting, stimulating, and evaluating. Taking time to decide what you want to say—and how you want to say it—may make the difference between getting your point across in a productive way...or not (Hanin, 1992).

I: Sometimes there is a tendency to avoid using "I" because it might appear boastful. It is important to understand that using "I" means that you are taking responsibility for what you say. It allows you to take ownership without putting anyone down.

You: Be cautious about using this word. Saying, "You are always the first to complain" can sound like an accusation. (A clear directive such as "I want you to..." is not usually a problem.)

They: The use of "they" can be an indirect way of speaking. If an athlete says, "They all feel this way" or "They all agreed we should take the day off training," you need to ask, "Who are 'they?'" Is it really the whole team, or just this athlete?

But: When an athlete or colleague says, "Yeah, but...," it almost invariably means she is not listening well and has already made a decision on the issue or problem. Or, at the very least, she is confusing two issues, and you need to help her deal with one at a time.

Always, Never: Seldom is anything "always" or "never." These words take on an emotional emphasis. "You always yell at me." "You never listen to me." These are emotional statements, laden with guilt, that do not encourage good communication.

Should, Ought: These are words that trap, and often signify finger pointing. "You should have known." "I ought to have been better." Athletes' bodies get physically tight when they hear or use these words because they start believing something is not right with them, and they begin to lose self-confidence.

Always pay attention to the words you use. Making the wrong choices may restrict your ability to communicate effectively and skillfully.

Resolve Conflict Effectively

Coaches regularly encounter situations that have the potential to escalate into a conflict. Athletes within your training group or on your team may not like each other. An athlete may not like your way of coaching. You may have difficulty in getting an assistant coach to do his job well. Your vision for the team may be quite different from that of the head coach. Perhaps you have problems with your club executive or the national office. These are just a few examples of the countless potential problems or issues you might face throughout your career as a coach.

The very nature of conflict is an interesting and sometimes misunderstood concept. Conflict is a natural occurrence in our lives, and some degree of conflict is often inevitable whenever two or more individuals come together. It is important to recognize and understand conflict and to seek, first of all, to prevent as much conflict as possible. When conflict occurs, you must work toward resolving it effectively.

Conflict can be constructive when it opens up discussion on issues of importance, when it results in solutions to those issues, and when it increases the involvement of individuals in the discussion. But conflict can be destructive when it begins to take too much energy and diverts focus from more important activities (like training and recovery), destroys an individual's sense of self-confidence, and polarizes a team into two groups (Copeland & Wida, 1996).

How does conflict occur? There are many ways that conflict might begin on your team, or between you and another coach, or between your club and provincial executive. One way that conflict begins relates to information. There is a misunderstanding, a miscommunication, or a lack of information. "I thought we were going to start at nine o'clock." "I meant to tell you I couldn't make it, but I forgot." "I thought the head coach was responsible for the entries." "I didn't know that was part of my job description."

Conflict also occurs over how things are to be done—the methods. If you want to run your training sessions in the morning with a certain level of intensity, and the head coach wants the intense sessions in the evening, you have a conflict. If you and your strength coach disagree over the kinds of strength training your team should be doing and the frequency, you have a conflict.

Conflict also occurs over what is to be done or achieved, such as goals for your team. You as the coach (along with many other individuals involved, such as parents, coaches, club executive, volunteers, and sport science experts) want to ensure that consensus is built around not only how your team will train or practice, but also what the long-terms goals are. If you think your team has the talent and tenacity to succeed internationally and the parents don't have the willingness or the financial resources to support the travel, you have a conflict.

Finally, conflict can escalate over differing values, and this is probably the most difficult type of conflict to resolve. For example, you may believe that athletes can compete successfully at the national and international levels and still get an education or hold down a part-time job, and in fact believe that this is a necessary element for a successful life after sport, but you are faced with a parent who actively encourages her daughter to do nothing but train. This may be a difficult conflict to resolve.

These are some of the ways that conflict might begin. The good news is that through learning and effectively using all of the skills of effective communication, you will be able to prevent a great deal of conflict within your team and with those you work with and for. When you listen well, when you speak clearly and concisely, when you are able to give and receive feedback and criticism well, and when you can share these skills with others on your team, you can prevent conflict. And when conflict or issues do arise, you will be able to manage them well and resolve the issues effectively, using those same skills. The more effectively you manage conflict, the higher the probability for group cohesion, which can have a high correlation with overall team success and satisfaction rates (Carron & Chelladurai, 1981; DiBerardinis et al., 1983).

What is most relevant in becoming a skillful communicator is that you take the time to reflect regularly on how you are doing in working with your athletes, their parents, your club executive, your sport organization, and your coaching colleagues. Develop your communication skills. Learn to listen well, not to fear what you might hear, to ask questions effectively, to speak clearly, and to give and receive feedback and criticism effectively.

Skillful communication is a flowing, ongoing process. The speaker, the listener, and the message are ever changing. For you as a coach, it is a continuous dialogue. You can't speak one time only with your athletes or your colleagues about an issue and assume that it will never come up again. Inevitably, it will. And new issues, concerns, and ideas will also arise.

Be generous in sharing communication skills with your athletes and colleagues. After all, if everyone you work with becomes more effective at communicating, all of you will be much more effective. And you will be "successful" as a coach—not only in terms of results, but also in developing thinking, independent, responsible athletes.

REFERENCES

Aggressive, *adj.* (2009). *Merriam-Webster's online dictionary.* Retrieved from http://www.merriam-webster.com/dictionary/aggressive

Assert, *trans. v.* (2009). *Merriam-Webster's online dictionary.* Retrieved from http://www.merriam-webster.com/dictionary/assert

Bandura, A. (1997). *Self-efficacy: The exercise of control.* New York: Freeman.

Bandura, A. (1986). *Social foundations of thought and action: A social cognitive theory.* Englewood Cliffs, NJ: Prentice-Hall.

Bradac, J.J., & Street, R.L., Jr. (1990). Powerful and powerless styles of talk: A theoretical analysis of language and impression formation. *Research in Language and Social Interaction, 23,* 195-242.

Bruner, B. (2008). Listening, communication & trust: Practitioners' perspectives of business/organizational relationships. *The International Journal of Listening, 22,* 73-82.

Carron, A.V., & Chelladurai, P. (1981). Cohesion as a factor in sport performance. *International Review of Sport Sociology, 16,* 2-41.

Copeland, B.W., & Wida, K. (1996). Resolving team conflict: Coaching strategies to prevent negative behavior. *Journal of Physical Education, Recreation, & Dance, 67*(4), 52-54.

DiBerardinis, J.D., Barwind, J., Flanningam, R.R., & Jenkins, V. (1983). Enhanced interpersonal relations as predictor of athletic performance. *International Journal of Sport Psychology, 14,* 243-251.

Elman, C.B. (2001). Sometimes it's all in what you're listening for. *Women in Business, 53,* 5.

Erickson, B., Lind, E.A., Johnson, B.C., & O'Barr, W.M. (1978). Speech style and impression formation in a court setting: The effects of "powerful" and "powerless" speech. *Journal of Experimental Social Psychology, 14,* 266–279.

Gray, R., & Robertson, L. (2005). Effective internal communication starts at the top. *Communication World, 22,* 26–28.

Halone, K.K. (2001). Relational listening. A grounded theoretical model. *Communication Reports, 14,* 59–72.

Hanin, Y. (1992). Social psychology and sport: Communication processes in top performance teams. *Sport Science Review, 1,* 13–28.

Hughes, L. (2002). How to be a good listener. *Women in Business, 54,* 17.

Imhof, M. (1998). What makes a good listener? Listening behavior in instructional settings. *International Journal of Listening, 12,* 81–105.

Lakoff, R. (1975). *Language and a woman's place.* New York: Harper & Row.

Latting, J.K. (1992). Giving corrective feedback: A decisional analysis. *Social Work, 37,* 424–430.

Lizzio, A., Wilson, K., & MacKay, L. (2008). Managers and subordinates evaluations of feedback strategies: The critical contribution of voice. *Journal of Applied Social Psychology, 38*(4), 991–946.

Passive, adj. (2009). *Merriam-Webster's online dictionary.* Retrieved from http://www.merriam-webster.com/dictionary/passive

Sparks, J.R., & Areni, C.S. (2002). The effects of sales presentation quality and initial perceptions on persuasion: A multiple role perspective. *Journal of Business Research, 55,* 517–528.

Sparks, J.R., Areni, C.S., & Cox, K.C. (1998). An investigation of the effects of language style and communication modality on persuasion. *Communication Monographs, 65,* 108–125.

Sullivan, P.J., & Feltz, D.L. (2003). The preliminary development of the scale for effective communication in team sports (SECTS). *Journal of Applied Social Psychology, 33,* 1693–1715.

Sullivan, P.J., & Gee, C. (2007). The relationship between athletic satisfaction and intrateam communication. *Group Dynamics: Theory, Research, and Practice, 11*(2), 107–116.

Timm, S., & Schroeder, B.L. (2000). Listening/nonverbal communication training. *International Journal of Listening, 4,* 109–128.

Laura Inward was Team Ontario's beach volleyball coach at the 2009 Canada Summer Games in Prince Edward Island.

PHOTO: JOHN SIMS, TEAM ONTARIO

UNDERSTANDING MENTORING AS A DEVELOPMENT TOOL FOR FEMALE COACHES

SIX

Dru Marshall and Dawn-Marie Sharp

Introduction

Mentoring is all the rage, and with good reason. In a productive mentoring relationship, mentor and protégé reap many benefits, from the sharing of personal and professional experiences, to contributing to a vibrant and confident future generation, to providing rewarding professional development opportunities.

Mentoring is occurring in a variety of circumstances and configurations, and has become standard practice in most professional environments in Canada, including sport. In this chapter, Dru Marshall and Dawn-Marie Sharp clarify what mentoring is and describe the qualities mentors and protégés need for a successful relationship. They analyze the many types of mentoring, explain options for the structure and the duration of the relationship, and describe the various types of mentors.

In examining the role of facilitated mentoring, which is widely used in Canada's coaching environment, the authors draw attention to the highly successful mentoring initiatives of the Coaching Association of Canada's Women in Coaching program, including its Online Mentor Program. They point out how the traditional reluctance of experienced women to serve as mentors and the dearth of qualified female coaches are creating a human resource dilemma. While they caution that mentors may not be able to solve every problem, under the right circumstances, mentors are a reliable and valuable source of potential solutions.

ALTHOUGH MANY ASSUME MENTORING to be a modern business trend, the roots of the practice are found in ancient times. Legend suggests that when Odysseus, the King of Ithaca, went off to fight in the Trojan War, he left behind his trusted friend and adviser, Mentor, to educate and look after his son Telemachus. Interestingly, in Homer's *Odyssey,* the goddess Athena disguises herself in Mentor's form to take over the training of Telemachus. Over time, the mentor has become a resilient archetype figure within literature that influences the present-day meaning of the word: "mentor" has come to connote a wise and trusted teacher and counsellor (Fishman & Lunsford, 2008). For much of the twentieth century, the use of mentoring as a human resource development tool was lost in a climate of social change and corporate restructuring. At one time thought to be reserved for a limited few who were "in the loop" or "in the network," mentoring has become only recently the focus of much research and discussion. This is in part because mentoring is being used across many disciplines, fields of work, and study to develop the next generation of professionals.

Mentoring is used in a variety of settings:

- In the not-for-profit sector. For example, Big Sisters matches young girls with adult mentors who serve as positive role models.
- In business, where one finds a range of mentor/protégé relationships, from informal contacts with a superior, to formalized matching within a company-recognized mentor program.
- In the academic area, in programs ranging from peer tutoring of students to formalized mentor programs for professors and administrators.

- In health and education, to enhance the transition from formal studies into practical settings for entry-level teachers, nurses, and specialized doctors.
- In the coaching arena, where we find examples of formalized programs like the Women in Coaching Long-Term Apprenticeship Program (LTAP), and more informal programs, such as the matching of National Coaching Institute candidates with mentor coaches in their sport.

Regardless of the setting, it appears that comparisons between non-mentored and mentored individuals generally yield consistent results: individuals with informal mentors report greater career satisfaction, career commitment, career mobility, and more positive job attitudes than individuals without mentors (Eby, Allen, Evans, Ng, & Dubois, 2008). Salmela (1996) suggests that one of the best ways to develop as a coach is to take advantage of the advice and actions of a mentor. Wickman and Sjodin (1997) suggest that all of us are where we are today because somebody, at some point in time, saw something in us that we may not have seen in ourselves.

A great mentor has a knack for making us think we are better than we think we are. They force us to have a good opinion of ourselves, let us know that they believe in us. They make us get more out of ourselves, and once we learn how good we really are, we never settle for anything less than our very best.

—THE PROMETHEUS FOUNDATION

The purpose of this chapter is to describe mentoring and the various forms it takes, to highlight key findings from research on mentoring, and to examine specifically the role of mentoring in the development of female coaches.

What is Mentoring?

MENTORING, IN ITS SIMPLEST FORM, is people helping people; it means helping, advising, teaching, counselling, sharing, instructing, and guiding another person. A mentor is someone who helps us learn the ways of the world (Wickman & Sjodin, 1997). Kram (1985) defines a mentor as an individual with advanced experience and knowledge who is committed to providing upward mobility and career support to a protégé.

Why Mentoring Works

MENTORING WORKS FOR a variety of reasons.

- Mentors have a tremendous amount of personal and professional experience. Through professional experience, the mentor has "inside knowledge" of an organization's norms, values, and procedures. Access to this knowledge allows the protégé the opportunity to develop more quickly than if she did not have access to the information and to receive support during her development (Roed, 1999).
- Mentor and protégé, if well matched, can create more energy and accomplish larger goals than can a single person alone. That is, two people together create synergy to accomplish things they might never have attempted as individuals (Bozionelos, 2004; Lentz & Allen, 2009).
- The mentoring process helps to perpetuate positive action. It allows the knowledge, expertise, secrets, tips, and tricks of a master, those that have allowed this person to be successful, to be passed on to the next generation—without the information finding its way into the public domain (Wickman & Sjodin, 1997; Parise & Forret, 2008).
- Mentoring is part of a naturally occurring transitional process. The relationship between mentor and protégé typically helps the mentor identify and address critical issues which provides a sense of making a contribution to future generations (Erickson, 1963), and helps the protégé meet early career needs for guidance, support, and affirmation (Eby et al., 2008). For many sport organizations, mentoring offers a cost-effective way to provide professional development opportunities for coaches.

- Mentors can foster a sense of belonging within a professional environment by facilitating relationships outside of the one-on-one mentor/protégé setting to increase the protégé's network (Eby & Allen, 2008). Furthermore, the mentor can assist in and promote the protégé's interaction within communities of practice, which in turn, may actively cultivate unmediated learning situations (Wright, Trudel, & Culver, 2007). This creation of a sense of belonging will increase the protégé's willingness to remain within an organization and may help to narrow the gender gap, which has become a significant ongoing concern for groups advocating for an increase of women in coaching (Ayers & Griffin, 2005; Dodds, 2005; Singh, Ragins, & Tharenou, 2009).

Successful Mentor Qualities

WHILE MENTORS ARE TYPICALLY important role models, being a mentor goes beyond role modelling. A mentor will actively engage in the protégé's professional development, whereas a role model holds a much more passive influence over potential protégés, in that they primarily set a good example and their actions and knowledge are, for the most part, maintained at an observable distance (Scheerer, 2007). The primary resource of a successful mentor is "inside knowledge," along with years of practical experience. Mentors should be able to identify and model professional behaviours and best practices, and should be able to communicate them to the protégé. Insider information allows mentors to open doors for protégés that would otherwise be closed (Blickle, Witzki, & Schneider, 2009; Scandura & Williams, 2004), and to help short-circuit errors that protégés might make. But although mentors open doors, they allow protégés to walk through themselves and be responsible for their own behaviour. In other words, successful mentors focus on the protégé's development and curb their own urge to produce a clone (Roed, 1999; Wickman & Sjodin, 1997). Positive mentors will allow and generate opportunities for the protégé to show resourcefulness. Mentors must be willing to share their learned knowledge, introduce the protégé to their professional network, facilitate discussion, encourage thinking, propose alternate solutions, be approachable, acknowledge ethical behaviours, be aware and manage situations to diminish the perception of power, and serve as a confidante/counsellor in times of professional and personal crises (Bozionelos, 2004; Coaching Association of Canada, 2008). A successful mentor can thus alleviate some of the intense isolation that a protégé feels in times of stress. Mentors must be able to provide constructive criticism in a non-judgemental fashion, and establish an environment where the protégé feels free to make mistakes without losing self-confidence. Finally, Eby and Allen (2008) state that one of the most critical aspects of a successful mentor is the value she places on committing to the mentor/protégé relationship.

Successful Protégé Qualities

DOUGHERTY AND TURBAN (1994) found a high degree of correlation between certain personality traits and successful protégés. These personality traits include an individual's belief that she could influence her own success, sensitivity to social cues, and overall level of self-esteem. Successful protégés must assume responsibility for their own professional growth and development and be dedicated to improving their level of knowledge (Eby et al., 2008; Poteat, Shockley, & Allen, 2009). It is also important for protégés to be able to articulate their needs clearly, ask for clarification in confusion, celebrate success, build on existing strengths, take measurable risks to explore new directions of thought and practice, attempt to understand the broader context of the profession (the "bigger picture"), take time to reflect on and enjoy the protégé process, and practice life-long learning (Coaching Association of Canada, 2008). In addition, Poteat, Shockley, and Allen (2009) found that successful protégés must respect the mentor's time, take action on the information provided by the mentor, show respect for the mentor's efforts to open new doors, and eventually pass on the gift of mentoring to a new protégé.

TABLE 1 SUCCESSFUL QUALITIES

MENTOR	PROTÉGÉ	ORGANIZATION
• Identifies and models professional behaviours.	• Believes that she can influence her own success.	• Provides clear expectations and accountability.
• Has years of practical experience.	• Is sensitive to social cues.	• Provides appropriate training for mentors.
• Possesses insider knowledge.	• Is dedicated to improving knowledge.	• Involves mentors in the matching process.
• Has strong communication skills and facilitates discussion.	• Has the ability to ask critical questions.	• Builds legitimacy within the organization.
• Is approachable.	• Has the ability to state needs.	• Generates greater commitment from the mentor.
• Acknowledges ethical behaviours.	• Builds on strengths.	• Optimizes compatibility and communication.
• Isn't interested in reproducing herself.	• Respects the mentor's time and efforts to share networks; acts on suggestions and opportunities provided.	• Provides resources.
• Shares knowledge and encourages thinking.		• Encourages time for meetings between a mentor and protégé.
• Has the ability to open doors/create opportunities.	• Attempts to see the bigger picture.	• Funds particular aspects of a program if required.
• Proposes and encourages alternate solutions.	• Has a strong sense of self-esteem.	• Creates opportunities where other mentors and protégés meet and learn from one another's experiences.
• Maintains confidentiality.	• Assumes responsibility for her own professional growth and development.	
• Creates an environment where errors are seen as learning opportunities.	• Practices life-long learning.	• Is aware of power dynamics.
	• Celebrates success.	
• Is aware of power relationships and management of power.	• Takes measurable risks to explore new directions of thought and practice.	• Provides visibility to the mentoring programs to ensure that the programs are not creating social constraints for the protégé.
• Provides constructive criticism without being judgmental.	• Takes time to reflect and enjoy the process of being a protégé.	
• Is committed to the mentor/protégé relationship.	• Passes on the gift of mentoring to a new protégé.	

Ayers & Griffin, 2005; Parise & Forret, 2008; Blickle, Witzki, & Schneider, 2009; Bozionelos, 2004; Coaching Association of Canada, 2008; Dougherty & Turban, 1994; Eby & Allen, 2008; Eby, Allen, Evans, Ng, & Dubois, 2008; Fishman & Lunsford, 2008; Lindley, 2009; Poteat, Shockley, & Allen, 2009; Roed, 1999; Scandura & Williams, 2004; Sheerer, 2007; Wickman & Sjodin, 1997

Successful Organizational Qualities

ORGANIZATIONS THAT FOSTER mentoring programs should provide clear expectations and accountabilities—for example confidentiality, responsibility for personal growth, and goal setting—for the mentor and protégé. Mentorship programs that provide appropriate training for mentors and involve the mentors in the matching process see greater success and legitimacy within an organization (Ayers & Griffin, 2005; Parise & Forret, 2008). The mentor becomes invested from the start because she can exercise some control over the selection of a protégé. As well, it is more likely that she will identify a protégé who is compatible, and so communication is optimized (Scandura & Williams, 2004). Organizations that provide resources, such as the opportunity and encouragement of time for meetings between a mentor and protégé, funding for particular aspects of a program if required, and creation of opportunities where other mentors and protégés can meet and learn from one another's experiences, tend to be more successful. Successful organizations are aware of power dynamics and encourage participants in mentoring programs to meet in more humanistic environments to enhance relationship building (Lindley, 2009). They also provide programs that are visible and accessible to all—so that programs are not perceived to be exclusive, and those who are involved do not become alienated in the workplace (Ayers & Griffin, 2005). Finally, because mentor/protégé relationships are frequently rooted in patriarchal activities, successful organizations continually ensure that the programs are not creating social constraints for the protégé (Fishman & Lunsford, 2008).

Good intentions are not enough to facilitate good mentoring.

—AYERS AND GRIFFIN, 2005

Benefits of Mentoring

THE BENEFITS ASSOCIATED with mentoring are shared among the participants—the mentor, the protégé, and the organization—and vary depending on the level of commitment of each participant.

Benefits for the Mentor

Wickman and Sjodin (1997) suggest that we all have an implied responsibly to future generations to impart knowledge to those who come after us. As the adage suggests, those who do not learn from history are doomed to repeat it. Passing on insider information should provide the mentor with a sense of personal satisfaction. Mentoring also serves to keep the mentor mentally sharp. It forces her or him to reflect on best practices, encourages creativity, and provides opportunities for continual learning (Bozionelos, 2004; Parise & Forret, 2008). Moreover, the opportunity to pass on knowledge becomes more valuable when the mentor involves the protégé in an applied sense, and a loyal protégé, in turn, can support and create greater productivity for the mentor (Bozionelos, 2004; Parise & Forret, 2008).

> *It is impossible to teach without learning something yourself.*
> —RALPH WALDO EMERSON

In some cases, the mentor finds that the experience triggers greater reflection on developing stronger ties and communication with peers, which builds better relationships and knowledge about the challenges within an organization as a whole (Patton et al., 2005; Singh et al., 2009), and a sense of enhanced career satisfaction for the mentor (Lentz & Allen, 2009). The mentor typically provides a variety of options for the protégé to consider. This can force the mentor to think outside of the box to develop options (Eby et al., 2006). As a result of reflecting on best practices, the mentor is forced to set an example, thus becoming a role model. Typically, peer recognition for the mentor is the result (Eby et al., 2006; Lentz & Allen, 2009).

Benefits for the Protégé

The rewards for the protégé are abundant. The following highlight only a few of the benefits that protégés experience. Doors are opened for the protégé that might otherwise be closed, which results in increased social interaction and networking and greater visibility that may lead to other opportunities (Blickle et al., 2009; Bozionelos, 2004; Day & Allen, 2004). The protégé receives assistance and advice on setting realistic career goals and strategies (Wickman & Sjodin, 1997). Mentors can help the protégé save time and money. The mentor has "been there before" and can help the protégé avoid errors (Day & Allen, 2004). Protégés typically report greater career satisfaction, more positive job attitudes, and greater career commitment (Blickle et al., 2009; Fagenson, 1989; Scandura, 1997; Mobley, Jaret, Marsh, & Lim, 1994; Colarelli & Bishop, 1990). Typically, if you are satisfied with your job and happy in your environment, your commitment and loyalty to the organization increases (Wickman & Sjodin, 1997). Mentor/protégé relationships provide legitimate involvement within an organization because protégés experience a greater sense of belonging, which produces greater retention of participants (Patton et al., 2005; Singh et al., 2009).

Benefits to the Organization

Because mentored individuals have greater career satisfaction and more positive job attitudes, organizations benefit from better trained staff and increased productivity. The training tends to be time efficient and cost-effective. There is increased communication among staff, creating a sense of stability within the organization. Insider information is handed down from one generation of worker to the next, resulting in a solid organization legacy (Blickle et al., 2009). More recent studies show that mentorship programs have led to building professional culture, where a community of practice is informally formed and shared knowledge within an environment stimulates professionals to engage more fully in their work (Patton et al., 2005; Singh et al., 2009; Wright et al., 2007).

TABLE 2 BENEFITS OF MENTORSHIP PROGRAMS

FOR THE MENTOR	FOR THE PROTÉGÉ	FOR THE ORGANIZATION
• Imparts knowledge to future generations. • Keeps the mentor mentally sharp. • Promotes reflection on best practices, encourages creativity, and provides opportunities for continual learning. • Results in greater productivity for the mentor, with the support of a loyal protégé. • Strengthens ties and communication with peers. • Enhances relationships and knowledge about the challenges within an organization. • Provides enhanced career satisfaction. • Positions the mentor as a role model. • Assures peer recognition.	• Provides greater opportunity for doors to be opened that might otherwise be closed. • Offers increased social interaction and networking. • Assures greater visibility leading to other opportunities. • Provides assistance and advice on setting realistic career goals and strategies. • Saves time and money. • Offers guidance to help avoid making unnecessary errors. • Ensures greater career satisfaction and commitment. • Increases the potential for increased commitment and loyalty to the organization. • Ensures legitimate involvement within an organization and a greater sense of belonging, which produces greater retention.	• Ensures better trained staff and increased productivity. • Ensures time-efficient and cost-effective training. • Increases communication among staff, creating a sense of stability within the organization. • Hands down insider information from one generation of worker to the next, resulting in a solid organizational legacy. • Builds a professional culture in which a community of practice is informally formed, and shared knowledge within an environment stimulates professionals to engage more fully in their work.

Blickle, Witzki, & Schneider, 2009; Fagenson, 1989; Bozionelos, 2004; Colarelli & Bishop, 1990; Day & Allen, 2004; Eby, Durley, Evans, & Ragins, 2006; Lentz & Allen, 2009; Mobley, Jaret, Marsh, & Lim, 1994; Parise & Forret, 2008; Patton et al., 2005; Scandura, 1997; Singh, Ragins, & Tharenou, 2009; Wickman & Sjodin, 1997; Wright, Trudel, & Culver, 2007

Categorizing Mentoring

FOR THE PURPOSE OF THIS CHAPTER, mentoring will be categorized by type, by the degree of structure and the duration, and by the type of mentor. It is important to note that mentoring relationships fall along a continuum, from those that are short term and informal in nature to those that are highly structured long-term partnerships. While many mentoring relationships are highly satisfying, some may be only marginally satisfying, dissatisfying, or at the extreme, dysfunctional or harmful (Eby et al., 2000; Ragins, Cotton, & Miller, 2000; Parise & Forret, 2008).

Kram (1985) suggests that mentoring relationships are fluid. She hypothesized that "[mentoring] relationships are dynamic and changing; while enhancing at one time, a relationship can become less satisfying and even destructive." Therefore, the matching of mentors with protégés becomes a key issue in mentoring relationships.

Types of Mentoring

There are three types of mentoring: supervisory, unstructured (informal), and facilitated (Coaching Association of Canada, 1998).

SUPERVISORY MENTORING
- typically takes place in a work environment and is considered to be a function of a supervisor's duties
- while this is a nice model in theory, it does not often work in practice, particularly in hectic and stressful environments, or if the program is not voluntary (Scandura & Williams, 2004)
- relies on the ability of the supervisor to communicate knowledge about the job; this, unfortunately, is not always guaranteed
- usually lasts a year or less, and keeps the relationship efficient and focused on specific outcomes (usually organizationally driven) (Parise & Forret, 2008)

UNSTRUCTURED (INFORMAL) MENTORING

- is the unofficial, natural pairing of two individuals, characteristically based on mutual values and trust (Scandura & Williams, 2004)
- is typically initiated by the protégé, by finding a trusted adviser or teacher whom she perceives can help her meet her personal and professional needs
- tends to last longer than a formal mentoring connection
- evolves and progresses into the needs of the protégé and mentor, whereas a formal mentor/ protégé union would be confined to more specific objectives (Dodds, 2005)
- has limited effectiveness because the mentor may not be aware of the role she is playing; that is, while the protégé sees the mentor as a role model, the mentor is unaware of her role in the partnership
- may be limited because it frequently does not cross barriers of social disparity like gender (women look for female mentors, men for male mentors), which can potentially hinder the capacity to advance a career

FACILITATED MENTORING, the style of mentoring endorsed by the Coaching Association of Canada requires

- a strategically planned mentoring program design
- facilitated matching of mentors and protégés
- developmental training for the mentors and protégés
- a no-fault termination clause
- a formalized career development plan and tracking system
- a co-ordinator, whose primary role is to implement the program, match the pairs, and then monitor progress, counsel, and evaluate

Degree of Structure and Duration

UNSTRUCTURED (INFORMAL) mentoring programs are characterized by a more personal, relaxed atmosphere. Typically, informal relationships develop by mutual identification, where mentors choose protégés viewed as younger versions of themselves, and protégés select mentors viewed as role models (Parise & Forrett, 2008). Many mentor/ protégé relationships are initiated as hierarchical. However, in an informal mentoring program, the relationship is fluid. The dynamics of the relationship change as the people involved progress. Both participants come to share a mutual contribution, and the perception of power dissolves (Patton et al., 2005; Poteat et al., 2009). Informal programs have been effective in enhancing job attitudes and career commitment.

Many organizations have attempted to replicate and build on the benefits of informal mentoring by developing formal, structured mentoring programs. Examples include the facilitated mentoring programs found at National Coaching Institutes or in many business mentoring programs, where protégés are matched to corporate mentors with organizational assistance or intervention. In some cases, mentor and protégé have not met before the match is made. Formal mentors typically enter a mentoring relationship to meet organizational expectations or to be good corporate citizens (Ragins et al., 2000). Therefore, formal mentors may be less likely to receive intrinsic reward, may be less intrinsically motivated to be in the mentoring relationship, and may be less personally invested in their protégé's development than an informal mentor (Poteat et al., 2009).

Unstructured mentoring relationships usually last between three and six years, with pairs meeting as often as desired or needed. Formal mentoring relationships, in contrast, are usually contracted to last six months to one year, with meetings being either sporadic or specified in a contract (Parise & Forret, 2008). Since formal mentoring relationships are typically shorter in duration, mentor influence on the protégé may be reduced. Wickman and Sjodin (1997) suggest that a person should enter into all mentoring relationships, whether as a mentor or protégé, with the assumption that they will be short term, as the future of a mentoring relationship is always uncertain.

While we know that informal mentoring programs improve work attitudes, little research has been done comparing work attitudes among protégés in formal and informal mentoring relationships. One glaring methodological issue in most studies is that researchers have failed to control for quality of satisfaction with the mentoring relationship when comparing informal and formal mentoring. In one of the few studies that did, Ragins et al. (2000) found that satisfaction with a mentoring relationship had a stronger impact on job and career attitudes than the presence of a mentor, whether the relationship was structure or unstructured. That is, individuals in highly satisfying mentoring relationships reported more positive work and career attitudes than non-mentored individuals, but the attitudes of those protégés in dissatisfying relationships were equivalent to those of non-mentored individuals. Good mentoring may lead to positive outcomes; bad mentoring may be destructive, and it may be worse than no mentoring at all.

Ragins et al. (2000) studied a national sample of 1,162 employees representing social workers, engineers, and journalists from professional associations involved in mentoring programs. Program purpose was found to be critical. In programs in which the purpose was to promote the protégé's career, there was a significantly stronger relationship to positive work attitudes than to programs in which the purpose was to orient new employees. Another key finding was that protégés in programs with mentors who were in the same department as the protégés expressed significantly less satisfaction with the mentoring relationship than protégés in programs with mentors from other departments. The authors hypothesized that mentors from other departments may provide fresher insights and a broader organizational perspective.

The gender differences that were represented in this study are also of great interest. Women who had formal mentors were less satisfied with their mentoring program than men were, and these women reported less career commitment than formally mentored men and non-mentored men and women. Ragins et al. (2000) suggest that formal programs may be less effective for women than men, and further suggest that although the selection of the effective mentors is important for all programs, it may be critical for programs aimed at women. Experienced women have traditionally been more reluctant to serve as mentors than their male counterparts. Some studies have suggested that women are sensitive to the overall risks of mentoring, particularly to the increased visibility one has as a mentor, and the potential reflection of failure if a protégé is unsuccessful. Wickman and Sjodin (1997) suggest we need to work towards creating environments where women do not feel threatened by the risk of a protégé's errors.

Organizations can facilitate the development of potential female mentors by making mentorship training options more available within their programs, and encouraging women to position themselves initially as secondary or peripheral mentors. Secondary or peripheral mentoring roles provide a base to develop mentoring skills and experiences. Success in these roles may encourage women then to evolve into primary mentoring roles.

It is important to develop more female mentors because there may be particular benefits for female protégés.

- A female mentor can ease the female protégé's feelings of isolation and fear of failure.
- She can serve as an unbiased "sounding board" for the protégé that does not take gender into account.
- She may have experienced the same barriers the protégé faces, issues that men may never experience or understand. She might be able to empathize better in difficult situations that arise because of gender barriers. Even if the situations encountered are not identical, other experiences have given shape to her perspective and appropriate problem-solving skills.
- She provides a model of what it means to be a woman in her organization, which nurtures the protégé's sense of belonging and purpose (Casto, Caldwell, & Salazar, 2005).

There are successful women who mentor and are inspired and motivated by such a relationship. Once a woman has had a positive experience with a mentor, there is a good chance that she will want to reciprocate the experience by mentoring someone else. However, because there are so few female mentors, it is important that they do not take on too many protégés. Protégés who compete for an individual mentor's attention may not receive the same breadth and intensity of support that they need or require for success (Brown, 2005; McGuire & Reger, 2003).

Protégés can also play a role in helping to develop mentors. Brown (2005) notes that many women passively wait for female mentors to appear. She argues that potential protégés have the agency to seek out actively women whom they regard as ideal mentors. However, it is critical that they are aware of their responsibility for enhancing the mentor's status as well as their own by publicly acknowledging the mentor's contributions, and sharing her success with her mentor (Casto et al., 2005).

Primary and Peripheral Mentors

It is important to note that protégés are not locked into interacting with a single mentor. The benefit of having more than one mentor means that the protégé has opportunity to weigh alternative perspectives and thus various options and multiple contributions to help shape her career development (Wright et al., 2007). Ayers and Griffin (2005) suggest that individuals interact with multiple types of mentors throughout their lives. Here are three types of mentors.

- A *primary mentor*, the one we think of as being more important, is likely to change throughout various stages of life and career, but is the person to whom we talk about a variety of issues (Wickman & Sjodin, 1997). Merlin was the primary mentor for King Arthur, for example, and Yoda was the primary mentor for Luke Skywalker.
- A *secondary* or *peripheral mentor* is an individual we go to for specific issues. A secondary or peripheral mentor tends to be a specialist in a particular area (Eby & Allen, 2008). In coaching, one may have a primary mentor who has been or is a coach in her sport or another sport, and one may have secondary mentors in a number of areas, such as physiological training, mental training, ethics, team

building, and technical and tactical training. Meetings tend to be more intermittent with secondary mentors, as they are typically set on an as-needed basis.

- A *momentary mentor* is an individual who is in your life briefly, who gives you a pearl of wisdom, and then is gone. Momentary mentors are people who make you stop and think, and sometimes cause you to view the world differently (Wickman & Sjodin, 1997; Eby & Allen, 2008; Singh et al., 2009).

Alternative Approaches

RECENTLY, MORE STUDIES have started focusing on power in mentoring relationships, and have provided an emphasis on building mutual respect, empowerment, and learning as opposed to more traditional and hierarchical models of mentoring (Bozionelos, 2004; Byrne, Dik, & Chiaburu, 2008; McGuire & Reger, 2003). Primarily, these approaches look at folding in co-mentoring and communities of practice with more traditional models of mentorship (McGuire & Reger, 2003; Singh et al., 2009; Wright et al., 2007).

McGuire and Reger (2003) highlight that there are benefits likely to be missed if a young professional denies herself an opportunity to be mentored by a person who has greater influence and experience within an organization or profession. Mentors can provide greater access to important resources, people, and "reflected power" (association to the mentor gives seemingly natural legitimacy to the protégé). In addition, McQuire and Reger believe that co-mentor relationships (those in which both parties are equal and share reflective practice) are particularly helpful for marginalized groups such as women. In their feminist approach, these authors found a number of benefits of supplementing the traditional method of mentoring with co-mentoring, including a greater focus on learning, rather than a competition for attention from a single mentor; an opportunity to balance power where participants are both teacher and learner; and a more balanced approach focused on celebrating successes with examining and fixing weaknesses.

A growing trend in coaching and teaching education is the development of communities of practice as an advanced form of mentoring and social learning (Erickson, Bruner, MacDonald, & Côté, 2008; Lemyre, Trudel, & Durand-Bush, 2007; Wright et al., 2007). Communities of practice foster a learning environment where power is more equalized by peer mentoring opportunities, social capital can be built, new knowledge is nurtured, and innovation is stimulated. Members of communities of practice have deep discussions about issues that professionals working toward common goals might face within a particular time and culture. A single mentor may not have experienced the breadth of issues, and so a community of practice provides additional value to the protégé. The benefits of communities of practice include problem solving, development of new capabilities, standardization of some practices, leveraging of best practices, talent development, and mistake avoidance.

No man is an island, entire of itself.
—JOHN DONNE

The annual National Coach Workshop is an excellent example of a community of practice where past and present Canadian team female coaches come together to support each other's professional development, and to build a stronger network (Robertson, 2009).

Mentoring and Coaching

COACHES LEARN HOW TO COACH through formal education programs, experience, observation, and through informal mechanisms. It is important to note that while mentoring enhances other types of training, it does not replace it. A mentor can open doors for the protégé, identify information and new technology, and assist in the development of skills required to maximize use of these resources, but ultimately success lies in the hands of the protégé. To be successful, a coach has to be able to access all the tools available, including technical, tactical, physiological, and psychological expertise, technology tools, and sport specific resources. A good mentor will help a coach to access these tools and demonstrate how to use them effectively. Mentors may not have the solution to every problem, but they should be able to help find the solutions. Individuals within a community of practice will likely provide further information and practices regarding tools that are available.

Expert coaches in Canada, Australia, France, the United States, and Britain have identified mentoring as one of the best ways to develop as a coach (Salmela, 1996; Wright et al., 2007). The twenty-two expert coaches in Salmela's 1996 study unanimously supported a mentorship program and also acknowledged their obligation to serve as mentors of other coaches. However, they also suggested that if mentorship was going to become a viable and standard part of training for professional coaches, mentorship programs had to be funded to a greater degree.

The youth coaches studied by Wright et al. (2007) suggested that interaction with other coaches (both peers and mentors) was more significant to their career development than the traditional information obtained in a coaching certification program. These coaches believed that formal mentoring programs would enhance their overall education experience. They noticed gaps in the formal certification process that were filled by discussion and observations of other coaches and mentors. Wright et al. identify the role of the coach as complex; coaching certification clinics cannot meet the needs of every coach, simply because they come from various backgrounds and experiences. The addition of a mentor coach can facilitate the specific personal development of the protégé coach more comprehensively, because the mentor understands the context. The mentor becomes a live resource in a learner-centred approach, as opposed to coaching courses that are somewhat limited by established curriculum-centred content, time, and geography.

While mentoring for high performance coaches has been a more traditional focus of the Coaching Association of Canada, more recently researchers and various sport bodies have been examining, developing, and implementing mentorship programs for community,

A coaching career often starts in the teen years, as shown by Kaleigh Boyer correcting the form of Adam Morrill.

PHOTO: MARIANN DOMONKOS

competitive, and varsity levels of competition (Erickson et al., 2008). Studies by Erickson et al. (2008), Lemyre et al. (2007), and Wright et al. (2007) propose that mentoring as a mode of learning for coaches may be isolating, stressing again that it is not meant to be the sole approach to training coaches. These authors recommend that a mentoring system should be established within the context of a community of practice. A co-operative organization that shares and invests in developing, retaining, and progressing the same pool of athletes and coaches is one possible environment in which to host a coaching mentor and protégé program.

Mentoring and Female Coaches

A number of mentorship programs have been developed in Canada for female coaches. From 1977 to 1998, the Coaching Association of Canada offered full-time coaching apprenticeships that provided $12,000 for living expenses to the apprentice, $3,000 for travel expenses, and $4,000 for a mentor coach salary. In its heyday, as many as twelve coaches per year were involved in this program.

The Coaching Association of Canada's Women in Coaching program has also offered numerous apprenticeships. For example, there have been apprenticeship projects attached to major games: a Common-wealth Games apprenticeship program in 1994; the Pan American Games apprenticeship program, directed at coaches in Saskatchewan and Manitoba, in 1999; and the 2005 Jeux de la Francophonie Appren-ticeship Program, which benefited coaches from abroad. There have been programs that have lasted longer, such as the National Team Apprenticeship Program that started in 2000, which involves a three-year commitment to six female coaches and includes mentoring. There have also been numerous innovative mentoring programs for developing coaches at the Canada Games level that have involved partnerships between provincial and national sport organizations, the Canada Games Council, and the Women in Coaching program.

The Pan American Games program marked the first time all of the female apprentice coaches were brought together as a group for profes-sional development and networking. While different doors might have been opened by their respective mentor coach, these apprentices had a chance to share their collective experiences and build a community of practice. The powerful learning environment and strong connections built within the group served each individual well as they furthered their development, many of them becoming national coaches in their own right. This practice of bringing coaches together to establish networks and communities of practices for coaches at the local, provincial, and national levels continues, but requires more study.

Data collected from the 2007 Canada Games apprentice coaches demonstrated that as a result of the apprenticeship program, coaches were exposed to new ideas and resources; had a coaching role rather than a managing role; pushed to obtain higher certification through the National Coaching Certification Program and higher education; extended their coaching network; became more reflective of their experiences; had a collective voice as well as an individual voice; and were part of a female coach community of practice (Croxon, 2007). Importantly, some of these developing coaches started seeing themselves choosing coaching as a career rather than just a hobby. As a result of their feedback, current Canada Games apprentice coaches also now receive the benefit of two professional development seminars focused on leadership, communication, advocacy, and planning. These seminars have included both apprentice and mentor coaches, have been well received by the participants, and have further helped to form communities of practice.

In each of the programs highlighted above, the matching of mentor coach to apprentice coach was facilitated by the national sport organizations involved in the apprenticeship program. Unfortunately, many of these organizations have human resource limitations. Mentor coaches should typically have more experience than apprentice coaches, and they should have a broad-based understanding of the requirements of both the apprentice's current position and potential future positions to which they aspire. However, a group of mentor coaches with these qualifications does not always exist. This can be a particular problem if female apprentices want female mentors, since the number of female head coaches declines when you reach the national level. There is some evidence to indicate that protégés with women mentors receive a greater amount of psychosocial and career developing support than they do from male mentors (Avery, Tonidandel, & Phillips, 2008). Therefore, the development of women mentor coaches is critical for the recruitment, development, and retention of female coaches at all levels of competition. Further development of communities of practice may help to address this issue. Regardless, much of the research on mentoring and communities of practice suggests that these programs have a notable impact on the prolonged retention of participants. Given that we have a decline in numbers of women coaching, particularly at the higher levels, resources should continue to be allocated for coaching development programs that include mentorship and community of practice components.

Mentoring Strategies

HOW MIGHT WE ADDRESS this human resource dilemma? A first and obvious strategy, and certainly one that is used frequently by national sport organizations, is to involve retired coaches in their coach development plans. In this way, there are opportunities to share the vast amount of information collected and wisdom developed by these individuals over many years of coaching. An immediate criticism of this suggestion might be that retired coaches may not be current in terms of technical and tactical knowledge. However, it is possible to get current technical and tactical information from other sources—coaches of the top competing countries in the world, for example, who might serve as secondary mentors for our female high performance coaches. While retired coaches may not have all the immediate answers, they likely have well-developed investigative skill sets that allow them to find the appropriate information.

A second strategy may be to have primary mentors from other sports. As Ragins et al. (2000) hypothesized about mentors from other departments, perhaps coaches from other sports would provide fresh insights and broader perspectives. After all, there is some communality in coaching, and this strategy definitely comes to life in communities of practice. However, this strategy may not be effective for developing our youth coaches, who may not be comfortable interacting with coaches outside of their sport association (Wright et al., 2007).

A third strategy involves careful and future consideration of how to best make use of communities of practice. Other professions, such as education and business, have successfully employed a community of practice model. We should study in more depth the lessons learned, and determine if there is further application to the coaching setting.

A fourth strategy is to enlist men in the mentoring process of female coaches. While some researchers have demonstrated benefits of a female/female mentor-protégé pairing, others have suggested value in mixed gendered pairings. Avery et al. (2008) note that men with organizational power who mentored female coaches did not make any notable contribution to the career movement of their female protégés. However, as the gendered relationship developed, commitment to common interests became more intense, and gendered differences became less of an obstacle. These types of relationships require further study as we work to develop more diversified leadership in coaching in Canada.

A final strategy involves the use of technology as a complementary strategy to those listed above. Technology such as videoconferencing, and tools such as Skype, open up the possibility for mentor/protégé matches in cities of different origins in a way that may not have been imagined before. The Online Mentor Program, another Women in Coaching initiative, matches inexperienced female coaches with mentors based on specific requests, primarily of a technical and tactical nature, from the protégé. This program has potential to be an additional, cost-effective method of coach development. However, the program will be only as good as the volunteer mentors who enlist. It is unlikely, though, that technology-based programs will replace those that involve regular interactions. Rather, they will always likely be an adjunct training/mentoring tool. As Wright et al. (2007) suggest, coaching is a social activity, and face-to-face interaction is critical in developing a relationship centred on trust. Therefore, matching potential online mentors and protégés may benefit from an initial or early meeting outside the online environment, and may require periodic face-to-face interactions. In addition, the mentor/ protégé relationship is more successful when the experience occurs within certain social and geographical boundaries. Without these boundaries, the context can become limited, and the benefits for both parties in the relationship can feel less profound and more superficial (Ayers & Griffin, 2005).

Overall, mentoring programs offer great potential for developing and retaining Canada's female coaches. Careful consideration, however, must be given to matching mentors with protégés, and should focus on the issues of shared values, mutual respect, and trust (Patton et al., 2005). Successful mentoring relationships work because attention is focused on the individual needs of both the mentor and the protégé. In the facilitated mentoring programs that are used widely in coaching, if relationships are not working, there should be procedures developed to allow the mentor, the protégé, or both individuals to terminate the relationship gracefully, without fear of repercussions. The time frame for these relationships should be flexible and not forced, and there should be opportunity, if possible, to shift mentors as the protégé grows and develops. Further research in the area of mentoring and coaching should be conducted, to ensure that we maximize the benefits of mentoring as a developmental tool.

REFERENCES

Avery, D.R., Tonidandel, S., & Phillips, M.G. (2008). Similarity on sports sidelines: How mentor/protégé sex similarity affects mentoring. *Sex Roles, 58,* 72–80.

Ayers, S.F., & Griffin, L.L. (2005). Chapter 5: PETE mentoring as a mosaic. *Journal of Teaching in Physical Education, 24,* 368–378.

Blickle, G., Witzki, A.H., & Schneider, P.B. (2009). Mentoring support and power: A three year predictive field study on protégé networking and career success. *Journal of Vocational Behavior, 74,* 181–189.

Bozionelos, N. (2004). Mentoring provided: Relation to mentor's career success, personality, and mentoring received. *Journal of Vocational Behavior, 64,* 24–46.

Brown, T.M. (2005). Mentorship and the female college president. *Sex Roles, 52*(9/10), 659–666.

Byrne, Z.S., Dik, B.J., & Chiaburu, D.S. (2008). Alternatives to traditional mentoring in fostering career success. *Journal of Vocational Behavior, 72,* 429–442.

Casto, C., Caldwell, C., & Salazar, C. (2005). Creating mentoring relationships between female faculty and students in counselor education: Guidelines for potential mentees and mentors. *Journal of Counseling and Development, 83,* 331–336.

Coaching Association of Canada. (2008). A report on the women in coaching 2009 Canada game apprenticeship program: Professional development workshop #1, February 22–24, 2008. Retrieved June 5, 2009, from http://www.coach.ca/eng/WOMEN/documents/REP_WiC_CGAPReport_EN_FEB08.pdf

Coaching Association of Canada. (1998). Mentoring workshop: Mentor journal.

Colarelli, S.M., & Bishop, R.C. (1990). Career commitment: Functions, correlates, and management. *Group and Organization Studies, 15,* 158–176.

Croxon, S. (2007). Women in coaching 2007 Canada games apprenticeship program report and recommendations. Ottawa: Coaching Association of Canada.

Day, R., & Allen, T.D. (2004). The relationship between career motivation and self-efficacy with protégé career success. *Journal of Vocational Behavior, 64,* 72–91.

Dodds, P. (2005). Chapter 4: PETE women's experiences of being mentored into post-secondary faculty positions. *Journal of Teaching in Physical Education, 24,* 344–367.

Dougherty, T.W., & Turban, D.B. (1994). Role of protégé personality in receipt of mentoring and career success. *Academy of Management Journal, 7*(3), 688.

Eby, L.T., & Allen, T.D. (2008). Moving toward interdisciplinary dialogue in mentoring scholarship: An introduction to the special issue. *Journal of Vocational Behavior, 72,* 159–167.

Eby, L.T., Allen, T.D., Evans, S.C., Ng, T., & Dubois, D.L. (2008). Does mentoring matter? A multidisciplinary meta-analysis comparing mentored and non-mentored individuals. *Journal of Vocational Behavior, 72,* 254–267.

Eby, L.T., Durley, J.R., Evans, S.C., & Ragins, B.R. (2006). The relationship between short-term mentoring benefits and long-term mentor outcomes. *Journal of Vocational Behavior, 69,* 424–444.

Eby, L.T., McManus, S.A., Simon, S.A., & Russell, J.E.A. (2000). The protégé's perspective regarding negative mentoring experiences: The development of a taxonomy. *Journal of Vocational Behavior, 57,* 1–21.

Erickson, E.H. (1963). *Childhood and society.* New York: Norton.

Erickson, K., Bruner, M.W., MacDonald, D.J., & Côté, J. (2008). Gaining insight into actual and preferred sources of coaching knowledge. *International Journal of Sports Science & Coaching, 3*(4), 527–538.

Fagenson, E.A. (1989). The mentor advantage: Perceived career/job experiences of protégés versus non-protégés. *Journal of Organizational Behaviour, 10,* 309–320.

Fishman, J., & Lunsford, A. (2008). Educating Jane. In Eble, M.F., & Gaillet, L.L. (Eds.). *Stories of mentoring: Theory and praxis.* West Lafayette, IN: Parlor Press.

Homer. *Odyssey.* Book II.

Kram, K.E. (1985). *Mentoring at work: Developmental relationships in organizational life.* Glenview, IL: Scott, Foresman.

Lemyre, F., Trudel, P., & Durand-Bush, N. (2007). How youth-sport coaches learn to coach. *The Sport Psychologists, 21,* 191–209.

Lentz, E., & Allen, T.D. (2009). The role of mentoring others in the career plateauing phenomenon. *Group and Organization Management, 34*(3), 358–384.

Lindley, F.A. (2009). *The portable mentor: A resource guide for entry-year principals and mentors.* California: Corwin Press.

McGuire, G.M., & Reger, J. (2003). Feminist co-mentoring: A model for academic professional development. *NWSA Journal, 15*(1), 54–72.

Mobley, G.M., Jaret, C., Marsh, K., Lim, Y.Y. (1994). Mentoring, job satisfaction, gender, and the legal profession. *Sex Roles, 31,* 79–88.

Parise, M.R., & Forret, M.L. (2008). Formal mentoring programs: The relationship of program design and support to mentors' perceptions of benefits and costs. *Journal of Vocational Behavior, 72,* 225–240.

Patton, K. et al. (2005). Chapter 2: Navigating the mentoring process in research-base teacher development project: A situated learning perspective. *Journal of Teaching in Physical Education, 24,* 302–325.

Poteat, L.F., Shockley, K.M., & Allen, T.D. (2009). Mentor-protégé commitment fit and relationship satisfaction in academic mentoring. *Journal of Vocational Behavior, 74,* 332–337.

Ragins, R., Cotton, J.L., & Miller, J.S. (2000). Marginal mentoring: The effects of type of mentor, quality of relationship, and program design on work and career attitudes. *Academy of Management Journal, 43*(6), 1177–1194.

Robertson, S. (2009). A report on the national coach workshop 2009. Ottawa: Coaching Association of Canada.

Roed, B. (1999). *Mentoring: A strategy for faculty growth.* Edmonton: University of Alberta, University Teaching Service.

Salmela, J.H. (1996). *Great job coach!* Ottawa: Potentium.

Scandura, T.A. (1997). Mentoring and organizational justice: An empirical investigation. *Journal of Vocational Behavior, 51,* 58–69.

Scandura, T.A., & Williams, E.A. (2004). Mentoring and transformational leadership: The role of supervisory career mentoring. *Journal of Vocational Behavior, 65*(3), 448–468.

Scheerer, C.R. (2007). Mentoring in occupational therapy: One state's status. *Occupational Therapy in Health Care, 21*(3), 17–30.

Singh, R., Ragins, B.R., & Tharenou, P. (2009). What matters most? The relative role of mentoring and career capital in career success. *Journal of Vocational Behavior, 75,* 56–67.

Wickman, F.T., & Sjodin, T. (1997). *Mentoring.* New York: McGraw-Hill.

Wright, T., Trudel, P., & Culver, D. (2007). Learning how to coach: The different learning situations reported by youth ice hockey coaches. *Physical Education and Sport Pedagogy, 12*(2), 127–144.

Wrestling coach Christine Nordhagen (L), a ten-time Canadian champion and six-time world champion, is a role model for young athletes aspiring to excel.

PHOTO: MARIANN DOMONKOS

POLITICAL ADVOCACY IN COACHING— WHY ENGAGE?

Rose Mercier and Dru Marshall

SEVEN

Introduction

Advocacy, which the *Nelson Canadian Dictionary* defines as "the act of pleading or arguing in favour of something, such as a cause," is an action that few female coaches engage in on their own behalf. Speaking out in support of their athletes, certainly; speaking out in support of themselves, rarely. In this chapter, Rose Mercier and Dru Marshall argue that for female coaches to advance their own cause and "become optimally effective"—and consequently tap into a fairer share of coaching positions with commensurate remuneration, not to mention respect—they must learn to become better advocates of the considerable value they bring to sport. In the male-dominated, politically driven world of sport, no one else is going to do it for them.

As the authors make clear, the focus of such political advocacy is not whether men or women are better equipped to be coaches—clearly such a discussion is as outmoded as female athletes being barred from distance events because of potential damage to the reproductive process. Rather, it is about valuing the differences, especially in the vital area of communication, and recognizing the unique skills and benefits female coaches bring to their athletes.

As well as explaining political advocacy, the authors provide a system map that guides the reader through the complexities of Canada's sport system. Understanding the system within which you work is critical to your political effectiveness.

The ability to advocate successfully is generally not an intrinsic aptitude but requires knowledge imparted and skill developed, and to this end, the authors urge that political advocacy be made part of the curriculum of Canada's coach education programs.

TRADITIONALLY, COACH EDUCATION programs have focused on improving technical and tactical understanding in coaches and enhancing sport science knowledge, particularly in the physical and mental domains. More recently, coaching process skills such as leadership, communication, conflict resolution, and planning have become part of coach education programs. While these skills can effectively be used in advocacy, one skill not usually included in these programs, but is becoming increasingly important, is political advocacy. It is our contention that coaches must acquire political advocacy skills to become optimally effective.

Why is political advocacy an important skill for coaches? Quite simply, sport is politicized. Questions such as who receives funding and how much, who gets to use the facilities and when, who receives new equipment, which team has a full complement of support staff, who makes decisions on coach selection, who decides when and where major competitions will occur, and what support is provided when coaches are away with the team are all political. Coaches need to understand the political environment within which they exist, and need to know how to advocate for their positions on issues.

Female coaches need to be strong advocates of the value they bring to coaching, the importance of having more female coaches, and the need for a coaching environment that makes more female coaches possible. These topics have been covered frequently and in depth in the *Canadian Journal for Women in Coaching*. In July 2001, Rose Mercier and

Penny Werthner wrote about the need for coaching models that value men and women equally, and that ensure women's experiences and perspectives are reflected in decision making. In May 2005, Werthner discussed differences between how men and women learn and communicate, and the resulting impact on coaching. In April 2008, Sheila Robertson addressed the importance of having an environment that enables women both to coach and to parent. In April 2009, Guylaine Demers addressed the importance of having female coaches working at the community level. The *Journal* tells the story of why women are needed in coaching. Female coaches need to carry these messages forward, be visible, and advocate on behalf of themselves and other female coaches.

None of this is to say that female coaches should advocate that women or men are better coaches; rather, men and women coach differently, and these differences are valuable and necessary for athletes. The life experiences and different worldviews that women bring to coaching and sport are essential in creating sport that is inclusive.

Although all coaches need political advocacy skills, learning them is particularly important for female coaches because sport has been and continues to be, despite many efforts, male dominated. This issue was made prominent at the first World Conference on Women and Sport, held in Brighton, England in 1994. The conference brought together policy makers and decision makers in sport from both the national and international levels, and was held specifically to examine the imbalance women face in their participation and involvement in sport. In the background to the Brighton Declaration on Women in Sport, the following statements were made:

> Sport and sporting activities are an integral aspect of the culture of every nation. However, while women and girls account for more than half of the world's population and although the percentage of their participation in sport varies between countries, in every case it is less than that of men and boys.
>
> Despite growing participation of women in sport in recent years and increased opportunities for women to participate in domestic and

international arenas, increased representation of women in decision making and leadership roles within sport has not followed.

Women are significantly under-represented in management, coaching and officiating, particularly at the higher levels. Without women leaders, decision makers and role models within sport, equal opportunities for women and girls will not be achieved.

Although some progress has been made since the declaration, we still have a long way to go. Since Brighton, the International Working Group on Women and Sport (IWG), which was also a result of the Brighton conference, organizes an international conference every four years. The conference is attended by women and men who make decisions or influence policy related to women and sport at all levels—all of them advocates. The conferences highlight progress and identify what further changes are needed to create a positive environment for women and sport. Female coaches need to be aware of the changes that are identified through this process, and other research.

Two recent studies—"Women in Coaching: A Descriptive Study" (Kerr, Marshall, Sharp, & Stirling, 2006) and *A Report on the Status of Coaches in Canada* (Reade et al., 2009)—identify important issues that female coaches should be informed about: the overall lack of women in coaching positions at the national, Canadian Interuniversity Sport, Canadian Colleges Athletic Association, provincial, and Paralympic levels, and the need to address the quality of life and job satisfaction of high performance coaches. Knowing what is wrong is the starting point of effective political advocacy.

What is Advocacy?

ADVOCACY IS PART OF A WIDER continuum of a communication process (McKee, 1992). It involves the selection and organization of information to create a convincing argument or message. When coaches are advocating for an issue, they must have a thorough understanding of it, and know what they want changed. Advocacy can then be accomplished by structuring a message using three questions (Dorfman, Wallack, & Woodruff, 2005):

1. What is wrong?
2. Why does it matter?
3. What should be done about it?

The results of effective advocacy can be seen in the 2009 initiatives of women who compete in ski jumping. Their efforts as advocates made their message clear about adding women's ski jumping to the Olympic Winter Games. Although they have not been successful for 2010, they have created a convincing argument.

Well-structured messages alone do not work. Coaches also need to organize and build their alliances. People need to be mobilized into action and, therefore, the establishment of important and meaningful connections with a network of people is critical. It is also necessary for coaches to educate those who are in positions of influence by providing them with well-structured messages. Coaches need to gain commitment from decision makers. For this to happen, coaches must understand where and how decisions are made. They must understand how to make use of the power they hold as individuals, as well as know who holds the power within their organizations.

What Types of Power Exist?

POWER IS OFTEN THOUGHT of in negative terms because it is associated with those who use the power that they have (as a result of being in a specific position) to their own advantage. Yet this type of power—positional power—can just as easily be used toward positive ends. It depends upon the intention with which positional power is exercised. This is the first important lesson about power: in and of itself, power is neither positive nor negative. The nature of power depends upon the way it is used. Power is useful when it is used to bring about positive change. If coaches want some control in their coaching careers, it is useful to cultivate the types of power that will enable them to accomplish their goals. Coaches have positional power. They use it to make positive choices for their athletes. Coaches also need to recognize those individuals who hold positional power within their organizations, and realize the value of cultivating relationships with them.

Early in a coaching career, coaches need to develop relationships with a variety of people in many different facets of sport. They should identify the people in their sports who are decision makers, or who know the decision makers. Coaches need to take advantage of opportunities and seek out occasions where they can meet people who play different roles in sport, even if they are not directly involved in the current coaching environment. Developing a network takes time and effort, and should be done in an intentional manner. The resulting associative power will pay dividends at different points in a coach's career. Coaches can use a Sport System Map (see Figure 2) to think about the different people with whom they may want to develop connections.

Possibly one of the easiest types of power to develop as a coach is expert power. Becoming knowledgeable and skilled in the strategy, tactics, science, and history of a sport establishes credibility, an essential element of being your own advocate. It is unlikely, however, that expert power will be sufficient for coaches to have optimal impact in their sports. Therefore, they need to develop an understanding of different types of power, and consider how to diversify the types of power they have available to them.

Female coaches can also develop power through a deep understanding of their importance to sport. The topic will invariably come up, mainly because women are still under-represented in the coaching ranks, and because strategies to recruit and develop female coaches continue to be introduced. Staying informed about issues such as those identified in the research earlier in this chapter is essential. One of the best sources of information about issues is the Women in Coaching section of the Coaching Association of Canada website. The answers to the Frequently Asked Questions are an invaluable primer.

Female coaches need to develop the type of power that makes them effective in advocacy by mastering the skills to speak to important

A thoughtful Brianne Law, Alpine Ontario coach at the 2007 Canada Winter Games in Whitehorse, Yukon.

PHOTO: JOHN SIMS, TEAM ONTARIO

issues in simple language that helps others quickly understand issues. Developing the abilities to analyze a situation and use language effectively will help them to challenge the way things are currently done; to name issues that need to be addressed, such as inadequate competition opportunities, unfair coach selection procedures, and inadequate working conditions; or to offer equally valid alternative explanations. In advocating for themselves, their athletes, and their sports, female coaches want to be in the position where they are naming what is important in a situation, and not leaving others to exercise the power of naming.

Another type of power they need to develop is enabling power; that is, the ability to help athletes and others make good choices, often related to their team's or an athlete's goals. This type of power involves empowering others through appropriate positive and critical feedback, and celebration of accomplishments of athletes and staff. As advocates, coaches can empower others by treating them and their ideas with dignity and respect, by developing mutually beneficial relationships, and by facilitating the successful resolution of conflicts. Empowering others requires a variety of skills. Communication skills will help a coach to express her ideas clearly, and to hear what others are really saying. Facilitation skills will help coaches to create processes for helping groups accomplish goals or solve problems together. Enabling power is an asset in any situation that involves groups of people trying to work together and, therefore, it should be nurtured.

A coach will become a more effective advocate when she develops the personal power that results from acting on deeply held values, and having a vision for herself, her athletes, and her sport. A coach's credibility as a leader grows stronger with clear beliefs and values, personal commitment, and self-confidence. Very few coaches can rely on their natural charisma; most of us need to work on creating a source of personal power by clarifying our values and aspirations for the future, and developing confidence in our ability to set course of action that is consistent with these.

In summary, here are six actions a coach can take to enhance her power quotient.

1. Develop a strong network based on solid personal relationships.
   a. Pay attention to who is in your network.
      - Are there individuals who support you through good times and difficult times?
      - Is there someone who will challenge your ideas or offer straight talk feedback?
      - Do you know individuals who understand the politics of your sport?
      - Are there experts you can call upon to test your ideas or help you solve a problem?
      - What types of skills exist among your network?
      - Can you call upon a wise person whose judgement you trust and who provides perspective on issues?
      - How many female coaches are among your circle of contacts who you can compare notes with, celebrate, or commiscrate with?
      - How many coaches do you know in your community? Your municipality? Your sport? In other provinces? In other countries?
   b. Nurture your network.
      - Look for opportunities to connect the people in your network with each other when there's an opportunity.
      - Acknowledge the support and help you receive—saying "thank you" is essential.
      - Recognize the accomplishments of the individuals in your network: a call, a note, an email on the occasion of an award, a new job, an election.
      - Keep learning about the people in your network: stay genuinely interested in their lives and what's important to them.
      - Ask permission—to follow-up at a later date, to refer them to someone else, to mention their name.

- Check in just to check in.

c. Be strategic about how you use social networking media.
- Start or join a Facebook group with a common interest.
- Follow the Twitter postings of people in your network.
- Post questions and see who answers.
- Think before you post.

2. Polish your skills in analyzing situations.
   a. Stay up to date with issues that are important to you.
   b. Read articles and journals, research, visit the Internet so that you understand perspectives that exist.
   c. Use this short analysis to frame an issue:
   - What specifically are you talking about? Can you give a "title" to the situation?
   - Who benefits and who loses from the way things are?
   - When is the situation problematic?
   - When do things get better or worse?
   - Reframe the issue as a question: How can we...?
   d. Uses the suggestions for the action below to talk to others.

3. Practice expressing your ideas in a clear and compelling fashion.
   a. Take a public speaking course.
   b. Join Toastmasters and learn how to make your point on an impromptu occasion, or when you have a chance to prepare.
   c. Write a "stump speech" about an important topic—something you can say when the occasion arises, and that gets better each time you use it.
   d. Make a habit of collecting stories and examples that help explain your ideas.
   e. Focus on three points: people remember things in threes.
   f. Use some common formulas to make your point:
   - (past, present, future) Yesterday it was like this...; today, this happens...; tomorrow we need...
   - (here, there, everywhere) In our community...; in the province...; for our sport...

- (perspectives) what I think; what she thinks: what is the common perspective
g. Stay current with the issues that matter to you. File articles. Save statistics.

4. Use an inclusive approach whenever practical.
   a. Think about who will be affected by your actions or decisions.
   b. Explain what you want to do and why, and ask those who will be affected about what matters to them in a situation.
   c. Let those whose opinions you asked for know what you did with their ideas, and what will happen next.
   d. Think about who else would benefit from being included in something, and ask him or her to participate.

5. Improve and refine your facilitation skills.
   a. Learn more about facilitation: Take courses. Read books. Subscribe to online journals.
   b. Consider taking the training to become a National Coaching Certification Program (NCCP) Learning Facilitator.
   c. Ask for feedback whenever you are leading a group. Use a short form that people can fill out quickly that asks: "What's one thing I did well as a facilitator?" and "What's one thing I could do better?"
   d. Ask an experienced facilitator if she will be your mentor as you improve your facilitation skills.
   e. Start a facilitation journal: Whenever you participate in a facilitated or chaired meeting, make notes about what the person did that you would like to incorporate into your facilitation practice. Take note of actions that you don't like and why.
   f. Look for occasions that need a facilitator, and volunteer.

6. Get clear about your personal values and coaching vision.
   a. Read Chapter 10 of this book: The Business of Greatness.

What Is the Circle of Influence in Sport?

JUST AS AN UNDERSTANDING of power is important for political advocacy, understanding the sport environment in which a coach operates is equally critical. Depending on their situations, coaches need to be aware of the many dimensions they need to think about to become politically effective.

We developed a Sport System Map (Figure 2) for a leadership seminar for federal/provincial/territorial Canada Games apprenticeship coaches. It has proven to be a useful tool for coaches in creating a plan of action.

There are five dimensions in this map. Coaches need to become familiar with the dimensions that affect not only where they currently coach, but also their coaching aspirations.

The *Single Sport Organizations* dimension includes those organizations that follow one sport. Typically, this dimension features a hierarchical nest of organizations from club to international level. Each level in the single sport organization is typically linked through membership to the next higher level.

The *Multi-Sport Organizations* dimension includes organizations that serve many sports, such as the Coaching Association of Canada, the Canadian Centre for Ethics in Sport, the Canadian Sport Centres, and National Coaching Institutes. It also includes organizations, such as Own the Podium, that determine funding support for high performance programs in national sport organizations. In this dimension, while there may be similar types of organizations at provincial/territorial or regional levels, they are not usually linked formally. There may be a loose relationship among organizations at different levels because of the nature of services they provide.

The *Educational Sport Federations and Related Agencies* dimension incorporates institutions and organizations that characterize the sport environment of coaches working in an educational sport setting (for example, Canadian Interuniversity Sport). This dimension features both the hierarchical nest of organizations and the associated organizations.

FIGURE 2   A SPORT SYSTEM MAP: DIRECTIONS

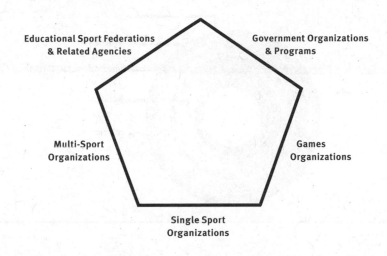

Educational Sport Federations & Related Agencies

Government Organizations & Programs

Multi-Sport Organizations

Games Organizations

Single Sport Organizations

Games Organizations encompasses those organizations, such as the Canadian Olympic Committee, the Canadian Paralympic Committee, Commonwealth Games Canada, or the Canada Games Council, that are the franchise holders and organizers for the various games.

Government Organizations and Programs is the dimension that includes various levels of government that are involved with funding, programming, and facilities.

Each of the five dimensions can be viewed from five different levels (Figure 3). Coaches can create a map of the organizations and individuals that need to be included in their sphere of connection by considering the different levels of a dimension, or by examining all dimensions at one level.

Different types of organizations can be found at each level. The following list is not intended to be exhaustive. Coaches may consider adding other organizations that are important in their unique situations.

LOCAL: coaches, clubs, leagues, municipal recreation departments, school athletic associations, local school boards, individual

FIGURE 3 A SPORT SYSTEM MAP: LEVELS

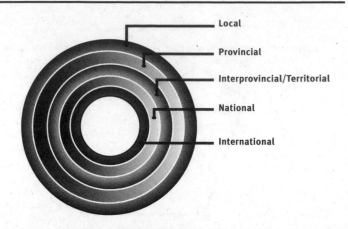

educational institutions with teams, sport schools, multi-sport events or clubs, local games or event organizers

PROVINCIAL/TERRITORIAL: provincial/territorial coaches, provincial/ territorial coaches associations, provincial/territorial sport organizations, provincial/territorial ministries responsible for sport, provincial/territorial coaching co-ordinators, provincial/ territorial sport federations, provincial multi-sport organizations, regional/provincial sport centres, provincial games societies, provincial university athletic associations, high school sport athletic associations

INTERPROVINCIAL: presidents' or executive directors' councils, interprovincial games societies, Interprovincial Sport and Recreation Council

NATIONAL: national sport organizations, Coaches of Canada, Canadian Olympic Committee, Canadian Paralympic Committee, Sport Canada, Canadian Heritage, Coaching Association of Canada, Canadian Association for the Advancement of Women and Sport and Physical Activity, Canadian Centre for Ethics in Sport,

Canada Games Council, Commonwealth Games Canada, Canadian Interuniversity Sport, Canadian Colleges Athletic Association, Physical and Health Education Canada

INTERNATIONAL: international federations, International Olympic Committee, International Paralympic Committee, World Anti-Doping Agency, Commonwealth Games Federation, Pan American Sports Organization, Fédération Internationale du Sport Universitaire, Commonwealth Heads of Government Meeting, Commonwealth Ministers of Sport, Comité International des Jeux de la Francophonie, Council of Europe, UNESCO, General Assembly of International Sport Federations

Coaches do not necessarily need to understand the full scope of organizations and individuals working at all levels, but it is useful to develop an appreciation of the myriad of relationships and jurisdictions that come into play in sport. Being effective advocates requires coaches to understand where decisions that affect them are made, to be aware of who makes those decisions, and to appreciate the context of a decision. None of these happen without intentional action on the part of the coach.

Conclusion

POLITICAL ADVOCACY IS AN important process for coaches to understand, particularly female coaches. To be effective advocates, they must be informed about issues, understand the personal and organizational contexts within which they are working, develop a strong network, and appreciate the goals and vision that they have for their athletes and program (Richey, 1991). We would argue that advocacy lessons should be taught in coach education programs. Advocacy takes courage, strength of character, and brains—and it is not optional if we are to change the current landscape in sport.

A list of political advocacy groups follows below:

- Coaching Association of Canada (CAC): Women in Coaching program
- Canadian Association for the Advancement of Women and Sport and Physical Activity (CAAWS)
- Égale Action (Montreal, Quebec)
- Centre for Sport and Law (Toronto, Ontario)
- InMotion Network (Edmonton, Alberta)
- PROMOTION Plus (Richmond, British Columbia)
- Women's Sports Foundation (United States)
- International Working Group on Women and Sport (Australia)

REFERENCES

Advocacy, n. (1997). *Nelson Canadian dictionary.* Nelson Thomson Learning. Toronto: Nelson Thomson Learning.

Brighton Declaration on Women and Sport. (1994). Retrieved from http://www.sportsbiz.bz/womensportinternational/conferences/brighton_declaration.htm

Coaching Association of Canada: Women in Coaching Website. (2008). Retrieved from http://www.coach.ca/eng/WOMEN/index.cfm

Demers, G. (2009). "We are coaches": Program tackles the under-representation of female coaches. *Canadian Journal for Women in Coaching, 9*(2).

Dorfman, L., Wallack, L., & Woodruff, K. (2005). More than a message: Framing public health advocacy to change corporate practices. *Health Education and Behaviour, 323*(3), 320–336.

Kerr, G., Marshall, D., Sharp, D.-M., & Stirling, A. (2006). *Women in coaching: A descriptive study.* Ottawa: Coaching Association of Canada.

McKee, N. (1992). *Social mobilization and social marketing in developing communities: Lessons for communicators.* Penang, Malaysia: Southbound.

Mercier, R., & Werthner, P. (2001). Changing the androcentric world of sport. *Canadian Journal for Women in Coaching, 1*(6).

Reade, I. et al. (2009). *A report on the status of coaches in Canada.* Ottawa: Coaching Association of Canada.

Richey, D. (1991). The process and politics of advocacy. *Journal of Physical Education, Recreation and Dance, 62*(3), 35–36.

Robertson, S. (2008). They never give up: Once a coach, always a coach. *Canadian Journal for Women in Coaching, 8*(2).

Werthner, P. (2005). Making the case: Coaching as a viable career path for women. *Canadian Journal for Women in Coaching, 5*(3).

Wrestling coaches Shelley Morton (L) and Lyndsay Belisle (R) offer advice during a break in the action at the 2009 Canada Summer Games.

PHOTO: 2009 CANADA GAMES—F. SCOTT GRANT

PART THREE

Advice

Long track speed skating star Kristina Groves thrives on Xiuli Wang's coaching style.

PHOTO: MIKE RIDEWOOD

COACHING AS A VIABLE CAREER PATH FOR WOMEN

Penny Werthner and Bettina Callary

EIGHT

Introduction

A fundamental question for sport has long been why we would need or want women in the coaching profession. And when women are encouraged to aspire to the highest levels of coaching, through programs such as the Coaching Association of Canada's Women in Coaching program and its National Team Apprenticeship Program, what is being done to ensure these women continue to progress long after their involvement in such initiatives is past? This chapter tackles the questions head-on.

Penny Werthner and Bettina Callary begin their investigation by examining recent findings in gender differences in communicating and learning. They then speak to leaders of several national sport organizations that have supported the National Team Apprenticeship Program.

The investigation strongly supports the case for women and high performance coaching, confirms the importance of apprenticeship programs for female coaches and their career prospects, and allows the reader to feel cautious optimism. The challenge is to build on the authors' findings by putting in place mechanisms to keep women in coaching once they reach the national team level.

As indicated by the recent increase in government funding, which reflects a multi-year commitment to sport, the timing is right. Every sector in sport unequivocally recognizes the value of the coach to performance. We foresee a future when female coaches hold national team positions not because it is the fair and equitable thing to do, but because of the skills they bring to the job, and the unique and valued contribution they make to athletic performance.

IN EXAMINING THE POSSIBILITY of women creating viable careers in the coaching profession, it is intriguing to note, as mentioned in earlier chapters, that while the number of girls and women participating in organized sport continues to increase, this is not the case for the numbers of female coaches. A fundamental question that underlies this exploration has been why would we want or need women in the coaching profession? And when we create programs for women in coaching, such as the National Team Apprenticeship Program (NTAP), what is being done to ensure that the women continue to progress long after their involvement with the program is past?

What Do the Numbers Continue to Tell Us?

RESEARCH CONTINUES TO DEMONSTRATE low numbers of female coaches at all levels of sport, in Canada, as well as in many other countries. Laberge's (1992) study of the employment situation of high performance coaches in Canada found that only one in five senior coaches were women. As noted in Chapter 2, in a recent study on coaches in Canada at the university, college, provincial, Canada Games, and national level of sport, entitled *A Report on the Status of Coaches in Canada* (Reade et al., 2009), only 26% of the coaches who responded were female. Only 20% of the coaches of carded athletes (athletes who are competing at the national level of sport and are funded by the Government of Canada) were female. In the United Kingdom, Norman (2008) reported that less than a quarter of all active coaches were women and cites similar numbers for Germany. Acosta and Carpenter (2008), in their longitudinal study on intercollegiate coaching in the United States, found that women comprised only 42.8% of head coaches of women's teams.

What Are the Issues Women Face?

CHAPTER 2 HAS DELINEATED MANY of the difficulties that women face in the workplace in general. In *Harvard Business Review*, Eagly and Carli (2007) explored the problem of the continuing lack of women in leadership roles, particularly in the business field, and suggested that women face problems at every phase of their working lives. They proposed the metaphor of the labyrinth to illustrate what confronts women at many different phases of their working lives. (See Dru Marshall's Introduction and Chapter 2 for further discussion of the labyrinth.) Eagly and Carli cited a large number of research studies to support the numerous issues and prejudices that women face, such as resistance to the style of women's leadership, the difficult balancing act between work and family life, and continuing wage discrepancies.

If we turn from women's working lives in general to the world of women and coaching, we find numerous research studies conducted on the issues faced by female coaches and, in some cases, suggestions for solutions to those issues. We know that coaching is a complex activity encompassing many diverse responsibilities, and long hours on the field or pool deck, and at competitions. In an article outlining the challenges that female coaches must overcome, and strategies for facilitating their development in coaching, Kilty (2006) describes a number of external barriers such as unequal assumption of competence (where a male coach is automatically assumed to be more competent than a female coach); hiring from a principle of similarity (individuals hiring someone like themselves—known as homologous

reproduction); homophobia; and lack of female mentors. She then
cites internal barriers such as perfectionism (female coaches being
too self-critical), lack of assertiveness, inhibition in promoting accomplishments, and the high stress of balancing work and personal life.
Kilty concludes with suggestions for coach education, and advocates
for mentoring programs for female coaches at both the individual and
institutional level.

Why Do We Need Female Coaches?

FROM A BROAD GENDER PERSPECTIVE, Pinker (2008) examines the
science of sex differences between women and men. She concludes
that differences do indeed exist, and not recognizing them only
devalues women's strengths and preferences. In exploring the nature
of women's working lives, she cites Catherine Hakim of the London
School of Economics, author of *Work-Lifestyle Choices in the Twenty-First
Century* (2000). Hakim states that we cannot ignore that many women's
histories have an "organic quality" about them, where the goal is a
moving target. "The feminine life story typically presents a smoothly
integrated stream of events in which everything they did was the
"natural" outcome of the situation at the time, the actions of others,
chance events" (Hakim, p. 16). Importantly, Pinker (2008) concludes by
stating that understanding that women may have nonlinear careers
allows us to create ways for women to opt back into a career. She cites
numerous companies that have attempted to build this kind of flexibility into the working environment. We should be thinking about
this for female coaches!

Indeed, precisely because of the differences between men and
women, and despite all the issues women face in coaching, we argue
that we need many more women to coach our young female athletes,
and perhaps even our young male athletes. To answer why, it is useful
to reflect on the qualities of an effective high performance amateur
sport coach, as well as on research into gender differences and
communication.

Plenty of anecdotal evidence and some recent research point to several specific and necessary qualities most successful coaches possess. Interviews with fifteen of Canada's best coaches at the Olympic level (four women and eleven men, with "best" based on the Olympic and world rankings of their athletes or teams) identified three key qualities that enabled them to succeed as coaches (Werthner & Trudel, 2009).

Firstly, all of these coaches, both women and men, spoke of being open to learning and seeking out mentors or experts in a number of areas to help them continue to learn. Initially, the focus of the learning tended to be in technical or strategic areas, and then it often turned toward a communication or team issue or conflict management area. What needed to be learned was consciously sought out by each coach, whether that learning took place with mentors, or through formal or informal learning situations. The coaches all saw this learning as a necessary and ongoing process. As one of the female coaches said in reference to mentors, "I have learned a lot from other coaches. I got paired up with another national coach, and I worked alongside him and it was awesome. But how we worked was left up to us, it wasn't really formal."

Secondly, the coaches spoke extensively about the importance of being open to listening to and learning from their athletes, particularly at this level of sport, in which the athletes are, for the most part, very aware and knowledgeable. As one of the female coaches said, "One of the important ways I have learned to be a good coach is by listening to my athletes. It is not through evaluation forms, but rather dialogue and listening to their comments and getting to know them."

Thirdly, each spent an immense amount of time in self-reflection (thinking about how things were going, what they needed to do differently, what they might be missing in the training or competition), and in enabling those around them—athletes and assistant coaches— also to reflect on these issues. "I am always analyzing the training program, thinking about how it is going, what I need to be changing."

These latter two key qualities also created strong, clear-thinking, independent athletes and, therefore, an environment where great sport performances occurred.

There has also been a vast amount of research on gender differences and how we, as women and men, communicate. An article in the *Canadian Journal for Women in Coaching* on the differences in gender communication and sport, based on the work of Deborah Tannen (2001), clearly delineates the differences between how women and men communicate, and why this is a significant consideration for coaches and their athletes. Tannen (1990), in her book *You Just Don't Understand: Women and Men in Conversation*, writes about the influence of linguistic styles on conversations and relationships. She states that language communicates ideas and, at the same time, negotiates relationships. There is no one best way to communicate, but being aware of your own personal communications "style," understanding the nature of gender differences in communication, and listening well to the styles and preferences of others is an important skill for coaches to acquire.

Why Gender Matters (Sax, 2005) rekindles the debate about the differences between how females and males learn and think. Sax suggests that girls' and boys' brains develop differently and that the sexes "hear" differently and respond to stress differently. The research that backs these claims needs to be closely examined, but anyone who has coached both female and male athletes knows that they must take into account differences between what each wants and needs in order to perform well.

Another research study regarding sex differences, which bodes well for women as coaches, is the work of Feingold (1994). He conducted a meta-analysis of personality traits. In looking for traits common to all people, and covering many personality studies in numerous countries over fifty-two years, he found that men, on average, were more assertive than women, no matter where they lived or level of education. Women were more trusting of others, gregarious, and nurturing, again regardless of country or level of education. Of course, this is not true of every woman and every man. However, we would certainly argue that, while women often still need to learn to be more assertive, the ability to be supportive and helpful with others is a crucial quality in working effectively with athletes.

It is important to take these various areas of research—the nature of women's working lives, gender differences in communication, specific issues facing female coaches, and coach learning—into consideration when trying to answer the fundamental questions of why we need women as coaches, and how we can keep them in the profession.

From the coaching research outlined above, it appears that the essential qualities of our "best" coaches can be learned and demonstrated by both women and men. This research is early evidence that all these skills or qualities are required at the highest levels of amateur sport to ensure excellent individual and team performances. Are women inherently better at possessing or honing these qualities? We do not know the answer definitively. But, to paraphrase Charlotte Whitton, a former mayor of Ottawa, women "are certainly not worse." Female coaches are often willing to seek out experts for help, are skilled at listening and "reading" their athletes, and are skilled at reflecting on their actions. We have observed many male coaches at the national and international levels, from Canada and from other countries, who have great technical sport skills but who dismiss female athletes' concerns and their need for greater dialogue and explanation in training. These coaches resort to yelling, sometimes harsh personal comments, and telling athletes that they are not tough enough.

It is our belief that technical skills are not enough to be an excellent coach. With only these skills, coaches do not consistently produce great performances, and they certainly do not create independent, responsible young individuals inside and outside of sport. They produce athletes who get angry, lose confidence, change sports, and often drop out. Does this mean that only women should coach female athletes? Perhaps not—we will sit on the fence on that one for a little longer. Certainly we have in Canada many excellent male coaches coaching female athletes very well, clearly understanding their needs and concerns. And these working relationships have resulted in many

Olympic medallists. We would not want to see that end! But we need many more female coaches in the sport system. Female coaches need to continue to work on these so-called "softer" skills, but what they also need is experience in coaching at world levels. They need that work experience to develop what Dorothy Leonard and Walter Swap (2005) called "deep smarts"—the valuable wisdom and instincts that come only from having lived through such situations as being on the floor at a national championship with two minutes to go and your team is up by just one point; being at the Olympics with one day to go before your athlete's heat and suddenly having to deal with a damaged boat; being at a provincial championship and finding that one of your athletes cannot compete due to an injury; or being at the FIS Freestyle World Ski Championships when the athlete competing ahead of your athlete crashes and breaks her neck.

The Coaching Association of Canada's Women and Coaching Programs

THE COACHING ASSOCIATION OF CANADA's programs for female coaches are helping women progress in the sport coaching process. The association provides funding for three programs:

- the National Team Apprenticeship Program, where selected female coaches are provided with funding (approximately $7,800 per year for three years) to take part in national team training camps, world championships, and for education and ongoing learning
- the National Coaching Institute scholarship program, where fifteen women each year are provided with $1,500 to attend an institute
- the Professional Development Program, which provides grants of $2,000 to national sport organizations or individual female coaches for special learning projects

The National Team Apprenticeship Program gives female coaches the opportunity to gain valuable experience and insight into national and international athletic experiences through mentoring, working with other high-level coaches, experiencing first-hand high performance coaching situations, and discussing topics with other high performance female coach apprentices. Additionally, the program encourages national sport organizations to identify their top female coaches, nominate them to the program, and continue to support them after the program is completed. The program provides structured mentorships that enhance learning in addition to giving female coaches the chance to gain international experiences through financial support that would otherwise not be viable. What this means is that female coaches are given the opportunity to commit fully to coaching and get the experiences to back up their interest and passion. Thereafter, their résumés speak for themselves.

Three coaches who have been through this program are Laryssa Biesenthal, Tobie Gorman, and Joanne Devlin-Morrison.

Laryssa Biesenthal is a former Olympic medallist in rowing who started coaching when she retired after the 2000 Olympic Games. She coached in the 2004 Olympic Games, and she is now Australia's senior women's coach, a definite loss for Canada (see Chapter 1). Brian Richardson, the high performance director of Rowing Canada Aviron during her apprenticeship, stated that the program provided "enormous value both to her and to our sport. The program gave Laryssa the opportunity to commit fully to coaching, which allowed her to get the experience needed to get a full-time job. Getting that experience and then getting hired is always the difficulty, and this program helps enormously. Amateur sport is still male-dominated, and so the opportunities are limited for women to gain those coaching experiences. NTAP has been tremendous for our sport. Certainly the individual has to have the ability, but Laryssa is a good coach. She can now stand on her own."

Tobie Gorman is a gymnastics coach with many years' experience operating and coaching in her own club. She developed two athletes, Heather Purnell and Melanie Banville, who qualified for the 2004 Olympic Games. Gorman was then selected by Gymnastics Canada to be an Olympic coach in Athens. Lise Simard, high performance director for Gymnastics Canada's women's program at the time of Gorman's apprenticeship, said, "The Coaching Association of Canada provided us with the money to help Tobie develop into an international-level coach. We certainly needed a good candidate, with a good attitude, willing to learn, and willing to share, and with Tobie we had that. But she was inexperienced at the world championship and Olympic levels, and we needed this program to help create ways to complete that learning. Plus, this program provides other experiences that we do not offer." Simard and Gorman both spoke of the value of the mentor coach, David Kenwright, and the national coach, Andrei Rodionenko. "Tobie had the unique opportunity to work with both these coaches as mentors, and each provided expertise at the Olympic level for her and her two athletes," said Simard. "As an example, David worked closely with Tobie despite the fact that their respective clubs and athletes were actually in competition with each other. It truly was a remarkable mentorship." Gorman felt that "both Andrei and David recognized my abilities and the abilities of my athletes. They each worked to help me. They gave me such an immense amount of their time, and they were so open to my questions. Importantly, they recognized how I needed to learn. They encouraged me and raised my self-confidence. Having both of these coaches work with me was such valuable learning."

Graham Barton, the high performance director of CanoeKayak Canada, noted that the program provides opportunities to educate female coaches at Level 4 of the National Coaching Certification Program, and opens the door for them to coach at national and international levels. Joanne Devlin-Morrison, who completed Level 4 at the National Coaching Institute in Calgary, coached at a number of international regattas, and found that the opportunities and learning were invaluable. "This program gave me opportunities I would not otherwise have had: learning at the National Coaching Institute and attending international regattas with the national team. As well, my mentor coach, Mark Granger, in his work with the men's kayak program, allowed me to observe and be part of the planning and work that goes into preparing for the Olympics." Barton, however, did emphasize that although a sport organization can help and encourage, ultimately it is up to the coach to decide whether she wants to continue and become an established head coach of a national team.

These are just three examples of the strong, skilled female coaches who have been part of the National Team Apprenticeship Program. Clearly, the program has helped these women continue to develop. It has created a learning environment with a structured mentor coach situation that has enabled the female coaches to have experts, both in coaching and in sport in general, with whom to interact on a regular basis. These mentors have played key roles by being open to sharing their knowledge and being excellent teachers and facilitators of learning. And without question, the national sport organizations have played an important part in the success of the coaches. Their willingness to identify top female coaches for the program has been crucial. We now need to ask sport organizations to continue to support their coaching work within the sport, because we continue to lose a number of our excellent coaches, women and men, to other countries on a regular basis. Clearly, from the perspectives of female coaches and their sport organizations, the elements of the apprenticeship program—the mentorship, the learning seminars, the opportunities to discuss issues and learn from other coaches, and the national and international coaching opportunities—while not perfect, are having some positive effects. Nonetheless, the comment voiced by Barton raises important issues. The support from the sport organizations, the Coaching Association of Canada, and the other female coaches in the National Team Apprenticeship Program is crucial, but the women must decide what they want to do, and must work hard to accomplish their goals. The barriers continue to exist, despite the help that is provided. It is not an easy path to get to and remain in high performance coaching.

How Can We Keep Women in Coaching?

HOW CAN WE KEEP WOMEN in the system once they start the process of becoming high-level coaches? The fundamental answer—so simple and yet so seemingly hard to do in Canada—is salaried coaching positions. We need look only to the university system, where coaches are paid, albeit not very well in many universities, to see a greater number of female coaches of women's teams and occasionally of men's teams. When we look at national teams, the number of female coaches still sits at about 17%, depending on the year. If we had the money in the national sport system to pay coaches well—an issue for male and female coaches at this level—we would be able to attract many more individuals to coaching.

Salaried positions are hugely important for female coaches because, whether we choose to admit it or not, women continue to bear the brunt of childcare and home care. With paid positions, coaching could become a viable and attractive career option. We would hear more women say, "I will train to be a coach." Certainly, with the increased monies in Canada's sport system because of the 2010 Olympic Winter Games, we have moved in this direction. Importantly, with coaching as a paid profession, we would be able to hold coaches accountable—in the best sense of providing constructive feedback and conducting effective performance reviews—ensuring they have all the qualities and skills necessary to be effective coaches. We could perhaps begin to value the communication skills, the listening to athletes, and the ability to manage conflict as much as we value the technical skills. All these skills must be in place for coaches to succeed at the Olympic level, and indeed, at all levels of sport.

The Coaching Association of Canada has played a key role in the process of increasing the number of female coaches. Its ultimate success, however, is tied to ensuring that the sport system clearly understands and appreciates the skills that women bring to coaching, and the still very real need for many more decently paid coaching positions.

REFERENCES

Acosta, R.V., & Carpenter, L. (2008). Women in intercollegiate sport: A longitudinal, national study: 1997–2006. *Women in Sport*. Retrieved June 22, 2009 from http://webpages.charter.net/womeninsport/2008/Summary/Final.pdf

Eagly, A., & Carli, L. (2007). Women and the labyrinth of leadership. *Harvard Business Review*, 63–71. Retrieved from http://www.hbr.org

Feingold, A. (1994). Gender differences in personality: A meta-analysis. *Psychological Bulletin, 116*(3).

Hakim, C. (2000). *Work-lifestyle choices in the twenty-first century.* New York: Oxford University Press.

Kerr, G., Marshall, D., Sharp, D.-M., & Stirling, A. (2006). *Women in coaching: A descriptive study.* Ottawa: Coaches Association of Canada.

Kilty, K. (2006). Women in coaching. *The Sport Psychologist, 20*(2), 222–234.

Laberge, S. (1992). Employment situation of high performance coaches in Canada. *Sport Canada Occasional Papers, 3*(1).

Leonard, D., & Swap, W.C. (2005). *Deep smarts: How to cultivate and transfer enduring business wisdom.* Boston: Harvard Business School Press.

Norman, L. (2008). The UK coaching system is failing women coaches. *International Journal of Sports Science & Coaching, 3*(4), 447–464.

Pinker, S. (2008). *The sexual paradox: Extreme men, gifted women and the real gender gap.* Toronto: Random House Canada.

Reade, I. et al. (2009). *A report on the status of coaches in Canada.* Ottawa: Coaching Association of Canada.

Sax, L. (2005). *Why gender matters: What parents and teachers need to know about the emerging science of sex differences.* New York: Doubleday.

Tannen, D. (2001). Understanding the differences between how women and men communicate. *Canadian Journal for Women in Coaching.* Retrieved from http://www.coach.ca/WOMEN/e/journal/may2001

Tannen, D. (1990). *You just don't understand: Women and men in conversation.* New York: Ballantine Books.

Werthner, P., & Trudel, P. (2009). Investigating the idiosyncratic learning paths of elite Canadian coaches. *International Journal of Sports Sciences and Coaching, 4*(3), 433–449.

Competing at the 2009 Canada Summer Games, Team Yukon benefited from its excellent coaches (L to R): head coach Mark Hureau; assistant coach Sarah Crane, making a point; Diedre Davidson, an apprentice coach through the Coaching Association of Canada's Women in Coaching program; and manager Kaeli Ritchie.

PHOTO: 2009 CANADA GAMES—F. SCOTT GRANT

DEVELOPING THE NEXT GENERATION OF FEMALE COACHES

Dru Marshall, Guylaine Demers,
and Dawn-Marie Sharp

NINE

Introduction

This chapter builds on the insights provided by Penny Werthner and
Bettina Callary in Chapter 8 by offering eight specific strategies for
developing the next generation of female coaches. That such strategies
are necessary is borne out by the figures in Tables 3 and 4. Beyond
suggesting ways of training upcoming female coaches, Dru Marshall,
Guylaine Demers, and Dawn-Marie Sharp provide suggestions for keeping
female coaches in their careers. The solutions offered in this chapter also
develop ideas set up in Chapters 6 and 7, and tie these themes together
in practical ways.

THE PREVIOUS CHAPTERS ALL POINT to the fact that, despite the
involvement of respected organizations like the Coaching Association of Canada and the Canadian Association for the Advancement
of Women and Sport and Physical Activity, there has been limited
success in helping female coaches. Women continue to confront a
dearth of coaching opportunities, feelings of isolation, and lack of

TABLE 3   NUMBER OF CERTIFIED COACHES (NCCP), OCTOBER 2007

	WOMEN	MEN	PERCENTAGE OF WOMEN
NCCP Level 1	76,594	181,028	30
NCCP Level 2	22,600	43,978	34
NCCP Level 3	2,830	6,927	29
NCCP Level 4	177	669	21
NCCP Level 5	10	81	11

Source: Coaching Association of Canada, 2007

professional and sustained development opportunities to enter the field of coaching (Mullins, 2008).

Recently, researchers have suggested that we may not have been targeting the right obstacles. Some scholars who have been concerned about the ineffectiveness of many strategies for female coaches—such as bringing more women into coaching, retaining them, and providing them with mentorship (Demers & Audet, 2007; Kerr & Marshall, 2007)—started to study the problem from a new perspective: feminist cultural studies. Kamphoff (2008) explains that "using a feminist cultural studies approach allows for women's experiences to be at the center of the research and the research is conducted for women, not on women" (p. 469). Leanne Norman (2008) is one of the researchers using this approach. She examined high performance coaches in the United Kingdom and her results showed the inadequacies of the coaching system in contributing to women's inferior status within the coaching profession. She reported "how the existing masculine culture of sport has shaped coaching opportunities and coach education strategies for the participants" (p. 451). The three themes that emerged from the data she collected with the female coaches of her study were (a) fewer opportunities; (b) feeling isolated with minimal support offered by their sport organization; and (c) flawed coach education that does little to facilitate women's personal and professional development. Interestingly, Norman suggests that rather than a "glass ceiling," female coaches experience

TABLE 4 CANADIAN COACHES AT THE OLYMPIC GAMES, 1996–2008

	MALE HEAD COACHES	FEMALE HEAD COACHES	TOTAL HEAD COACHES	PERCENTAGE OF FEMALE HEAD COACHES
Beijing, 2008	20	2	22	9
Torino, 2006	23	4	27	15
Athens, 2004	25	2	27	7
Salt Lake City, 2002	11	3	14	21
Sydney, 2000	27	3	30	10
Nagano, 1998	14	4	18	22
Atlanta, 1996	15	1	16	6
Totals	**135**	**19**	**154**	12

Compiled by the Coaching Association of Canada. Statistics are derived directly from official Canadian Olympic Committee team handbooks, and include post-publication edits where possible/available. Coaches are categorized according to the position declaration in the handbook.

a narrow "bottle neck" path in which the higher the women climb, the fewer their pathways become, and they are excluded from positions of power. She concludes by saying that increasing the number of female coaches does not mean they will be valued or that pathways to powerful positions in coaching will be available to them.

We think there are some important parts to Norman's analogy of a "bottle neck," namely that as a female coach rises through the ranks, fewer opportunities exist. However, the "bottle neck" analogy implies a high volume of coaches getting to a narrow area and being stymied. We believe Canada has a narrow development pyramid for female coaches, and so the "bottle neck" analogy is imperfect. In Canada, there are only a few high-level opportunities. Consequently, women either remain at lower levels by choice, or drop out before reaching their full potential as coaches. Regardless, it is clear that more research is required in this area.

According to Mullins (2008), this new line of research allows us to understand that the most potent barrier for female coaches is the "social construct of sport as a male-dominated profession translating to fewer opportunities for women, and social isolation or lack of institutional support for those women who break through the male-dominated ranks" (p. 465). Therefore, if we want to help female coaches, we have to tackle that barrier in particular.

The Importance of Female Coaches

FROM THEIR LONG HISTORY of studying women in sport, the Tucker Center for Research on Girls and Women in Sport suggests three major reasons for increasing the number of female coaches (2009). Firstly, research indicates that children and youth benefit when females hold positions of power. Messner (2009) argues that today's boys are moving into a world where they will have women co-workers and possibly women bosses, so they need to experience the full range of women's leadership abilities. Conversely, without female coaches as role models, girls may devalue their own abilities, report lower self-efficacy, accept negative stereotypes, fail to realize their own potential, and limit their sport career aspirations. Female coaches are more likely to encourage female athletes to enter coaching (Werthner, 2005). Secondly, women in positions of leadership have the potential to be a mechanism for change. The visibility of women in leadership positions helps create social change and challenges the social construction of gender. Ultimately, for those within and outside sport, the presence of female coaches sends an important message that the sporting arena is an inclusive one (Kerr, Marshall, Sharp, & Stirling, 2006). Thirdly, there is the potential for self-fulfillment for women, particularly in a lifetime commitment to physical activity.

If we look at our own experiences as coaches, we realize that women have typically had different experiences in sport than men. As a result, women can relate better to the experiences of female athletes. Moreover, women's experiences in sport have made sports more inclusive to female and male athletes, particularly with female athletes becoming increasingly more involved in "men's" sports. For instance, the number of girls playing ice hockey tripled between 1998 and 2005 (Ifedi, 2008). Often the male and female versions of a sport differ because of different athletic attributes or tactical approaches. These differences have an impact on the way a sport is played. Women who have been involved as athletes in women's sport truly understand the sport and why the particular techniques and tactics are used specifically in the women's game. However, while we have more women than ever before competing in sports that were traditionally played by men, such as ice hockey and soccer, male coaches are still coaching female athletes.

As men continue to hold positions of power, gender inequities and stereotypes are reproduced. There have been positive changes at the athlete level, but not at the coach level. Women need female role models. See Chapter 8 for a further exploration of why we need more female coaches.

Strategies

TO DEVELOP THE NEXT GENERATION of female coaches, we suggest eight strategies. While the list is not exhaustive, we hope it provides food for thought:

1. Identification of coaches to nurture
2. Identification of female athletes with the potential to coach
3. Retention of current coaching situations
4. New paradigms of coaching
5. Development of networks
6. Mentoring (see Chapter 6)
7. Political advocacy (see Chapter 7)
8. Development of negotiation skills (see Chapter 11)

Strategy 1. Identification of coaches to nurture

One apparently simple way to develop the next generation of high performance female coaches is to identify and nurture those coaches who have the potential to develop to the upper ranks. Identification of potential high performance coaches is comparable to the process that coaches use for athlete selection.

Young female coaches interested in developing into high performance coaches need

- a strong dedication, desire, and commitment to personal excellence
- solid leadership and communication skills
- well-developed coping skills
- an ability to demonstrate athlete improvement
- open-mindedness
- the desire to move up the coaching ranks

We suggest this is an "apparently" simple method because identifying the next layer of coaches in a system is often easier said than done.

Politics often enter into the picture with different interest groups pushing their candidate of choice, so it is important to think critically about who identifies the next layer of coaches. It is best to build a committee formed of different interest groups. The committee should include someone with "big picture" vision, a person who understands the needs of the sport as well as the needs of coaches. Preferably, this individual should not be seen as having ties to any particular stakeholder group. Committee members should include individuals representing various stakeholders, such as provinces/territories, clubs, and universities and colleges. Some organizations may even consider including a player representative within the mix, because the players have yet another perspective. Moreover, the experiences that a player gains while on the committee can influence her decisions for future involvement in the sport. In other words, a positive experience on a forward-thinking committee could be a potential recruitment and retention strategy.

In addition, choices for coach selection should be based on agreed-upon criteria and strategies that are put in place for each identified coach. These strategies should be unique, depending on the coach's life circumstance and level of development. If a choice cannot be made between two coaches, both should be given opportunities to display their coaching attributes so that the next level of decision is performance-based.

Two cautionary notes:

1. In some sports, the idea of providing women with an opportunity to coach at an advanced level is not considered; therefore, women in these sports are dealing with systemic problems that must be handled by broader policies. Therefore, gender equity policies may have to be developed within organizations.

2. Sometimes choices are made, and the selected coaches are seen as the "anointed ones" within their sport's coaching community. As a result, the road is made a little bumpier for that person. Fortunately, if the individual can make it through this initial political minefield, she will have become well trained to do the higher level coaching jobs.

Along with broad political issues in coach identification, there are also issues at the coach level. Many younger female coaches may not even be considering a career in coaching. Their reasons range from seeing high performance coaching jobs as something they may never achieve, to seeing those jobs as being undesirable because of the political pressure and work involved, to perceiving a lack of opportunity. Therefore, the identification process should involve identifying coaches at a variety of levels, with appropriate strategies to help in the development. For example, a developmental club coach may not be ready for an offshore experience with a national team and all that entails, but she may benefit from an experience at a national development camp in combination with a provincial team experience. Some coach identification strategies have failed because a younger coach is put into an experience for which she is not yet ready. This can result in one of two extreme situations. From the coach's perspective, the stresses are too great, the experience is not enjoyable, and she quits. From the association or club perspective, there is a lack of success with the athletes and, therefore, they do not want the coach around. We do not put athletes into situations we think they are not ready for; we should use the same care with coaches.

On a personal note, we believe high performance coaches have a responsibility to identify and develop the up-and-coming coaches. They can act as role models for the job. They can offer support, encouragement, and advice for coaches in any position, because typically they have an understanding from a personal perspective of where a younger or less experienced coach is coming from. They can generate excitement and enthusiasm for the sport and the job. One of us learned, for example, that although coaching a national team was one of the toughest things she had ever done, the position also afforded her the richest learning environment to date. She highly values learning experiences, so "selling" people on being a top-level coach is easy for her. While the costs are high, the benefits are greater. Probably most importantly, national coaches, with the support of the national sport organization, can help provide opportunities, through annual planning, for developing coaches in both on- and offshore training and competition ventures. These opportunities should become part of the strategies for developing coaches. They may also become part of a broader program for an individual coach, as in an apprenticeship program.

CRITICAL QUESTIONS FOR STRATEGY 1:

1. Where can we find potential new coaches?
2. Who should identify new coaches?
3. How should coaches be identified?
4. How can coaches with potential be nurtured in your sport, and who should be involved in the nurturing?
5. What types of resources do I need to develop coaches with potential?

Strategy 2. Identification of female athletes with the potential to coach

Another strategy to help develop the next wave of female coaches is to identify high-level athletes with coaching potential. Coaching is not for every athlete, but there are those who have the skill set to develop into excellent coaches. Traits these athletes possess include intelligence, an ability to strategize, a positive and enthusiastic attitude, passion for their sport, a high energy level, and great communication skills. High-level athletes who become high performance coaches have a distinct advantage over coaches who have not been athletes: they know how athletes think and feel during competition because they have been there before. However, again we must be careful about how quickly we push athletes into the coaching realm.

Laurie Eisler is the present coach of the University of Alberta's Pandas volleyball team. The Pandas are the seven-time Canadian Interuniversity Sport champions. Eisler has a number of alumni involved in coaching roles with her program (Canada West Conference, 2009). She says, "At times we push people who have finished their playing careers into coaching

I concur with this perspective. Over my twenty years of coaching at the university level, I have involved thirteen of our alumni as assistant coaches; two have gone on to coach at other Canadian Interuniversity Sport institutions, two at National Collegiate Athletic Association institutions, and six have been involved with coaching at the provincial level. In all cases, when they first started coaching, they were amazed at the amount of work behind the scenes, and some of them lost interest within a year or two. I have learned through the years that people need to be introduced to coaching on a gradual basis. I have had coaches involved in our program for as long as thirteen years. The legacy continues as the present coaching staff of the Pandas field hockey team consists of three alumni of the team. Those who have been gradually introduced to coaching, and given more responsibility over time, recognize the beauty of the job.

—DRU MARSHALL

too quickly." She believes athletes who have finished their playing careers need a gradual introduction into the coaching arena. "Athletes who have played at a high performance level typically need a break. Few are going to want to continue making the sacrifices that are necessary to coach at that level. You need a lot of time and energy, and you also need to get some balance."

CRITICAL QUESTIONS FOR STRATEGY 2:

1. What should I look for in a potential coach?
2. Which of my athletes exhibit the characteristics in Strategy 1?
3. How will I nurture and develop these identified athletes to become coaches?
4. How can I best be a role model for these individuals?
5. What other resources and opportunities can I identify and recommend for these individuals?

Strategy 3. Retention of current coaching situations

Another important strategy is the further development and retention of women who are currently in coaching positions. Coaching needs to be seen as a viable career choice for a woman. High performance female coaches need to be hired—with salaries and benefits packages that are commensurate with their capabilities and responsibilities. As noted earlier, the current representation of women coaching at the international level of competition is low, and the numbers have, in fact, decreased. Strategies, such as the Sport Canada policy goal,[1] must be put in place to develop more high performance female coaches. Those women who have made it to that level should have comparable situations to those of their male counterparts. For the most part, this has not yet happened. Here is one illustrative example.

.Tracy David, one of Canada's premier soccer coaches, is currently coaching at the University of Victoria. At one time in her career, national team head coach Even Pellerud appointed her as an assistant coach with the national youth teams program. However, progress in her coaching career has been neither simple nor effortless.

As a player, David established herself at an international level. She won six national club championships in ten years with the Edmonton Angels, and played on the national team from 1986 to 1990. In 2003, she became the second female to be named to the Canadian Soccer Hall of Fame, in recognition of her accomplishments and contributions to the game (University of Victoria, 2008). To date, David has successfully gained multiple coaching positions and experiences to prepare her for coaching with the national women's soccer teams, including sixteen years with the University of Alberta and eight years with the University of Victoria. She has won several CanWest conference titles and three Canadian Interuniversity Sport championships. In 2005, she coached British Columbia to the gold medal at the Canada Games. Moreover, she has obtained her B License (Level 4), and completed her master's degree in coaching studies.

With all these qualifications and experiences, David still faces barriers based on gender. The Canadian Soccer Association continues to hire men to coach developmental teams and for national select competitions at the provincial level. These opportunities are ideal for women's coaching development, but few women are appointed. The problems for female soccer coaches in Canada are compounded by the androcentric nature of the

In my own situation, I had to decide between two careers. After having spent twenty years with our national team program, doing jobs from regional coaching right up to head coach of our national team, I had to choose between a job at the University of Alberta and one as the full-time head coach of the national team. I had held the position for five years on a part-time basis while working as a professor. One of the things I had fought for was a full-time position with the national team. When this came to fruition, the salary level and benefits package were not comparable to my situation at the university. While this was only one factor, it made my decision to stay at the university easier. I cannot help but think, though, of the time and money that both Field Hockey Canada and I have invested in my coaching career.

—DRU MARSHALL

game in this country—females essentially have no voice on the association's board of directors or technical committee. As a result, they feel isolated, powerless, frustrated, and discouraged. If implemented, Sport Canada's new policy could change these practices, but clearly, more political advocacy needs to be done at the high performance level. In the soccer example, advocacy work would have to be done from outside the sport since women feel they have no voice. Optimistically, the Canadian Soccer Association began an initiative in 2009 to increase the number of female coaches certified to coach provincial and national teams (Canadian Soccer Association, 2009). In 2008, they appointed Carolina Morace of Italy to succeed Pellerud as head coach of the national team.

This example illustrates that we have a ways to go in making coaching a viable career option for women. There is hope on the horizon in the form of Sport Canada policies, initiatives from the Coaching Association of Canada (particularly the Women in Coaching program), and in the infusion of money that the federal government has committed to coaching.

CRITICAL QUESTIONS FOR STRATEGY 3:
1. How can I support female coaches who are currently coaching in my sport?
2. What resources, both human and otherwise, are required for this support?
3. Where can I access these resources?
4. How can I ensure that each of these female coaches has a supportive network? What doors do I need to open for them?
5. How can I ensure that professional development opportunities are available so that their personal knowledge base is increased and their confidence is built and/or maintained?

Strategy 4. New paradigms of coaching

It is apparent that something may be wrong with the current paradigm of coaching. Research is scarce when it comes to studies of coaching employment.

A study conducted by Cunningham and Sagas of assistant coaches in the National Collegiate Athletic Association (NCAA) shows that more than two-thirds of the female assistants surveyed anticipated leaving the profession before age forty-five, compared with 15% of the males surveyed (Anderson, 2001). More recent research by Cunningham and Sagas (2003) found that women stay in coaching for an average of only five years. Drop-out and retention are issues for female coaches. As Mercier (2000) stated, "It takes a supportive employment environment and creativity—to find workable solutions."

To reiterate, common reasons for coach drop-out and lack of retention are burnout, lack of financial incentive, lack of experience, family conflicts, discrimination, fighting the old boys' network, and expectations to succeed. We need to be aware of these factors as we develop new paradigms for women in coaching. The *Canadian Journal for Women in Coaching* provided compelling stories from twenty-one women who have tried to continue coaching while raising families (Robertson, 2007). Many have a conflict between their family and their coaching commitments, but almost all have figured out solutions to make it work, including job sharing.

Laurie Eisler found a creative solution that allowed her to coach while she had two children. She started coaching university volleyball in 1991. She had her first child during the 1996–1997 season, and her second during the 1999–2000 season. Lorne Sawula, a male coach with great experience, was hired as an assistant coach of her team during the 1996–1997 season. Although Eisler was initially intimidated by his involvement in her program, and worried that her athletes would think less of her compared to him, she knew the opportunity to work with someone of his calibre was too great to pass up.

In fact, the athletes benefited because they had two perspectives from two wonderful communicators. Sawula took over the team as head coach when Eisler went on her second maternity leave, and she rejoined the team at the end of that season in which they won their sixth consecutive national title. As their relationship evolved, Sawula and Eisler became co-coaches. They were hugely respectful of one another and confident in each other's abilities. They shared the same philosophy, but used different methods and words to communicate their messages. They both recognized there were many ways to do the same thing. They created an environment in which the athletes felt comfortable asking for clarification.

Eisler believes one key to making the situation with Sawula work was the internal support system that has developed. "Coaching is a lonely profession. With Lorne, I have unconditional support. We don't necessarily agree on everything, but there is always support." Another key to success in this situation was the apparent lack of ego of both of the coaches. In a study of the top fifty business leaders in the United States, Neff and Citrin (1999) found that an ability to keep egos in check was a common characteristic of these leaders. A third key to this success story was the athletes themselves. They learned to be tolerant, accommodating, and accepting of individual differences.

The final key, and an important piece of the new paradigm puzzle, is the role the University of Alberta, its athletic department, and its athletic director played. For example, Eisler requested that her team practice during the day, in order to accommodate her family situation. The Faculty of Physical Education and Recreation moved classes to accommodate this request, and athletic director Ian Reade was willing to make a controversial decision, based on a women's issue, to move practice to the middle of the day. It was a coach-friendly decision by an organization, and this will be important in the future paradigms for coaching. Eisler's example and the stories of the twenty-one women told in the *Journal* demonstrate that workable solutions are possible. We need to be creative in our approach and look at different situations for female coaches so that coaching is seen as a truly viable career option.

CRITICAL QUESTIONS FOR STRATEGY 4:

1. What other possibilities exist that would allow this coach to stay in coaching?
2. Is there a possibility for a job-sharing situation?
3. Can practice times and/or the competition schedule be altered to allow the coach to continue?

4. Can daycare be provided during practice and/or competition times? Can family travel with the coach?
5. Is the employment status appropriate for the coach? Is the pay level appropriate? Are the benefits available/appropriate?
6. Is the coaching environment welcoming to women?
7. Are the expectations for this coach realistic?

Strategy 5. Development of networks

Another strategy to develop the next generation of female coaches is to encourage informal networks. The programs that bring groups of like-minded coaches together provide a wonderful opportunity for coaches to meet and then interact over a period of many years. We are sure those women will stay in contact throughout their coaching careers on an informal basis and will help one another through difficult situations.

The Women in Coaching program has facilitated the development of a number of informal networks for national-level coaches and developing coaches. For example, the National Coach Workshop is an annual professional development event. While the event itself is only three days, female coaches connect with other like-minded individuals and develop their professional support networks. The Canada Games Apprenticeship Program, a partnership of Women in Coaching, the provincial-territorial governments, provincial sport organizations, and the Canada Games Council, encourages the development of female coaches through a series of professional development workshops and mentoring. A coaching support network is one of the outcomes of this program. Women generally do not spend as much time as men developing informal networks; networking is an important skill for young coaches to learn, and is an important investment of time.

CRITICAL QUESTIONS FOR STRATEGY 5:
1. Is the coach connected to a network?
2. Are there any existing networks which female coaches could join?
3. Could the coach create her own network? What does the coach need in her network(s)?

4. How can I help the coach develop her network(s)?
5. How can this coach develop and maintain her networking skills, and what role should I play in this development?

Strategy 6. Mentoring

A critical part of any coach's development is mentoring. Mentoring is becoming increasingly common in a variety of fields, from business to academics. Many university programs offer mentorship programs for young academic staff as they learn the ropes of being employed in the university environment. Medicine has implemented mentoring into its practice and has seen young doctors advance into fields that previously had difficulty with recruitment. Education research is finding that mentor and protégé teachers are benefiting from building mentor/protégé relationships that facilitate faster development and confidence of new teachers (Patton et al., 2005). Likewise, researchers working with coach education and development have been taking a greater interest in the benefits of mentorship/apprenticeship programs that can take theory and classroom learning into practice (Lemyre, Trudel, & Durand-Bush, 2007; Wright, Trudel, & Culver, 2007; Salmela, 1994). For an in-depth discussion on mentoring, please refer to Chapter 6: Understanding Mentoring as a Development Tool for Female Coaches.

I believe strongly in this model. As a young coach starting out in a high performance system, I was fortunate to have a group of mentors that included two experienced coaches in my own sport, two high performance coaches from outside my sport to provide perspective, two communications experts, and two leaders in sport administration. While my sport organization paired me with two senior coaches on an informal basis, I set up the rest of my "mentoring team." My mentors have never met one another, but I am sure they would have an interesting conversation!

—DRU MARSHALL

CRITICAL QUESTIONS FOR STRATEGY 6:

1. What kind of mentoring does the coach need, and in what areas?
2. Is the coach committed to being involved in a mentoring relationship?
3. What is my potential to be a mentor? Should I be a mentor to this individual?
4. What other types of mentors need to be identified? Where can I find other mentors?
5. Should the coach be involved in a formal mentoring program, or a more informal program?
6. Are there formal mentoring programs available for this coach?

Strategy 7. Political advocacy

All of us have a voice, be it at the local, provincial/territorial, national, or international level, in furthering the case of women in coaching. As a result of powerful voices, we see the development of policies for women in sport at the Sport Canada level. The members of the Coaching Working Group, a committee struck to examine coaching in Canada for the secretary of state for Amateur Sport, included six current or former national head coaches who are women (Sport Canada, 2008). Such coaches can serve as advocates for improving the lot of future coaches. University coaches can lobby for policies, salaries, and situations that are gender equitable. Organizations have to demonstrate a willingness to provide support to women during various stages of the life cycle, and differently than they may for men. Groups advocating for the awareness of girls and women in physical activity are growing both nationally and provincially, and include the Canadian Association for the Advancement of Women and Sport and Physical Activity, Égale Action in Quebec, PROMOTION Plus in British Columbia, and InMotion Network in Alberta.

Policies regarding workload and daycare provision during training are two examples of changes being brought about by political advocacy. Sport and politics go hand in hand, and we all have a responsibility to speak to ensure that the next generation of coaches has a viable situation. Individually we all have voices, and collectively we can make a difference. See Chapter 7: Political Advocacy in Coaching—Why Engage? for a more detailed discussion.

CRITICAL QUESTIONS FOR STRATEGY 7:

1. Is the coach aware of the advocacy groups for women in sport?
2. Does the coach speak about critical issues for women in her sport when presented with an opportunity?
3. Does she know how to use her personal and positional power to affect change?
4. Does she know the key influencers and decision makers in her sport? Does she have meaningful communication with them regularly?
5. Does she know how and where decisions are made in her sport? Does she know who holds the power?
6. Does she have access to training and development of advocacy skills?

Strategy 8. Development of negotiation skills

We need to work at improving the skill set of all female coaches, including negotiation skills. Coach education programs typically focus on technical, tactical, physical, and mental development, along with communication and leadership skills. They tend not to focus on negotiation skills for contracts, job situations, and conflict resolution. Typically, coaching contracts are not negotiated very often, so it is important to get it right the first time around. Women have to be demanding in contract negotiations; they need to consider carefully what they need to do the job, and they should be creative in their approach to putting together full-time career coaching positions.

For further information on contracts, read Chapter 11: Contracts and Contract Negotiations. The resolution of conflicts through negotiation is a critical skill for a coach to possess. Positive conflict resolution begins with effective communication. For more about communicating clearly, please refer to Chapter 5: Communicating with Clarity: Guidelines to Help Female Coaches Succeed.

CRITICAL QUESTIONS FOR STRATEGY 8:

1. Can the coach communicate her needs effectively?
2. Is the coach aware of all the possible outcomes and variables in a situation?
3. Can the coach identify a win-win situation if in conflict?
4. Is the coach aware of her personal values?
5. Does the coach know her own worth?
6. Is the coach open minded?
7. Is the coach well prepared and a careful planner?
8. Is the coach an active listener?

NOTE

1. In 2007, Sport Canada initiated a review of its 1986 *Sport Canada Policy on Women in Sport*. The purpose was to identify contemporary issues facing women in sport and to recommend any necessary adjustments to the federal government's policy objectives for women in sport. The new policy has not been launched yet, but one area of emphasis will be a focus on women in key sport roles, especially female coaches (Sport Canada, 2008). A specific objective will be "to increase and maintain the number of women becoming and continuing to be fully active within Canadian sport as coaches" (Sport Canada, 2008).

REFERENCES

Anderson, K. (2001). Where are all the women coaches? *Sports Illustrated for Women,* 86–91.

Béliveau, S. (2008). Making it happen—Here's how. *Canadian Journal for Women in Coaching, 8*(3). Retrieved August 25, 2008, from http://www.coach.ca/WOMEN/e/journal/index.htm

Canada West Conference. (2009). CIS winter championship history. Retrieved June 1, 2009, from http://www.canadawest.orgpdf/CHAM_cis_winterhistory.pdf

Canadian Soccer Association. (2009). Women in coaching initiative 2009. Retrieved June 4, 2009, from http://www.canadasoccer.com/coaching/programs/20090316_Women's_Initiative_2009_BLicense-NationalCourse_EN.pdf

Craig, C.L. (1997). *The contribution of coaching in Canada*. Ottawa: Coaching Association of Canada. Retrieved June 4, 2009, from http://www.coach.ca/eng/certification/documents/REP_Contribution-of-coaching-1997.pdf

Cunningham, G.B., & Sagas, M. (2003). Occupational turnover intent among assistant coaches of women's teams: The role of organizational work experiences. *Sex Roles, 49*(3/4), 185.

Demers, G., & Audet, M. (2007). What we know about the experiences of women beginner coaches. *Canadian Journal for Women in Coaching, 8*(1). Retrieved August 25, 2008, from http://www.coach.ca/WOMEN/e/journal/dec2007/index.htm

Ifedi, F. (2008). Sport participation in Canada, 2005. *Statistics Canada: Culture, Tourism and the Centre for Education Statistics Research Papers.* Retrieved June 4, 2009, from http://www.statcan.gc.ca/pub/81-595-m/81-595-m2008060-eng.pdf

Kamphoff, C. (2008). The UK coaching system is failing women coaches: A commentary. *International Journal of Sports Science & Coaching, 3*(4), 469–471.

Kerr, G., & Marshall, D. (2007). Shifting the culture: Implications for female coaches. *Canadian Journal for Women in Coaching, 7*(4). Retrieved August 25, 2008, from http://www.coach.ca/WOMEN/e/journal/october2007/pg4.htm

Kerr, G., Marshall, D. Sharp, D.-M., & Stirling, A. (2006). *Women in coaching: A descriptive study.* Ottawa: Coaching Association of Canada.

Lemyre, F., Trudel, P., & Durand-Bush, N. (2007). How youth-sport coaches learn to coach. *The Sport Psychologists, 21,* 191–209.

Mercier, R. (2000). Being professional about your employment. *Canadian Journal for Women in Coaching, 1*(1). Retrieved June 5, 2009, from http://www.coach.ca/WOMEN/e/journal/sep2000/index.htm

Messner, M. (2009). Including more women coaches in youth sports: Why it matters. Retrieved June 17, 2009, from http://www.momsteam.com/getting-more-women-coaches-in-youth-sports-why-it-matters#1xzzoI9yPrCLr&D

Mullins, A. (2008). The UK coaching system is failing women coaches: A commentary. *International Journal of Sports Science & Coaching, 3*(4), 465–467.

Neff, T.J., & Citrin, J.M. (1999). *Lessons from the top. The search for America's best business leaders.* New York: Currency Doubleday.

Norman, L. (2008). The UK coaching system is failing women coaches. *International Journal of Sports Science & Coaching, 3*(4), 447–464.

Patton, K. et al. (2005). Chapter 2: Navigating the mentoring process in research-base teacher development project: A situated learning perspective. *Journal of Teaching in Physical Education, 24,* 302–325.

Robertson, S. (2007). Coaching and motherhood: Staying in the profession. *Canadian Journal for Women in Coaching, 7*(2). Retrieved June 5, 2009, from http://www.coach.ca/WOMEN/e/journal/april2007/pg1.htm

Salmela, J. (1994). Tracing the roots of expert coaches: Searching for the inspiration. *Coaches Report, 1*(1), 9–11.

Sport Canada. (2008). New Sport Canada policy on women in sport. Discussion session, July. Ottawa.

Tucker Center for Research on Girls and Women in Sport. (2009, Spring). Wanted: Female coaches at all levels of sport. Tucker Center, University of Minnesota newspaper.

University of Victoria. (2008). Women's soccer coach Tracy David. *Vikes Athletics.* Retrieved June 2, 2009, from http://www.vikes.uvic.ca/teams/index.php?sportid=21&do=coach

Werthner, P. (2005). Making the case: Coaching as a viable career path for women. *Canadian Journal for Women in Coaching, 5*(3). Retrieved March 31, 2009, from http://www.coach.ca/WOMEN/e/journal/may2005/index.htm

Wright, T., Trudel, P., & Culver, D. (2007). Learning how to coach: The different learning situations reported by youth ice hockey coaches. *Physical Education and Sport Pedagogy, 12*(2), 127–144.

Coach Siobhan McLaughlin (centre) talks tactics with pairs rowers Mariel Boomgaardt and Samantha Kayser, with apprentice coach Jen Marsh (right) paying close attention.

PHOTO: JOHN SIMS, TEAM ONTARIO

THE BUSINESS OF GREATNESS

Rose Mercier

TEN

Introduction

Tapping into her own successful business experiences, Rose Mercier
has produced an invaluable guide by which female coaches can (and
should) conduct their professional lives in order to get the maximum
benefit from their chosen career. So often driven by passion for the
sport they coach, female coaches, more often than not, forget all about
caring for themselves. They ignore the importance of operating within a
well-thought-out framework consisting of a career plan, solid business
practices, and a well-defined vision based on carefully articulated values.
A strength of this chapter is the many questions the author poses,
questions that are essential to defining a career path that should lead to
excellence in every facet of life.

This chapter is relevant to all female coaches, not just the
"professional" or paid coach. We know beyond doubt that the capacity
to coach well is not strictly the purview of the professional. Many of our
successful female coaches operate as volunteers. Often the salary is the
only distinguishing feature between professional and volunteer—they
share commitment, skill, education, and a consuming desire to have
their athletes achieve their potential and derive the maximum from

sport. Therefore, as the author stresses, building your coaching career on effective business practices should be common to all. As she frankly acknowledges, such practices are all too easily put on the back burner; there are so many more pressing details to manage, even for someone as scrupulous as she.

THIS CHAPTER DRAWS ON MY OWN experience as a self-employed consultant to identify business practices that can be used by female coaches, whether they are self-employed, salaried, or volunteer.

I have been a self-employed consultant for nearly fifteen years. My business has been successful by many standards, more so than I might ever have imagined in the tentative first days of 1995. I had only the sketchiest business plan when I started and, fortunately, an initial contract. I had a lot of work experience, a fairly extensive network in the field in which I intended to work, and a strong desire to carve my own path. And as I often say: The good news is that I have always been busy, and the bad news is that I have always been busy. No doubt that may sound a lot like your career. While I continue to enjoy the confidence of clients and celebrate their successes and progress, and there always seem to be new and interesting opportunities, I have from time to time been nagged by a feeling that I should take the time to plan where I am going next. Lately, the desire to set a revitalized direction has intensified. I have acted on that feeling and embarked on planning for the next phase of my business. In so doing, I am discovering both those practices that have helped build my business, and those that I need in the future. I believe that the lessons of this journey are as relevant to any female coach who wants to succeed as they are to me.

In his book *Good to Great* (2001), Jim Collins introduces the Hedgehog Concept, which explains how good to great companies, in contrast to other companies, base their strategic decisions on the following three dimensions:

1. a deep passion about what they do

2. a deep understanding of what they can do better than any other company
3. the knowledge of what generates sustainable cash flow and profitability (p. 95–119)

This way of describing what distinguishes great companies from good companies has helped me in analyzing my business. Although it is possible to operate in the same way throughout a career or the life of a business, chances are that many of you, like me, are not satisfied in the long run with maintaining the status quo. In my experience, if you are self-employed, you subscribe to a set of fairly demanding standards of your own making. I have always been intrigued by the possibility of excellence, so I have developed my own way of looking at the three dimensions of strategic success.

It is not a direct application because, obviously, I am not a large corporation. However, I believe that it is essential to look for lessons in other fields. What I learned from the Hedgehog Concept[1] is that great companies focus on the activities that ignite their passion, know what they can be the best at in the world, and know how to generate sustained, robust cash flow and profitability. This might seem a big stretch in thinking for a one-person business, whether self-employed or in the employ of someone else. However, here are the business practices that I have created from this idea.

PRACTICE 1: Decide what work you are passionate about and follow that passion. If you deeply enjoy introducing children to basic movement skills, continue coaching in this context. If you are only excited about coaching when you are working with athletes who are resolutely committed to personal excellence, then search for those types of coaching opportunities. I know what gives me energy in consulting, and there are many things—supporting volunteer leaders to make significant changes within an organization they deeply love, working with coaches who want to be more effective leaders, helping organizations to create clear directions for a desired future. However, the common factor is the passion I have for working with others to help realize new possibilities. Do you know what you are truly passionate about? What gives you energy? What do you procrastinate about doing? Avoiding or putting off certain things provides a good hint about where not to focus your coaching business.

PRACTICE 2: Discover what you can be best at. You might want to be the "best in the world" in a particular aspect of coaching, or you may want to discover how you can stand out from whatever crowd you are in—all the coaches of your sport, in your community, province, region, country, or the world—or how to become a recognized authority in a particular area. You don't need to be "the best" right now, but take a hard look at where you can become outstanding. For example, is there a particular coaching expertise that is missing in your sport where you have the capacity to excel? Equally important, what can you *not* do better or *not* stand out in the crowd by doing? My quest for business renewal has offered up several insights about new areas where my business can be unique and where I believe that I can be truly outstanding; these areas also require a significant commitment to professional development in new knowledge. It is not enough merely to identify the areas where you can perform well as a coach; you need to do the work. A critical business practice for me—and you—is the continuing development of existing and new competencies.

PRACTICE 3: Understand how your career or business generates sustainable income. What is the formula that will enable you to continue coaching? Where are the possible areas of income? If you are coaching in a sport where it is possible to earn your living, determine the different ways that generate income: salary, lessons, workshops, resources, equipment, and so on. What is the most important source of a sustainable income, and what factors influence the level of income? If you are a volunteer coach or receive a seasonal honorarium, you still need to understand

Coach Amy Caskey and the Team Ontario synchronized swimmers celebrate their silver medal at the 2007 Canada Winter Games.

PHOTO: JOHN SIMS, TEAM ONTARIO

how you can sustain your ability to coach. It is essential that there is equity between the time and experience you invest and what you receive in return. Our first inclination is to measure equity in financial terms: Are you paid what your experience and competence are worth? Pay is certainly an important indicator, but it is not the only one. If you are a volunteer coach, how do you ensure that there is an equitable return for your time? Do your athletes and their families show respect for the commitment you are making to them? Does the club board, school administration, municipality, or township ensure that there is a safe coaching environment with necessary facilities and equipment? Is there recognition of your efforts? Are you able to coach in a way that challenges you? If there are imbalances in these areas, or if you only partly apply your ability, or if you repeat the same coaching experience over and over, you will eventually feel a sense of inequity.

The above are starting points in thinking about your coaching career, but if you do not go from thinking about how to operate your business to organizing your ideas into a written plan, then it is unlikely that you will become the coach you want to be. Coaches know how essential it is for an athlete to have specific goals and a written plan for achieving them, and yet it is not common practice for coaches to do the same for themselves. Imagine how curious it is for a consultant who helps organizations to craft strategic plans to not have a written plan of her own.

It is not always easy to do what we know is necessary. This is another key idea from Jim Collins's *Good to Great* that I hold as an essential business practice: You need to exercise the discipline to work out a strategy in a rigorous fashion. That means taking the time to work through all of the stages of a sound planning process and write them down. And then it requires the discipline to pursue the strategy. Imagine taking the time to prepare a sophisticated annual plan, with its interrelated micro-cycles, and then improvising every practice. That's not good coaching practice, and simply thinking about what you might do isn't good business practice. No, it isn't easy. It is, however, what distinguishes exceptional business practice from the ordinary.

Planning

I'D LIKE TO SHARE THE ELEMENTS of the planning process I use with organizations as well as the one I have been using to re-focus my business. You don't need to take a week off to complete this plan. I worked on mine in short sessions over a six-week period, and then took another six weeks to complete it. Soon I started to experience a different level of focus in work.

The starting point is clearly identifying values that guide your coaching business. What do you believe are the fundamental principles that should characterize how you coach? There are several different ways to clarify values. A simple way to start is to write down a list of ten values. Review these and then select the five most important. You can, if you wish, try to choose two or three from the list of five. There is no right answer about the number of values you should have; you have as many as you have. I usually suggest that somewhere between three and seven should do it; even the largest corporations in the world have only a handful of core values. Besides naming the value, it is important to explain what the value really means. For example, one of the core values of my business is respect. I explain this value as follows: "I believe that organizations are first and foremost people working together where everyone deserves to be heard and valued. I believe that personalities are the spice of organizational life. I believe that differences among people—their experiences, points of view, values—are a rich source of knowledge."

This explanation is a clear and constant reminder of how I want to work. It reminds me that I need to choose ways of working that are consistent. It also signals to clients what they should expect. Values become your lines in the sand; they tell you where compromise is not a choice. They also give you energy. When you finish this part of your plan and you show it to close friends, they should recognize you in your statement of values. Values are the most enduring part of your business plan.

Once your values are clear, you can start to work on your vision. A vision expresses your long-term aspiration for the future of your coaching business. It should answer the question of why you are coaching. I like visions that are short-term, qualitative statements that are motivating and resonate with you whenever you read them. There are many ways to create a vision (others might call it a purpose or mission), and you can find a way that works for you. In 2008, the American Express Members Project commercial featured great examples of personal visions that absolutely capture the work that individuals do:

- Live life on the edge. (A surfer)
- Tell unforgettable stories. (Martin Scorsese)
- Use laughter to help children learn. (Jim Henson)
- Encourage people to dance to their own tune. (Ellen DeGeneres)

Once you have a clear vision, you can develop a strategy that helps you plan how to accomplish the major changes that are necessary to move toward your vision. The plan I have been working on has four strategic goals and eight objectives. They express specific changes I intend to make over the next five years. The vision for my business is that clients are excited and optimistic about their future and maintain the forward momentum they build during our consulting relationship. I decided that to accomplish this vision, there were four strategic goals I needed to pursue.

1. Implement business practices that optimize consulting time.
2. Enhance the means to secure and maintain clients.
3. Pursue the advancement of qualifications, skills, and knowledge.
4. Focus on physical health and mental energy.

In each of those areas, I have some specific objectives, for which I identify specific tactics I need to take in the current year. For example, the first of two objectives for the strategic goal, "Implement business practices that optimize consulting time," is to "Ensure technology facilitates business." I expect this will continue to be an objective for the next four years. However in the current year, I identified four specific tactics that were needed:

- Replace laptop and set up wireless connection.
- Update software/data security.
- Backup client material.
- Archive out-of-date material.

These may seem obvious but, like many self-employed individuals, it is easy to stay so busy with the day-to-day that the obvious is overlooked. I am happy to report that all of these have happened. Writing things down gets things done.

A Harvard study of MBA graduates is often used to illustrate the power of writing down your goals. In 1979, MBA graduates were asked about the goals they now planned to accomplish. A very small number, 3%, had clear, written goals and specific plans to accomplish them. Thirteen per cent had goals but had not written them down. However, 84% had no specific goals. When the same graduates were interviewed in 1989, the researchers found that the 13% with goals, even though they were unwritten, were then earning double the salary of the 84% without goals. Notably, however, the 3% with written goals and an action plan were earning on average ten times as much as the other 97% of graduates (Brusman, 2006).

Of course, not everything I want to accomplish over the next four years is quite so straightforward and will involve significant investment of my time and some resources. However, I am confident about my ability to achieve my goals.

You will choose strategic goals that fit your vision. There are many valuable ideas in the other chapters of this book. For example, if one of your strategic goals is to "establish work conditions that optimize your coaching," there are several tactics in Chapter 11 that might help you.

Your plan doesn't need to be complicated or long. In fact, I like to think that you can capture a plan for someone who is self-employed on a single page. If your plan doesn't make you gulp a bit, it may not result in sufficient change. Operating from a plan is the business practice that will make the most difference to realizing what you want to achieve as a coach.

There are other business practices that have helped me maintain my business over the past fifteen years. The principle behind each practice remains the same, even if it takes on a different form depending on whether you are self-employed, salaried, or a volunteer. Here are the practices that inform my business.

1. Manage the business of your coaching.

a.   Make the nature of each working agreement explicit. Preferably, write it down. This is essential for new relationships. What results are you responsible for delivering? What resources will the other party supply? When does the relationship start and finish? When will payments be made? What expenses are covered? These are essential components to any agreement if you are self-employed, but even if you are a volunteer, it is still valuable to be clear about the scope of your responsibilities, your expectations, the expectations of the group you are coaching, and the conditions under which you will be working.

b.   Establish a regular time to complete ongoing business transactions. Issue invoices, complete expense claims, complete your bookkeeping, or turn your receipts over to an accountant at the same time of week or month. Stay up to date with GST payments, quarterly tax payments, and insurance.

c.   Get professional advice when important issues arise. If you aren't sure whether to incorporate, what type of insurance you should have, or what expenses are tax deductible, look for advice. Check with colleagues for references, and look within your circle of friends for expertise.

2. Look after yourself.

a.   Protect your health and energy. This is one of the things women seem to let go of easily. I know from experience. It is easier to put the needs of your athletes or your clients ahead of your exercise class or a healthy lunch. However, we are not very effective in our roles of supporting and leading others if we compromise our energy. We lose focus, sometimes so incrementally that we don't realize it until we reach a state of burnout. Taking a part of each day for yourself is essential business practice, even if some days it is only for a short period of time.

b. Pay attention to friends and family.

c. Develop your resilience for change. Understand that change is happening all the time and that we resist both negative and positive change. Look for the opportunities, and be curious about possibilities. Adopt an attitude of the glass being half-full.

3. Expand yourself.

a. Allocate time and funding for your own professional development, maintaining your professional network, learning new skills, and reading current material.

b. Use mentors to help you develop professionally. Mentors are a powerful way to learn to operate effectively in a role. Mentors can also enhance your effectiveness in a specific area.

c. Develop networks. Too often we think of networking as collecting business cards from people we think might be able to help us in the future. I have a friend who is brilliant at developing networks, and I have learned an essential truth about networking from her: in networking, you should focus on creating connections and opportunities for others. Doing this inevitably brings new contacts back to you.

4. Choose how you present yourself and your business.

Branding is a concept that has a lot of currency these days. It's useful to think about your brand character—how you distinguish yourself from other coaches. What are the objectives that capture what is unique about you? You can use this concept to help you create a logo, business cards, and a website. You can also use it to help choose what you wear to a club meeting or a coaching conference. Something I grow increasingly conscious of is that everything I do, say, write, or wear tells people something about who I am. You can, of course, be obsessive about this; however, a measured approach toward being conscious about how you represent yourself is sound business practice.

5. *Take advantage of resources available to develop your business.*

a. Women are among the fastest-growing group of self-employed. Industry Canada has reported that the number of women who head companies in Canada has doubled since 1990. As a result, women partially or wholly own nearly half of Canadian small businesses.

b. There are likely resources available in your community, such as the economic development agency, the chamber of commerce, or business networks, that may have grants or other resources that can help you develop your business.

c. The Canada Business (Government of Canada) website will help you identify the federal and provincial government programs, services, and resources that may be of interest to you.

d. Visit the Women in Coaching section of the Coaching Association of Canada website on a regular basis and stay up to date about apprenticeship programs and other opportunities that may be appropriate avenues to pursue, depending on the vision you develop for your coaching.

e. Remember that resource programs come and go. This type of information changes frequently. Go back to the websites you have found, and search for new ones.

Having a business, being self-employed, or fulfilling a role as a volunteer coach can be both rewarding and challenging. At an early point in my business, I worried about how to have a balanced life. However, as my business has evolved to become an integral part of my life, I have recognized that my ideal is a blended life, where business, family, friends, and community co-exist in a comfortable fashion. Having clear values, a motivating vision, and a crisp strategy helps keep the various parts of life working in harmony. Sound business practices support the achievement of personal, business, and coaching goals, and reduce the anxiety that is caused by feeling out of control or always behind schedule. I hope that by sharing some of what has helped me achieve success, I have offered you some ideas for managing the business side of your coaching life.

NOTE

1. "Hedgehogs...simplify the complex world into a single organizing idea, a basic principle or concept that unifies and guides everything." (Collins, 91)

REFERENCES

Brusman, M. (2006). "The art of goal." Retrieved from http://www.working resources.com/professionaleffectivenessarticles/article.nhtml?uid=10060

Collins, J. (2001). *Good to Great*. New York: HarperCollins.

National softball coach Lori Sippel advises runner Erin Cumpstone during Canada Cup play.

PHOTO: COURTESY OF SOFTBALL.CANADA

CONTRACTS AND CONTRACT NEGOTIATIONS

Hilary Findlay

ELEVEN

Introduction

It is generally acknowledged that few female coaches have an appropriate understanding of their contracts (if they are lucky enough to have one), or of what should be included in a contract. Clearly, female coaches need to learn how to ask, or negotiate, for things that they believe are important in contracts. In this chapter, contract expert Hilary Findlay describes the important difference between an employee and an independent contractor and the resulting differences in contract. She covers factors such as the job description, the performance review, term of the contract and renewal, compensation, and termination. Also provided is an Employment Contract Checklist that emphasizes clauses that must be seriously considered, whatever the nature of the contract. "Contracts and Contract Negotiations" is an important addition to ongoing efforts to provide information that improves the quality of the coaching experience for women.

CONTRACTS! THE MENTION OF THEM often turns people away. Nonetheless, contracts for coaches are a necessity, particularly for those coaches who have made coaching a career or are engaged in coaching activities at the high performance level. As Sheilagh Croxon and Dru Marshall wrote in their 2004 article for the *Canadian Journal for Women in Coaching*, "Part of being a professional is having a solid working contract with the organization that employs you" (Croxon & Marshall, 2004). As well, volunteers or part-time coaches often think contracts don't apply to them, but they do. They, too, should have at least some minimal written confirmation of their basic job description, if not simply to outline the scope of authority and potential liability of the coach, then to ensure the parties have a mutual understanding of the role of the coach within the organization, league, club, or institution.

One could think of the contract as wrapping paper around the coach's relationship with the organization or club. It is best when the paper fits neatly and seamlessly—wrinkles, tears, or just not enough paper cause problems. Coaches can take a number of steps to avoid problems. Firstly, there should be a contract, or some form of *written* agreement, whether formal or informal, between the coach and the sport organization.[1] The coach should understand what each clause of the contract means and its consequence, and then should ensure that all the clauses work together to reflect accurately the coaching relationship and understanding of the coach's position.

This chapter is based on the article by Croxon and Marshall (2004), extending the commentary and updating the data using *A Report on the Status of Coaches in Canada* (Reade et al., 2009). Croxon and Marshall's article drew on a survey done by Marshall in 2003, wherein she interviewed eighteen national team coaches (nine males and nine females) and inquired about their contract situations. At the time, all but one coach was working under some form of written contractual arrangement. In 2009, the subsequent survey by Reade et al. looked specifically at the current job status of Canadian coaches of high performance athletes. Survey responses from 819 high performance coaches representing fifty-six sports were analyzed. High performance coaches were defined as national, provincial, and Canada Games coaches, as well as coaches from universities and colleges; 26% of the 819 coaches were female. This dropped to 20% when only coaches of carded athletes were considered. Employers of the coaches were also surveyed. Of the ninety-four employers responding, thirty-five were from national sport organizations, thirty-five from universities, and twenty-four from colleges.

Before looking at findings from the two surveys and how they reflect on the content of coaches' contracts, it is useful to look at how coaches can contract. That is, what is the nature of the legal relationship, or relationships, they can enter into? The nature of the relationship directly affects the way in which the contract is written. The essential substantive elements of the contract—term, compensation, job description, performance review, and provisions for termination—may be the same between different kinds of contracts. However, how each element is framed and set out in the contract will vary depending on the nature of the relationship the coach has with the sport organization. This can have both advantageous and punitive effects depending on the nature of the contracting relationship. It is in the best interests of the coach to understand the nature of the working relationship and get it right in the contract, and then make sure the contract reflects the agreement of the coach with the organization.

The Two Forms of Working Relationships

THERE ARE TWO APPROACHES to employment for coaches: an employee of a sport organization, or an independent contractor. Both relationships are governed by contract, but the substantive content of the contract is drafted differently because the legal status of the coach is different within each form of working relationship.[2] For an employee, the relationship exists between the individual coach and the organization, or can be expressed as that of a person working for the organization. For an independent contractor, there is an intervening entity between the employee and the worker; the contract is between the organization and the corporate entity of the coach—not the coach herself (even though the coach may be the only person behind the corporate entity).

The differences in the two relationships are important, not only in drafting the contract, but in terms of responsibilities and potential liabilities of the coach, and financial considerations attached to the position.

It is not always a simple matter to determine the form of the working relationship. A case heard by the Tax Court of Canada illustrates the difficulty. In *Puri v. Minister of National Revenue*, Jannine Puri and Rae Anne Hesketh were figure skating coaches with the Campbell River Skating Club. Both taught figure skating to club members one or two hours a day in addition to teaching many private lessons. Although the club provided the skating facility through a rental arrangement with the municipality, the coaches provided their own music and stop watches, and also co-ordinated their coaching schedules from home offices. Both earned the majority of their incomes by teaching private lessons that had nothing to do with the club. In fact, their working arrangement was common in figure skating circles across Canada. Nonetheless, the court found that they were *employees* of the club with regard to the time spent teaching club members, not *independent contractors*, as both they and the club had originally defined the relationship.

Many coaches work several jobs simultaneously. In a number of sports, the pattern reflected in the Puri case, in which the coach has individual clients (typically entering "personal service contracts" with such clients) and also works with a club or sport organization, is not unusual. Many other coaches engage in non-sport jobs to supplement the coaching income. Reade et al. (2009) noted that less than half, or 47.6% of coaches, had only one coaching position and considered themselves full-time coaches. This increased to 62.2% of coaches of carded athletes, very few of which were women.

Coach as an Employee

The coach as an employee may work on a full- or part-time basis.
Either way, the coach is paid a regular wage, with income tax, employment insurance premiums, and government pension plan contributions withheld by the employer. An employee may participate in the
employer's benefits and private pension program, and may negotiate other benefits including vacation periods, maternity leave, and
employer-sponsored opportunities for continuing education,
among others.

Coach as an Independent Contractor

The coach as an independent contractor is essentially self-employed
and provides her services to a club or organization for an agreed-upon
fee. In other words, the coach is still an employee, but is self-employed
by her own company, not through the sport organization, and then
contracts out her services through her own company to others. The
contracting agent is the individual coach as a corporate entity, not
as an individual. She must disassociate herself as an employee of the
sport organization when contracting with the organization—she is
an employee of her own corporation, which, in turn, is contracting
with the sport organization. As an employee of her own corporation,
her role is very different, although the tasks may be similar to those of
an employee of the sport organization. This reality often lulls coaches
into treating the two forms of employment, that of the employee and
that of the independent contractor, as the same—which they might
be if one looked only at the substantive nature of the coaching duties.
But they are not the same from either a legal or a financial perspective.
This difference needs to be reflected in the coaching contract in order
to reap the benefits and avoid the disadvantages of the working relationship. There are advantages and disadvantages.

Confusing the Two

Each form of working relationship requires a different form of contract. Not only is it important to have a contract to set out each party's
understanding of the working obligations, it is also important to

understand that the contract needs to include certain elements that reflect the true nature of the actual working relationship. Barring a clear and concise contract, the relationship may wreak unanticipated legal and financial consequences if the coaching relationship is misinterpreted.

Which Form of Working Relationship Should You Choose?

THERE ARE ADVANTAGES and disadvantages to each form of working relationship. The coach may have a choice and an opportunity to structure the relationship in accordance with one or the other form of working relationship. On the other hand, the relationship may be obvious and have little room for manoeuvring. The distinctions are legal. They may seem to have no relevance from a practical perspective—but they do. It is important to understand the distinction. The financial and legal implication of each form of working relationship falls into three main categories: personal liability; taxes, benefits, and pensions; and termination. The following discussion of these categories will give some indication as to what clauses one might expect to include (or not include) in contracts for each form of working relationship.

Personal Liability

Generally, the employer is responsible for the wrongful acts of employees working within the scope of their employment duties. This is at least one reason for putting in place a clearly written job description, setting out the scope of the employment or volunteer duties. The employer is also held responsible for damages caused to others while performing the work of the sport organization. The underlying rationale for this legal principle is that the employee is seen to be engaged in beneficially assisting the enterprise of the employer, and the employer should, therefore, have responsibility for the way in which that work is done. As well, the employer typically has the resources (usually insurance) to pay any such damages for the negligent conduct of the employee, whereas the employee may not.

The liability situation for the independent contractor is quite different. The independent contractor is her own employer and is responsible for her own negligent acts. Instead of having the protection of the employer's liability insurance policy, the independent contractor may be personally liable for damages flowing from her own actions. As a result, the prudent independent contractor may wish to purchase liability insurance.

Taxes, Benefits, and Pensions

This issue is primarily financial. An employer is responsible for withholding certain payroll deductions on behalf of the employee, including income tax, employment insurance premiums, old age pension, and, in some provinces, health care premiums. Employers may also pay workers' compensation premiums for their employees. For hourly workers, employers are required by provincial and territorial employment law to pay overtime wages, or to provide time off in lieu of extra time worked. Employers are also required to pay wages on statutory holidays when the employee does not work, and to provide the employee with the minimum number of paid holidays per year. Some employers may also contribute to additional benefits for employees, such as extended health care insurance programs and retirement savings plans.

An independent contractor has none of these benefits provided. She does not get paid overtime or holidays. She is not covered by workers' compensation, and in many cases must pay her own health care insurance. She is also responsible for funding her own benefits and pension programs. All these "benefits" must be calculated as part of the contract fee, if possible.

Tax advantages may be, however, a consideration for the independent contractor, particularly if the individual is operating through an incorporated company. This tax advantage occurs for two reasons. First, many ongoing expenses that arise as part of the business enterprise can be offset against income (that is, deducted from the income) before taxes. Costs of equipment, travel expenses, insurance costs, and bookkeeper expenses—even parking tickets if assessed within the course of legitimate business activities—are examples of expenses incurred in the pursuit of business and may be deductible.[3] Second, it may be possible to access a lower income tax rate because corporate income is taxed at a lower rate than personal income. Determining the actual effective tax rate will, however, usually require professional advice. Of course, the tax advantages that may accrue to the independent contractor must be balanced against the time and cost of ongoing record keeping and filing of remittances that go along with them.

Termination

The third issue relates to job security. Under provincial and territorial law, an employer must have "cause" to dismiss an employee with no notice. Lacking "cause" as defined by law, an employer can still terminate an employee at any time, but only if the employer provides proper notice of the termination as set out in the applicable employment standards legislation, or the employment contract, or provides a payment in lieu of such notice, known as a "severance" payment.

The relationship between the independent contractor and the employer, on the other hand, is governed exclusively by the terms of the contract the parties have negotiated. Parties, for example, may agree to include provision in the contract for either party to terminate the working relationship on thirty days notice to the other. If, however, there is no such term, any dispute about termination is typically dealt with as a breach of the contract. The concept of "severance" is not a part of contract law (that is, it is only a part of employment law), and so would not be part of any termination of a contract between an independent contractor and the employer.

In conclusion, each form of working relationship stems from, and is governed by, a different area of law. This means that while contracts are typically used to set out the details of the working relationship,

Patricia Howes, the head coach of the Royal Military College Varsity Fencing Program, encourages Adrienne Sukunda at the 2007 Canada Winter Games in Whitehorse, Yukon.

PHOTO: JOHN SIMS, TEAM ONTARIO

they must be carefully written to reflect the particular form of relationship. In other words, while they will address much of the same content such as remuneration, job description, length (term) of the contract, and termination provisions, they will do so using significantly different language and from different perspectives. Keeping the nature of the relationship clear is very important.

Puri v. Minister of National Revenue identified the difficulty of the parties in determining the nature of the coaches' working relationship. It closely reflected the court's decision in *Whistler Mountain Ski Club v. Minister of National Revenue*, which found individuals retained to teach lessons in alpine ski racing to members of a non-profit ski club were employees, not contractors, even though they were not supervised during their teaching, provided private lessons to others independent of the ski club, and supplied their own equipment for the job. This was the same conclusion in the case of *Moose Jaw Kinsmen Flying Fins Inc. v. Minister of National Revenue*, where the court found that a swim coach who had been earning a modest honorarium for some twelve years was an employee and not a contractor. How does one determine the nature of the working relationship? That is the subject matter of the next section.

Determining the Nature of the Working Relationship

FOUR TESTS, OR FACTORS, are typically used to determine whether an individual, or in this case, a coach, is an employee or an independent contractor.[4] No single factor is definitive of the nature of the relationship; instead, the factors are used in combination and are applied to the circumstances of each individual case. At the end of the day, the focus is on the true nature of the relationship, regardless of what it might be called in a contract. Nonetheless, the factors can help to frame the coaching contract in terms of what a coach may wish to include or not include in the contract.

The four tests are

- the control test
- the integration test
- the financial risk test
- the specific task test

Each test is discussed below.[5]

CONTROL: The greater the degree of control and independence
the coach has in the workplace, the more likely she would be
considered an independent contractor. Several factors, such as the
authority to make significant decisions, hire assistants, define
the scope of the work, set one's own schedule, or terminate the
working relationship, will influence the degree of control which
she has.

INTEGRATION: This test examines whether the tasks performed by
a coach form an essential part of the organization's day-to-day
business. If the tasks are "integral" to the business, it is likely
that an employee relationship exists. In the cases about the figure
skating, alpine ski, and swim coaches described previously, the
courts found the coaching/teaching activities were integral to the
core activities of the respective sport clubs.

On the other hand, if the tasks are not integral to the regular
daily operation of the business, this is a strong argument that
an independent contractor relationship exists. This test is also
influenced by whether the coach provides the same or similar
services to other employers at the same time. If the worker
does provide similar services to others, this is evidence that
the contractor is truly independent. (However, this should
be contrasted with the skating, skiing, and swimming cases.
Depending upon the individual circumstances, a coach can be
an employee in some circumstances and, simultaneously, an
independent contractor in others. This simply emphasizes the fact
that no single factor is definitive of the nature of the relationship,

and that the factors are used in combination and are applied to the circumstances of each individual case.)

FINANCIAL RISK: This factor deals with the possibility of financial risk. It has several facets, including control, ownership of tools or equipment, chance of profit, and risk of loss. The matter of control has already been discussed above. The second facet is particularly important: does the coach supply her own equipment and supplies, or is she entirely reliant upon the employer to supply her with all of the equipment and supplies necessary to complete the task to be performed? An independent contractor would likely pay for her own equipment and supplies (and claim them as an expense against taxable income), whereas an employee would have these supplied by the employer. Similarly, an independent contractor would likely include within her contract a certain amount for administrative expenses (including out-of-pocket expenses such as meals, travel, and accommodation), often called "disbursements." An employee, on the other hand, would be reimbursed by the employer for out-of-pocket expenses, or the employer would pay directly for such expenses.

Self-employment as an independent contractor creates, by its very nature, the opportunity for profit and the risk of loss that employees do not normally have to consider. For example, if the coach performs competently, she will be rewarded financially under the terms of the contract, and conversely, if her work does not satisfy the terms of the contract, contract payments may be withheld. Likewise, the coach working as an independent contractor would not get paid if she were unable to complete the work due to illness, adverse weather conditions, or other factors beyond her control.

SPECIFIC TASK: This final test relates to whether the work is project-specific or ongoing. An employee relationship generally exists where an individual provides services to an employer over a longer period of time, without any reference to a specified result or task (although this does not preclude inclusion of performance targets in the employment contract or a separate document). Contractors are typically hired for a shorter time period, to achieve a specific result or to do a specific task.

The main elements of the coaching contract, and how they are drafted, are very much dependent upon the form of the particular working relationship. Table 5 gives examples of differences in terminology of the same clause between an employee's contract and that of an independent contractor.

Elements of the Coaching Contract

THE SECOND PART OF THIS chapter looks at five specific clauses central to the coaching contract. Regardless of the form the coaching relationship takes—employee or independent contractor—all coaches should have clear, concise, and complete contracts. No two contracts will be precisely the same, but they will have some common elements.

Just over one-third, or 36.7%, of coaches responding to the survey by Reade et al. (2009) were working without a formal written contract. All but one in the Marshall survey (Croxon & Marshall, 2004), which looked only at national team level coaches, was working without a formal contract. Of those with formal contracts in the 2009 survey, it is not clear the actual status of coaches as either employees or independent contractors, which would have an important effect on the nature of the clauses contained in the contracts and their interpretation. In the Marshall survey, of the coaches with formal contracts, nine were hired as employees and eight as independent contractors. Interestingly, given the view of the court in the tax cases quoted earlier, it would appear that most coaching positions with sport organizations, including national sport organizations, would be viewed as employment relationships, regardless of the contract the parties might negotiate between themselves.

The next section provides an overview of five main clauses of any coaching contract, including the job description, performance review, term of the contract and renewal, compensation, and termination. Findings from the Marshall survey (Croxon & Marshall, 2004) and the survey by Reade et al. (2009) will be incorporated into the discussion.

Job Description

The job description is often given little attention in the employment contract and is usually not developed in much detail. Perhaps this is because people feel it is obvious, or they are prepared to defer to the expertise of the coach. Regardless, a complete and accurate job description will prevent many potential problems. A job description sets out the general duties or list of responsibilities the coach agrees to complete. But a good job description does much more; it bounds the legal responsibility, or liability, of the coach, clarifies levels of compensation, and establishes levels of seniority. In effect, the job description defines the employee's value to the organization. It *should* also form the foundation for the performance review. Put another way, the performance review should review what the coach has been asked to do as set out in the job description.

The independent contractor will still want the nature of the coaching assignment to be part of a contract; however, instead of listing general duties or responsibilities, she will want to have a discrete list of specific *tasks* she is responsible for completing and the timeframe within which to finish the work. As discussed previously, independent contractors are hired to perform specific tasks over a set time because of their expertise in the area. These tasks are often referred to as "deliverables," as opposed to a job description (see Table 5).

A job description should not be pulled out of the air or be done "intuitively," but should be based on a careful *job analysis* (MacLean, 2001). A job analysis involves examining a job position and job-related tasks from the perspective of the needs and goals of the organization. Depending on the organization's situation, needs, and resources, the position of "coach" may be broadly or narrowly defined. We often

TABLE 5 EXAMPLES OF DIFFERENCES IN TERMINOLOGY OF VARIOUS CLAUSES

EMPLOYMENT CONTRACT	INDEPENDENT CONTRACTOR
Description of job duties	*Deliverables*
Term of agreement	Term of agreement
Compensation, benefits, holidays	Compensation
Supervisory relationship	Reporting relationship
Performance appraisal	
Termination and severance	Termination

think of coaching as a single job. In fact, many different tasks can go into the job of being a coach, including recruiting athletes, reporting to the sport organization, liaising with parents, planning training regimes, organizing facilities and equipment, developing team selection criteria, selecting teams, and doing all the administrative work that accompanies a competitive schedule, among other tasks (Centre for Sport and Law, 2001).

The job description needs to be clear and concise, and it should fully set out the scope and substance of the job. Ideally, it should identify the position (including title and level of seniority); summarize the major functions and activities of the job; define the coach's relationships (including who the coach will work with and report to); describe the responsibilities and duties of the coach; define the authority of the coach (for example, the types of decisions the coach can make and budgetary limits on decision making); set standards of performance such as standards or markers for achievement; and outline the working conditions (including travel requirements, overtime, and weekend work). It should also outline job specifications, including personal requirements such as abilities, skills, experience, education, level of certification, and other qualifications (Centre for Sport and Law, 2001). Coaches may be involved in the development of the job analysis but if not, should encourage and negotiate the content of such a description to be incorporated into the contract (typically by reference with a copy included as an appendix to the contract).

Sixty-seven percent of coaches responding to the Reade et al. survey (2009) had a formal written job description; however, 77.6% of coaches having a job description reported not having seen the description before executing the contract. Almost 30% reported never having seen the description, even after executing the contract. Please note that all job descriptions should be included in the contract, or as an appendix to the contract, and the full contract should be carefully read by the coach before execution.

Interestingly, most coaches working with a job description were satisfied with the nature of the description, but felt it overly ambitious in light of either level of salary or allocated hours of work. Approximately half the employers interviewed expected coaches to work beyond a normal work week without compensation. In fact, "salaried" employees are exempt from overtime pay. Therefore, it is important that coaches ensure job descriptions are realistic and reflect the job to be done, and that salaries are consistent with such expectations.[6] Hourly workers, on the other hand, are subject to overtime provisions of provincial/territorial employment standards legislation; therefore, the contract should include some provision for overtime work and pay. (Hourly workers should be familiar with the applicable legislative provisions regarding overtime work.)

Performance Review

Performance reviews are critical to coaches as they form the basis upon which major decisions are made, including decisions about continued employment, contract renewal, salary increments, and entitlement to potential bonus arrangements. They also directly reflect on the continuing credibility and reputation of the coach. Yet this area is often overlooked, both in coaches' contracts and in practice. The contract should be very specific about how the coach's performance will be evaluated. It should specify not only what criteria will be used in the evaluation, and how it will be weighted, but also who will carry out the evaluation, at what times, and in what format (that is, written or verbal).[7] The criteria should relate back to, and reflect, the job description and should state whether the performance review process provides the coach with an opportunity for input or feedback. The single most common oversight in this whole area is not setting out the evaluation criteria and process at the outset of the coaching relationship.

Over a third of coaches in the Reade et al. survey (2009) reported they were never evaluated. The flip side is that approximately two-thirds of coaches were evaluated. While the survey did not ask coaches if they were aware of the basis of their evaluation, it did ask employers how coaches were evaluated. Verbal feedback from supervisors and written assessments of athletes were the most commonly used sources of information. Athlete performance results were used, but not as frequently, and written reports from the coaches even less frequently. The coach should be part of the process to determine the basis of the performance evaluation and, ideally the process should be included in, or appended to, the contract.

Coaches need to enter the working relationship with eyes and ears wide open. As the goals and objectives of the sport organization change, they need to ensure the terms of their contract reflect these changes. The goals and objectives of the organization at the time the coach originally negotiated her contract may have changed. In these instances, it may be appropriate to revisit the contract and renegotiate certain terms, particularly those relating to performance review (Centre for Sport and Law, 1997). The time to address the evaluation process is at the time of negotiating the contract, not after the evaluation has occurred.

Term of the Contract and Renewal

Employment contracts are either of a specified term (fixed term contracts) or of an indefinite period (no specific ending date). Thirteen of the seventeen contracts in the Marshall survey were fixed term contracts. One might expect to see terms for renewal in those contracts. There would not be a need for such a provision in contracts with no end date; in fact, such a provision is at odds with the very nature of the contract (Centre for Sport and Law, 2004). Nonetheless, six of the contracts with renewal clauses were to be renegotiated on an annual basis, and ten were to be automatically renewed at the end of the term.[8] (The remaining coach wasn't sure if there were any renewal provisions in the contract.) For those being renewed automatically, one might question whether they were to be renewed on the same terms, if the entire contract was open renewal, or if only certain terms were open for re-negotiation. Identifying certain terms for re-negotiation, such as compensation, would be most appropriate. Establishing a date for such negotiations also would give the parties time to negotiate before the end of the contract period.

Compensation (Including Benefits)

Salaried employees negotiate an annual salary, hourly workers negotiate an hourly rate, and independent contractors negotiate a remuneration based on the specific contract. Compensation clauses, however, should deal with more than simply the pay the coach has negotiated. In an employment situation, they should include all forms of compensation negotiated with the employer, including, for example, regular salary; overtime pay for hourly employees; future increments in pay, whether fixed in advance or performance-based; bonus structure, if appropriate; parental leave and benefits (extended medical, holiday structure and pay, and the employer's contribution to a pension) (Centre for Sport and Law, 1997). Negotiations regarding benefits typically relate only to full-time employees.

For the independent contractor, the contract should specify not only the amount of payment negotiated but frequency of payment; for example, monthly, at certain milestones (trying to avoid a payment schedule reflective of an employment relationship), and reimbursement for out-of-pocket disbursements such as mileage, travel, accommodation, supplies and materials, and telephone expenses. (These disbursements should be invoiced to the sport organization as part of the regular payment schedule—often coaches working as independent contractors ask the sport organization to include travel expenses as part of the team's travelling expenses or ask for an advance. These sorts of actions are more indicative of an employee relationship.) The contractor may wish to negotiate a bonus package or other reward structure for achieving certain performance objectives.

It is interesting (and disturbing) to note that in the Marshall survey, twice as many males as females negotiated a benefits package as part of their contract. Of course, it needs to be noted that significantly more females than males were hired as independent contractors (seven females and two males were hired as independent contractors, whereas two females and six males were hired as employees), for which a benefits package in the contract would be antithetical to the nature of the working relationship. Nonetheless, when females were hired as independent contractors, they were typically paid an honorarium, while their male counterparts negotiated a fee for services. Unfortunately, the Reade et al. survey results did not break down income figures by gender.

Termination

Termination for independent contractors is defined exclusively by the contract. If specific reasons or terms for early termination are not set out in the contract by either party, then there are no grounds on which to terminate the contract early (other than a buy-out of the contract by the employer), and early termination is tantamount to a breach of the contract. Most contracts should have a thirty- or sixty-day notice period upon which either party may terminate the contract. The notice period is dependent upon the circumstances of the parties. Having a notice period allows both parties to make any necessary arrangements before the end of the contract.

Termination of the employee is fundamentally governed by employment standards legislation (although it may be altered by an employment contract, so long as the employment contract does not offer less than the legislation). There are three ways an employee can be terminated: without cause, with cause, or by constructive dismissal. Aspects of the first two forms of termination can be addressed in an employment contract. Employees terminated without cause are entitled to either a notice period before termination of the employment, or pay in lieu of such notice, also known as "sever-ance." The length of notice can be negotiated in the contract, failing which the applicable statutory notice provisions, which are typically minimal, will apply. In a short-term contract, the failure of the contract to refer to a notice period may not be significant. For coaches with longer-term contracts, this may be an important issue. Notice provisions in the contract can apply both ways, with the employee also being required to give notice of an intention to leave the employment relationship. Such provisions in the Marshall survey typically ranged from thirty to ninety days.

In the case of termination for cause, the parties may agree, as a term of the employment contract, what will constitute "cause." Such terms typically relate to (im)moral, (un)ethical, or illegal conduct, or significant conflict of interest. Most often, the employer will attempt to broaden the application of "cause," while the employee will wish to narrow it. The third form of termination, constructive dismissal, refers to situations where unilateral changes made to the contract alter the terms of employment so radically that it bares little resemblance to the original agreement made by the parties. In such extreme cases, the employee may consider the contract to have been terminated and, as such, may be entitled to some amount of compensation.

Marshall and Croxon (2004) noted that of the seventeen contracts reviewed by Marshall, none had a mandatory "cure" period, whereby a coach would have the opportunity to cure (remedy) a mistake or breach of the contract, rather than simply triggering the employer's immediate option to terminate the contract. Such a clause is a useful addition to both the employment contract and the contract of an independent contractor, and can help to maintain good and continuing relations between the parties.

Conclusion

CROXON AND MARSHALL commented in 2004, "A lot of work needs to be done in the area of developing solid contracts for high performance coaches in Canada." The Reade et al. survey (2009) suggests that much work still needs to be done, and not just with the national team level coaches studied by Marshall. Coaches are typically at the height of their bargaining power at the time of hiring. Indeed, Marshall's study noted a dearth of candidates for high performance coaching positions. The time to negotiate a fair and equitable contract is at the beginning of the relationship, before signing the contract. To ensure the contract reflects the coaching relationship (whether as an employee or an independent contractor) and includes all the appropriate provisions, coaches need to educate themselves to understand the full scope of the job description; research salary or other compensation level; speak with other coaches about their contracts; and use the resources of any professional coaching associations. Ensuring a proper contract is a task not to be overlooked or sloughed off.

Employment Contract Checklist

HOW COMPREHENSIVE the employment contract will be depends on the nature of the relationship. Some will require extensive, detailed contractual provisions, while others may not. In the following checklist, clauses that are bolded should be seriously considered, regardless of the nature of the contract. This checklist is not necessarily comprehensive; every contract should fit its own circumstance. Having a lawyer review your contract is always advisable.

1. **Date of agreement and hiring**

2. Parties
   a. Names and addresses

3. Relationship to be established
   a. Employee
   b. Independent contractor

4. Statement of hiring/employment

5. Time to be devoted to business
   a. Overtime (if hourly)
   b. Length of contract
   c. Hours per day/week

6. **Duties, responsibilities, and obligations**
   a. Critical skills employee brings to the position; specific duties; reporting relationship
   b. Employer's right to change duties/reporting relationships/ add duties from time to time—is notice of changes necessary/ appropriate?
   c. Employee agrees to be bound by employer's rules and policies

7. Location of employment
   a. Options to change

8. **Duration of contract**
   a. Fixed term/indefinite duration (with termination provisions)
   b. Renewal

9. **Compensation (including benefits)**
   a. Wages/salary
   b. When paid
   c. Increases in compensation
   d. Commission/bonuses
   e. Overtime (if appropriate)
   f. Vacations (statutory and other)
   g. Meal/car allowances

10. Expense accounts
    a. Employee/employer to pay
    b. Permission required before incurring certain expenses?
    c. Receipts to be filed?

11. **Review periods/process**

12. Restrictive covenants
    a. Non-competition (geographic area, time, definition of competition)
    b. Non-solicitation
    c. Confidentiality
    d. Exclusive service to employer
    e. Return of company property

13. Property rights of employer
    a. Copyright, trademarks, patents
    b. Waive moral rights

14. **Termination of contract**
    a. Cause/no cause
    b. Termination by employee (length of notice)
    c. Probation period

15. Rights arising on termination—return of property (credit card, equipment)

16. Modification of contract
    a. By employee/employer
    b. Effect of modification of one term on the rest of the contract

17. Employer protection
    a. Indemnification
    b. Liability insurance
    c. Bonded

18. Breach of contract
    a. What constitutes breach by either side

b. Remedy for breach—damages, legal fees, injunctive relief (restrictions)

19. Dispute management
    a. Mediation
    b. Arbitration

20. Severability

21. Entire Agreement Clause

22. Notice provisions

23. Governing law

24. **Signature (witness)**

RESOURCES
- Coaching Association of Canada
- Provincial and national coaching associations (see Appendix 2)
- Centre for Sport and Law
- Law firms with expertise and experience in the area of employment law

NOTES

1. A contract is simply a mutual agreement between parties. It does not have to be written but, if there is a dispute, having a written confirmation of the terms of the agreement is the best proof of the agreement. It can be formal or informal, long or short, depending on the circumstances and needs. Understanding the scope and complexity of the contractual relationship will help determine what form the actual contract should take.

2. Although the substantive content of each form of contract may be the same or similar, how they are expressed or reflected in the contract changes to reflect the legal nature of the contract.

3. Note that travel expenses can be deducted as an expense against income before taxes. This means that the independent contractor, not the sport

organization, must pay those expenses herself (although such expenses should be calculated into the contract fee).

4. *Wiebe Door Services Ltd. v. Minister of National Revenue.*

5. A fuller description of the tests and practical suggestions to assist in structuring the working relationship towards one form of working relationship or the other can be found in *Legal Issues in Sport: Tools and Techniques for the Sport Manager* (Corbett et al., 2008), p. 114–140.

6. Many professions publish salary scales so that members of the profession can judge appropriate salary levels.

7. Timing is critical—an evaluation immediately at the end of a disappointing season or event will clearly be tempered by that outcome. Yet the appraisal typically is, or should be, so much more than the season's or event's performance outcome.

8. In other words, and oddly, a number of the indefinite term contracts included renewal provisions.

REFERENCES

Centre for Sport and Law. (2004). Coaching contracts: Do you know what yours says? *Coaches Report, 11*(1).

Centre for Sport and Law. (2001). Job descriptions. *Coaches Report, 7*(4).

Centre for Sport and Law. (1997). Employment contracts for coaches. *Coaches Report, 3*(3).

Corbett, R., Findlay, H.A., & Lech, D.W. (2008). *Legal issues in sport: Tools and techniques for the sport manager.* Toronto: Emond Montgomery.

Croxon, S., & Marshall, D. (2004). Contracts and contract negotiations. *Canadian Journal for Women in Coaching, 4*(2).

MacLean, J. (2001). *Performance appraisal for sport and recreation managers.* Toronto: Human Kinetics Press.

Moose Jaw Kinsmen Flying Fins Inc. v. Minister of National Revenue [1988], F.C.J. No. 21 (F.C.A.)

Puri v. Minister of National Revenue 1998, CanLII 473 (TCC)

Reade, I. et al. (2009). *A report on the status of coaches in Canada.* Ottawa: Coaching Association of Canada.

Whistler Mountain Ski Club v. Minister of National Revenue unreported, 95-1723 (UI), August 2, 1996 (TCC)

Wiebe Door Services Ltd. v. Minister of National Revenue [1986], 3 F.C. 553 (F.C.A.)

Sophia Radecki honed her coaching skills with the Coaching Association of Canada's Women in Coaching Canada Games Apprenticeship Program.

AFTERWORD

Dru Marshall

So—AFTER MUCH RESEARCH, discussion, and sharing of personal experiences, where do we find ourselves? We know that the participation of girls and women in sport has increased, and that women have had tremendous success on the national and international stages. Despite this increase in participation, we know that a gender gap in leadership still exists in sport—even though accumulated evidence suggests that diversity in leadership is a critical factor for success.

We have analyzed this picture through a variety of lenses and perspectives. We know that women have the capacity to be excellent coaches who are leaders and role models. We also know that those women who have made it to the top of the coaching profession have experienced more obstacles and barriers along the way than their male counterparts, and that frequently they have done so at a heavier personal cost, and for fewer dollars. The obstacles for female coaches and female leaders in general that we have identified include stereotyping of and resistance to the leadership style of women; a variety of forms of discrimination; harassment and bullying; exclusion from social networks; a lack of female role models and mentors; decreased opportunities for coaching as a viable career choice; and the androcentric nature and structure of sport in general. We also know that those who make it to the top experience social isolation and typically lack support.

We have identified a number of strategies to overcome these obstacles, and have written entire chapters on important skill sets for female coaches, including communication, mentoring, and advocacy. We know we have to do a better job of identifying the talent pool of upcoming coaches, and we recognize that we should look to the athletes we currently coach as a first step in this identification process. We need to increase our understanding of the importance of negotiations, and of advocating on behalf of others and ourselves for change. We know we need to do a better job of developing networks, and using the information those networks can provide to make us more effective as coaches. We know we need to support women once they are put into coaching positions. Retired successful women, whether from the business, academic, or sport worlds, have important experiences to share, and we should consciously involve them in the current development of younger coaches. They can advocate in different and more direct ways, since they have no fear of losing a position. Ultimately, we need to examine new paradigms for women in coaching—and ensure that young women see coaching as a viable career opportunity.

It is no longer fair or just to say that women are not qualified for top jobs. Clearly they are. We know that diversity in leadership teams works. We are not suggesting that women take over all leadership positions, or all high-level coaching positions—but we are arguing for rapid closure of the gender gap in leadership. We hope aspiring coaches find the information in this book valuable as they navigate their own personal leadership labyrinths. The authors have collectively committed to helping and supporting future female coaches who want to become leaders—we encourage others to join us.

A Five-Point Collaborative Strategy for Change

A Plan to Improve Opportunities for Women to Succeed in the Coaching Profession

An Initiative of the Coaching Association of Canada's Women in Coaching Program

(May 2007)

The Current Climate

ON THE PLUS SIDE...

In recent years, as the participation of girls and women in sport in Canada has skyrocketed, barriers have tumbled and opportunities have proliferated. Women are now found in every aspect of sport, from the playing fields to the boardrooms, as administrators and officials, at the grassroots level through to high performance.

On the coaching side of sport, some progress has been made, thanks to national initiatives by the Coaching Association of Canada through its Women in Coaching program, the Canada Games Council (whose equity policy is having a major impact on the development of young female coaches), and the Canadian Association for the

Advancement of Women and Sport and Physical Activity (with its ongoing programs to raise awareness of women and sport). Initiatives by the Canadian Colleges Athletic Association, Canadian Interuniversity Sport, and Coaches of Canada are also making a difference.

A core group of women are finding ways to stay in the coaching profession and have children. At the 2006 Olympic Winter Games, four female coaches collectively produced eight of Canada's twenty-one medals. More female athletes are making a successful transition to coaching. Data from the 2007 Canada Winter Games reveals a rise in the number of female coaches from 165 in 2003 to 180 in 2007.

In short, Canadian sport is changing, albeit slowly.

Learnings from the Strategic Think Tank

WHILE COACHING HAS BEEN positively affected by the participation explosion, participants in the Strategic Think Tank, held during the 2007 Women in Coaching National Coach Workshop, agreed that women who choose to coach continue to face serious challenges.

The Strategic Think Tank identified a number of areas of concern:

- Female coaches function without an overall plan for their professional development that includes realistic targets, goals, accountability, and evaluation.
- There is no minimal baseline data by which progress can be tracked.
- There is little linkage to or shared information about programs and initiatives that are designed to create change.
- Few professional development pathways exist.
- Mentoring is hit and miss.
- There is a lack of networking opportunities, especially for new, young female coaches.
- Career mobility is hampered by conflicting personal and professional priorities.

- Too often, female coaches are offered short-term programs that come with rigid timeframes and unrealistic goals, making momentum impossible.
- Sport organizations fail to spotlight female role models.
- There is a lack of access to information that is critical to professional success.

The Strategic Think Tank then laid the groundwork for a Five-Point Collaborative Strategy for Change, consisting of specific actions that address these concerns. Three Guiding Principles focused the discussion to develop the Strategy.

Guiding Principles

ENSURE that female coaches currently in the Canadian sport system are celebrated and their employment opportunities increased.

ENSURE that there are opportunities to build on the good work done to date by linking all the partners into an overall, co-ordinated vision for women in coaching, recognizing that no single agency can effectively address women in coaching issues.

ENSURE collaborative action and co-ordinated policies and efforts by government ministries, the education system, the sport and recreation sectors, local governments, not-for-profit organizations, the volunteer sector, the corporate sector, and current coaches.

The Situation

A RECENT BASELINE STUDY commissioned by the Coaching Association of Canada confirmed the overall lack of women coaching at the national team and Olympic levels while uncovering some encouraging signs of upward movement, particularly at the university and Canada Games levels.

The study was triggered by statistics recorded at the 2004 Olympic Games, where women accounted for 50% of Canada's medals, 53% of Top-8 finishes, but only 10.5% of coaches accredited by the Canadian

Olympic Committee. Similarly, at the 2006 Olympic Winter Games, women accounted for 67% of Canada's medals, but only 14.7% of Canada's accredited coaches.

These statistics authenticated the long-standing perception that, while the successes of Canada's female athletes have risen substantially, the number of women in coaching positions has not increased at even close to the same pace.

The study's findings confirm that women are under-represented within the coaching ranks, despite the large increase in female athlete participation and achievement. Without equal representation of female coaches in the sport system, the sporting experience has not reached its full potential for both genders.

Taking Action: A Five-Point Collaborative Strategy for Change

ACHIEVING THE GOALS of the Five-Point Collaborative Strategy for Change requires actions in five strategic priority areas, leading to a made-in-Canada Women in Coaching model.

1. Promoting Collaboration through Strategic Partnerships and Capacity Building

The collaboration, partnership, and integration of regional, provincial, and national initiatives must be strengthened. This requires investments and systems that enable and co-ordinate the mechanisms necessary to achieve the Five-Point Collaborative Strategy for Change.

Actions:

ESTABLISH an Advisory Council for the Coaching Association of Canada's Women in Coaching program and hold a strategic meeting at the annual National Coach Workshop.

DEVELOP a strong Women in Coaching Network, consisting of leaders from varying sectors, including the corporate world and multi-sport organizations, to empower and support female coaches.

SEEK new resources from diverse sectors, including related professions and international organizations.

INCREASE opportunities for women to develop as high performance coaches.

DEVELOP a higher profile for Women in Coaching on the Coaching Association of Canada's website and ensure that it is linked to all lead organizations.

ENSURE that national sport organizations are seen as champions of Women in Coaching in partnership with provincial sport organizations and local sport organizations, and that they work closely on Women in Coaching solutions with key multi-sport organizations.

DEVELOP targeted approaches to partnerships that provide resources, both through value-in-kind and direct funding, and further the Women in Coaching social marketing strategy.

2. Public Education and Communication

Investments in public education efforts need to provide information, generate discussion, and influence attitudes and values around female coaches in order to create a climate conducive to social and behavioural change.

Actions:

ESTABLISH a Women in Coaching Clearing House consisting of a data bank, a resource bibliography, job opportunities, services, general information, and Best Practices.

DISSEMINATE Women in Coaching "Success Stories," new initiatives, and Best Practices.

PROMOTE the capacity of local, provincial, national, and multi-sport organizations.

MAKE a concerted effort to increase media exposure for female coaches, including targeting media messages for and about the 2010 Olympic Winter Games female coaches.

GUARANTEE access to training and proactive hiring practices.

3. Research, Monitoring, and Transfer of Knowledge

Research is essential to understanding and applying effective strategies and current trends in policies, plans, and practices to improve the situation for Canada's female coaches. Research will provide a base of knowledge that supports investments aimed at increasing the number of female coaches at all levels.

Actions:

FORM research partnerships and commission position papers that review the literature on the major issues facing Women in Coaching, and publicize the facts revealed by the review.

RESEARCH, analyze, and publicize successful examples of systemic change.

DEVELOP a database of female head and assistant coaches with Canadian Interuniversity Sport, the Canadian Colleges Athletic Association, and national and provincial sport organizations, and monitor career progress.

4. Public Policy

Governments at all levels must provide leadership and collaborative efforts to design and implement effective public policy that removes barriers and encourages women to pursue a career in coaching.

Actions:

TAKE an active role in the review of Sport Canada's Women and Sport Policy.

TAKE an active role in the Status of the Coach review.

ENCOURAGE national sport organizations to examine their policies regarding Women in Coaching.

ENSURE that the plans of national sport organizations contain commitment statements that support the career aspirations of their female coaches and that these statements are supported by budgetary line items.

PROMOTE, within existing programs, the importance of matching, flexible salary grants based on research.

5. Best Practices

Identifying and creating Best Practices is critical to bringing Women in Coaching into mainstream Canadian culture with the resultant recognition of and support for the value female coaches bring to sport at all levels so that the Canadian sport system is informed and practices systemic buy-in.

Actions:

CREATE mentorship systems at the college, university, provincial, and national levels.

INVESTIGATE the feasibility of bilateral agreements at the provincial/territorial level that include a Women in Coaching component.

ENSURE that granting programs at the national level, such as True Sport, include priority criteria related to Women in Coaching.

DEVELOP linkages with the Canadian Olympic Committee and AthletesCAN.

IDENTIFY and recognize national sport organizations whose policies and funding support Women in Coaching initiatives.

ENCOURAGE linkages between the Canadian Colleges Athletic Association, Canadian Interuniversity Sport, the provincial/territorial coaching associations, and the Canada Games Council.

DEVELOP strategies to encourage re-entry into the profession and examine business practices that could be applied to encourage this.

WORK to enhance the capacity of provincial sport organizations.

ENSURE access to training and proactive hiring practices.

Potential Research Topics

THE STRATEGIC THINK TANK identified potential research topics that could be the responsibility of several Women in Coaching partners and could include

- tracking and evaluating the career paths of National Team Apprentice Program coaches and Canada Games Apprenticeship Program coaches
- investigating whether or not women head coaches attract female athletes to coaching
- investigating whether or not a change in the coach gender ratio contributes to the decrease in girls' participation, and if a change in the coach gender ratio contributes to the decrease
- examining whether female athletes who are coached by female coaches have different experiences of sport, have different perceptions of the values of sport, and are more likely to choose a coaching career
- surveying Canadian Interuniversity Sport, the Canadian Colleges Athletic Association, and national and provincial sport organizations regarding their hiring policies. Include questions on the percentage of their funding that goes to girls and women, and how many female athletic directors, executive directors, CEOs, COOs, and technical directors are women
- investigating the feasibility of the resurrection of the National Coaching School for Women as a fast track mechanism for identified young female coaches
- developing benchmarking and measurable targets for national sport organizations, through the National Coaching Certification Program consultants

International Initiatives

THE FOLLOWING ORGANIZATIONS provide information on international works in progress.

- International Working Group on Women and Sport (IWG)
- WomenSport International
- United Nations Educational, Scientific and Cultural Organization (UNESCO)
- International Olympic Committee (IOC)

- International Association of Physical Education and Sport for Girls and Women (IAPESGW)

"Taking Action: A Five-Point Collaborative Strategy For Change" was developed by Marion Lay, Sheilagh Croxon, and Sheila Robertson. The Strategy reflects the discussion at the Strategic Think Tank, held during the 2007 Women in Coaching National Coach Workshop.

APPENDIX 2

Provincial and National Coaching Associations

Coaches of Canada
Wayne Parro, Executive Director
108 - 3 Concorde Gate
Toronto, Ontario M3C 3N7
Tel. 416-426-7023
Fax 416-426-7331
Website: www.coachesofcanada.com
Email: info@coachesofcanada.com

Coaches of Canada, Manitoba Chapter
David Telles-Langdon
c/o University of Winnipeg
515 Portage Avenue
Winnipeg, Manitoba R3B 2E9
Tel. 204-786-9248
Fax 204-783-7866
Email: d.telles-langdon@uwinnipeg.ca

Canadian Ski Coaches Federation (CSCF)
Peter Goodman, Managing Director
220 - 4900 Jean Talon West
Montreal, Quebec H4P 1W9
Toll-free 1-800-811-6428
Fax 1-800-811-6427

Website: www.snowpro.com/cscf/e
Email: coach@snowpro.com

Canadian Swimming Coaches and Teachers Association (CSCTA)
Chris Hindmarch-Watson, Executive Director
519 - 4438 West 10th Avenue
Vancouver, British Columbia V6R 4R8
Tel. 604-317-5756
Fax 604-608-5674
Website: www.csca.org

Coaches Association of British Columbia
Gordon May, Executive Director
200 - 3820 Cessna Drive
Richmond, British Columbia V7B 0A2
Tel. 604-333-3600
Fax 604-333-3450
Website: www.coaches.bc.ca
Email: info@coaches.bc.ca

Coaches Association of Ontario (CAO)
Susan Kitchen, Executive Director
108 - 3 Concorde Gate
Toronto, Ontario M3C 3N7
Toll-free 1-888-622-7668
Fax 416-426-7331
Website: www.coachesontario.ca

Coaches Association of Prince Edward Island (CAPEI)
Cheryl Crozier, Executive Director
P.O. Box 302
Charlottetown, Prince Edward Island C1A 7K7
Toll-free 1-800-247-6712
Website: www.coachespei.ca

Coaches Association of Saskatchewan (CAS)
Mark Bracken, Executive Director
1870 Lorne Street
Regina, Saskatchewan S4P 2L7
Tel. 306-780-9313
Fax 306-781-6021
Website: www.saskcoach.ca
Email: coach@sasksport.sk.ca

Coaching Manitoba

Greg Guenther, Director of Coaching
200 Main Street
Winnipeg, Manitoba R3C 4M2
Toll-free 1-888-887-7307
Fax 204-925-5916
Website: www.coachingmanitoba.ca
Email: coaching@sport.mb.ca

A Decade of Articles from the *Canadian Journal for Women in Coaching*

http://www.coach.ca

2000

"Being Professional About Your Employment" by Rose Mercier. Shows female coaches how to be professional, mixing practical tips and ideas that make the reader sit up and take notice. (September)

"In Their Own Voices: Women Coaches Raising a Family" by Sheila Robertson. Tells the personal stories of seventeen women, every one a dedicated, educated, passionate coach, and seeks to address the high fallout rate by searching for supportive commonalities. (November)

2001

"Communicating with Clarity: Guidelines to Help Female Coaches Succeed" by Penny Werthner. Spells out the specific skill sets a female coach must possess in order to become an effective communicator, and how to develop and use those skills when working with athletes and colleagues. (January)

"Developing the Next Generation of Female Coaches" by Dru Marshall. Suggests strategies to address the low number of women coaching national teams. (March)

"Understanding the Differences Between How Women and Men Communicate" by Penny Werthner. Explains how well-developed listening skills allow a coach to distinguish between words heard and what is really being said. Also covered are integrating the highly skilled athlete into the team, the "how" and "when" of asking questions, and the rituals of apologies, feedback, and opposition. (May)

"Changing the Androcentric World of Sport" by Rose Mercier and Penny Werthner. Enumerates what must change if the sporting world is to become a healthier, more caring environment for women, changing from an environment pre-occupied with men and the activities of men, to one that is inclusive and satisfying. (July)

"A Practical Lesson About Developing Women Coaches" by Rose Mercier. How an apprenticeship program for female coaches offered during the 2001 Jeux de la Francophonie in Canada proved to be a resounding success, fostering deep relationships and boosting confidence and leadership abilities. (September)

"Mentoring as a Development Tool for Women Coaches" by Dru Marshall. Explores what mentorship is, describing the qualities mentors and protégés need for a successful relationship, analyzing the many types of mentorship, explaining options for the structure and duration of the relationships, and describing various types of mentors. (November)

2002

"Applying Systems Thinking to Understanding Canadian Sport" by Rose Mercier. Unravels the complexity of Canadian sport in order to develop strategies that can make changing "the system" possible, offering six practical steps to put system thinking into practice. (January)

"Staying the Course: Candid Observations of Women Coaches on the Trials and Tribulations of Their Profession" by Sheila Robertson. Reveals timely insights into the reality of sport in Canada. (March)

"First Annual Women's National Team Coach Retreat" by Dru Marshall. Identifies the problems faced by female national team coaches, beginning the work of resolution, and founding a personal support system. (October)

"Laurie Eisler: Lessons Learned from a Champion Coach" by Laurie Eisler with Sheila Robertson. Hard realities discussed with candour. (December)

2003

"Decision Training: An Innovative Approach to Coaching" by Joan Vickers. Explains the Decision Training approach, demonstrating the value in enabling coaches to train their athletes to be more self-reflective, make their own decisions, become more self-reliant, and be better prepared for competition. (February)

"Tales of Transition: From Star Athlete to Career Coach" by Sheila Robertson. Examines the absence of significant numbers of retired high performance athletes from the coaching professions through discussion with three of the best who are making a name for themselves as full-time, paid professionals. (April)

"The New National Coaching Certification Program and Its Implications for Women Coaches" by Guylaine Demers. Describes Canada's revised coach education program along with a thorough analysis of the environment in which female coaches work in Canada, the implications of the changes, potential advantages and disadvantages for female coaches, and possible impacts. (July)

"Analysing the Impact of the Women in Coaching Apprenticeship Program" by Rose Mercier. Explains why the program was developed, its evolution, and the expectations and obligations of each partner and participant. The article includes the insights of five participants and one mentor coach, demonstrating that this is a vital and effective program. (October)

2004

"Contracts and Contract Negotiations" by Sheilagh Croxon and Dru Marshall. Addresses the shortfall of information on contracts and contract negotiations, expanding understanding of what should be included in a contract and demonstrating how to ask for things you believe are important. (January)

"Meet Marion Lay, Sport Leader Extraordinaire" by Sheila Robertson. Profiles one of Canada's most innovative sport leaders, whose lifelong commitment to the betterment of sport has brought her acclaim and awards, nationally and internationally. (April)

"Justifications for Unethical Behaviour in Sport: The Role of the Coach" by Ann Dodge and Brenda Robertson. Addresses the justifications varsity athletes offer for engaging in unethical behaviour and the role of the coach, both as a source of motivation for unethical behaviour and as an advocate for ethical practices. (May)

"Why Female Athletes Decide to Become Coaches—or Not" by Guylaine Demers. Provides observations of female athletes and coaches on what attracts or dissuades young female high performance athletes to or from coaching. (July)

"An Olympic Coach's Journal" by Laryssa Biesenthal. Reflections on Biesenthal's experiences up to and including the 2004 Olympic Games. (November)

2005

"Olympic Experiences: A National Coach Speaks Out" by Kelly Hand. A frank and moving account based on a speech delivered at the Women in Coaching Luncheon at the 2004 Petro-Canada Sport Leadership sportif. (February)

"Making the Case: Coaching as a Viable Career Path for Women" by Penny Werthner. Addresses the fundamental questions of why Canada would need or want women in the coaching profession, and what is being done to ensure that female coaches continue to progress. (May)

"Political Advocacy in Coaching—Why Engage?" by Rose Mercier and Dru Marshall. Argues that for female coaches to advance their own cause and become optimally effective, they must learn to become better advocates for the considerable value they bring to sport. (July)

"Inside China: A Canadian Coach's Perspective" by Cindy Thomson. Analyses first-hand the strengths and weaknesses of China's sport system, with provocative comparisons to the Canadian system. (December)

2006

"Homophobia in Sport—Fact of Life, Taboo Subject" by Guylaine Demers. Assesses a situation that should and must be discussed if the sport world is ever to become an environment that welcomes everyone, regardless of race, colour, creed, or sexual orientation. (April)

"Reflections of a Winning Coach: Behind the Scenes with Melody Davidson" by Melody Davidson with Sheila Robertson. Learn first-hand about the planning, hard work, trials, and tribulations that combined to produce the team that won the women's hockey gold medal at the 2006 Olympic Winter Games. (July)

"Women's Leadership in American Sport: Progressing or Backsliding?" by Sheila Robertson. Examines why the numbers of female athletic directors in the United States are in decline despite the optimism generated by Title ix, exposing the reality female sport leaders face. (October)

2007

"Why Growing Numbers of Canadian Women Coaches Are Going South" by Kelley Anderson. An expatriate coach's perspective on the steady drain of a vital resource—Canada's female coaches—told through personal stories. (January)

"Coaching and Motherhood: Staying in the Profession" by Sheila Robertson. Finds ways to combine career and motherhood without stepping away from coaching for prolonged periods, or forever. (April)

"Developing Female Leadership in the Canadian Sport System: Recommendations for High-Level Sport Organizations" by Josée Martel. Draws from an assessment of the barriers to more equitable female leadership, and provides seven well-reasoned recommendations that could change the face of Canadian sport for the better. (July)

"Shifting the Culture: Implications for Female Coaches" by Gretchen Kerr and Dru Marshall. Dissects the status of female coaches and draws compelling parallels with other sectors in society, along with recommendations for shifting the very culture of sport. (October)

"What We Know About the Experiences of Women Beginner Coaches" by Guylaine Demers and Marie-Hélène Audet. Reports on a study that helps to develop a comprehensive, realistic picture of the working lives of female coaches. (December)

2008

"They Never Give Up: Once a Coach, Always a Coach" by Sheila Robertson. Focuses attention on female coaches who have been tested, challenged, or shoved aside, yet who persevere, each driven by a powerful desire to coach: women with children, women with different ways of making it work, women with the highest of ambitions, women devoted to community coaching—above all, women who excel at coaching. (April)

"Making It Happen—Here's How" by Sylvie Béliveau. Understanding sport's potential as an instrument for positive change. (July)

"The Business of Greatness" by Rose Mercier. Stresses the importance of female coaches operating within a well-thought-out framework consisting of a career plan, solid business practices, and a well-defined vision based on carefully articulated values. (October)

2009

"We Are Coaches: Program Tackles the Under-Representation of Female Coaches" by Guylaine Demers. Describes a bold initiative for training women to become community coaches. (April)

"Female Coaches' Experience of Harassment and Bullying" by Gretchen Kerr. Examines the touchy subject, calling for more research in order to find solutions and bring about change. (July)

CONTRIBUTORS

BETTINA CALLARY is a PHD candidate at the University of Ottawa under the supervision of Drs. Penny Werthner and Pierre Trudel. She is conducting research on the biographies of Canadian female coaches to explore the multitude of experiences throughout their lives that have contributed to their learning and coaching development. Her research has extended to explore how sport organizations can take a lifelong learning perspective in developing coach education programs. Her master's research involved an intervention aimed at developing coach and athlete awareness of how they wanted to feel and the strategies that allowed them to feel that way. Callary is also an alpine ski coach and course conductor for the Canadian Ski Coaches Federation. She has a National Coaching Institute diploma in high performance coaching, was the head coach for the Canadian men's ski team at the International University Sports Federation (FISU) World University Games, and has worked with Canada's and Argentina's World Cup ski teams in addition to junior teams in Canada and Australia.

DIANE M. CULVER, PHD, is an assistant professor at the University of Ottawa's School of Human Kinetics. She obtained her PHD in Education from the university in 2004 and was a senior coaching consultant for the Coaching Association of Canada before coming to the School of Human Kinetics in July 2007. Her research interests are in the area of coaching and coach education, informal learning and changing everyday practices, and qualitative research methods, especially participatory research. She has published in several journals and has a chapter in *The Sports Coach as Educator*, edited by Robyn Jones. Culver is the co-ordinator of the Coaching Association of Canada's Research Committee. Her previous working experience includes coaching for the Canadian National Ski Team and the New Zealand Olympic Ski Team. She consults with athletes and coaches, facilitating the enhancement of their performance.

GUYLAINE DEMERS, PHD, has been a professor at the Department of Physical Education of Laval University since September 2001. She is the director of the undergraduate competency-based coach education program. She takes particular interest in issues of women in sport, coach education, and competency-based training. She was actively involved in the development and implementation of Canada's competency-based National Coaching Certification Program. She is the chair of Égale Action, the Quebec association for the advancement of women in sport and physical activity, and is on the board of the Canadian Association for the Advancement of Women and Sport and Physical Activity. Demers also sits on the Coaching Association of Canada's Coaching Research Committee and on the editorial board of the *Canadian Journal for Women in Coaching*. She is leading an extensive research project into the early years of female coaches' experience in coaching with the Coaching Association of Canada's *We Are Coaches* program. In 2007, she was named one of Canada's Most Influential Women in Sport and Physical Activity. She was a coach for nearly fifteen years and was also the technical director of the Quebec Basketball Federation. She is helping Qatar's women's sport committee develop a sport system for girls and women.

HILARY A. FINDLAY, PHD, LLB, is an associate professor in the Department of Sport Management at Brock University. She is a co-founder and director of the Centre for Sport and Law, a consulting company that has been offering services and practical resources on organizational governance, risk management, and other legal issues to Canada's sport community for over seventeen years. She is one of the authors of *Legal Issues in Sport: Tools and Techniques for the Sport Manager*. Findlay teaches courses in sport law, contract drafting, intellectual property and licensing, and negotiation techniques. Her research centres on dispute resolution systems in sport, particularly structural and procedural elements of dispute resolution processes and the way in which people experience the dispute resolution process (how fair they perceive it to be). As chair of the Ontario University Athletics appeals committee, she sits on that organization's dispute panels. She is also a member of the Canadian Centre for Ethics in Sport Ethical Issues Review Panel. Findlay continues to represent clients primarily in disputes before arbitral panels and in relation to human rights issues. Along with her colleagues at the Centre for Sport and Law, she writes a regular magazine column addressing a variety of legal issues affecting the sport community.

GRETCHEN KERR, PHD, is a professor in the Faculty of Physical Education and Health at the University of Toronto, a position she has held for the past twenty years. She also serves as the associate dean of undergraduate education, overseeing the undergraduate program in Physical and Health Education, including the Concurrent Teacher Education Program. Kerr's research focuses on two broad areas of interest: the psychosocial health of young people in sport, and the experiences of women in coaching. Her recent publications address young, elite athletes' experiences of emotional abuse in sport and include a review of coaching positions held by women in Canada. Her specific interests in harassment, abuse, and bullying within sport have led to numerous publications as well as leadership positions and advocacy work within the sport community. She serves as the harassment officer for Gymnastics Ontario and Gymnastics Canada. Additionally, she chairs the Ethics Committee for Gymnastics Ontario, a group that focuses on developing educational initiatives to enhance ethical conduct within the gymnastics community. Kerr also sits on the Coaching Association of Canada's Research Committee and on the editorial board of the *Canadian Journal for Women in Coaching*.

DRU MARSHALL, PHD, is deputy provost at the University of Alberta. She has a distinguished twenty-eight-year career with the university, serving in a number of senior administrative capacities, including the Faculty of Physical Education and Recreation's first vice-dean. An exercise physiologist, she is a scholar in the area of childhood obesity and children's fitness. Her work in the area of childhood obesity focuses on measurement, the impact of measurement, and the role of physical activity in the treatment of obesity. Marshall has a keen interest in women in coaching. She has an extensive and distinguished career in coaching at the university, provincial, and national levels, spanning more than twenty-five years. A National Coaching Certification Program Level 5 certified coach, she served as head coach of the University of Alberta's Pandas Field Hockey Team from 1981 to 2001, the National Women's Junior Field Hockey Team from 1986 to 1996, and the Women's National Team from 1996 to 2001. Her coaching skills have been recognized extensively at local, provincial, and national levels, most notably when she was given the 3M Canada Coach of the Year Award in women's team sport in 1994. In 2004, Marshall was named one of Canada's Most Influential Women in Sport and Physical Activity. She was also presented with an Herstorical Award for her outstanding contribution to the furtherance of women's sport. She continues to make an outstanding contribution to the development of women's sport in Canada through teaching and research, mentoring coaches at all levels of the sport continuum, and serving on numerous provincial and national advisory committees. She is the author of numerous peer-reviewed articles and is a frequent presenter at academic conferences. Marshall holds a Bachelor of Physical Education from the University of Manitoba and a Master of Science and PHD from the University of Alberta.

ROSE MERCIER, BPE, MBA, is a Kingston-based consultant in leadership development and organizational transition who has had a long involvement in sport. She competed in swimming and athletics, graduated from the University of Alberta with a degree in physical education, and coached club swimming in Ottawa before starting a twenty-year career in sport administration. Mercier worked as the director of education with Swimming Canada from 1976 to 1984. There, she was responsible for developing a variety of innovative coaching education programs. She was the director general of the Canadian Cycling Association from 1984 to 1990; a policy analyst with the International Relations and Major Games Directorate within Fitness and Amateur Sport from 1990 to 1992; and the director of the Tait McKenzie Institute for the Canadian Sport and Fitness Administration Centre from 1992 to 1994. Self-employed since 1995, Mercier's consulting work focuses on facilitating organizational transition, strategic planning, and leadership development in sport, other non-profit organizations, and the public sector. She works with a variety of clients; however, her real passion lies in her continuing relationship with sport organizations, including the Coaching Association of Canada, the Canadian Curling Association, Football Canada, Athletics Canada, Swimming Canada, Cowichan 2008 North American Indigenous Games, Speed Skating Canada, Aboriginal Sport Circle, Cross Country Alberta, Ringette Canada, Sport Canada, and various federal/provincial/territorial working committees. She earned her MBA at Concordia University's John Molson School of Business.

SHEILA ROBERTSON, BA, has worked as an editor and writer with Canada's sport community for over thirty years. The founding editor of *Champion* magazine, she was also the founding editor of *Coaches Report* magazine and its lead writer from 1993 to 2005. She is the founding editor of and a writer for the *Canadian Journal for Women in Coaching* and is the editor of several sport-related books. She was an author and editor for *Canadian Woman Studies: Women and Girls and Sport and Physical Activity*, a York University publication; the author and editor of numerous publications for the Canadian Association for the Advancement of Women and Sport and Physical Activity; and the editor of numerous manuals on long-term athlete development. Robertson has written many profiles of leading coaches and is a regular columnist with a national coaching magazine. She is also the author of *From Montreal to Kumamoto* for the International Working Group on Women and Sport, and the editor of a series of articles on service excellence for a Crown corporation. She attended three Olympic Games, working in communications for the Canadian Olympic Team, and has been a delegate to several international women in sport conferences. In 1995, she was the recipient of the Canadian Sport Award for Communications. In 2005, Coaches of Canada established the Sheila Robertson Award to recognize a sport organization that demonstrates a consistent approach in valuing and recognizing the role of the coach internally and to the media and the public. She is a graduate of the University of Manitoba.

DAWN-MARIE SHARP, MA, received her diploma in High Performance Coaching from the National Coaching Institute-BC (NCI-BC). Recently, she completed a Master of Arts in Coaching Studies at the University of Alberta and is pursuing further graduate education in sociology. She has significant playing, coaching, and administrative experience with women's rugby and has had success at all levels. She has won the Southern Alberta Championship and the Alberta Provincial Division II Championship as an athlete, and the Canadian Championship in 2003 as an assistant coach. In 2004, she was appointed as a coach to the National U-23 Women's team and was the manager of the national women's team that won the inaugural International University Sports Federation (FISU) women's rugby sevens championship.

SHAUNNA TAYLOR is a PHD candidate at the University of Ottawa under Drs. Penny Werthner and Pierre Trudel and a sport psychology consultant at the Ottawa High Performance Centre. Her current research investigates ways coaches learn to coach athletes with a disability in the Paralympic system in Canada. Her master's research in the 1990s, with Dr. Terry Orlick, looked at ways children can learn to manage their stress, and she continues to use these findings and techniques in her own life and in coaching youth soccer teams. For the past fifteen years, Taylor has consulted in the mental preparation and support of athletes at all levels, from local clubs to varsity and the national and Olympic level. She is the sport psychology consultant for the BodySense Program, a disordered-eating prevention program for athletes sponsored by the Canadian Centre for Ethics in Sport. She is part of the sport science team supporting Canada's Olympic and Paralympic athletes for Vancouver 2010. She became a consultant with the Coaching Association of Canada in September 2009.

PENNY WERTHNER, PHD, is a professor in the School of Human Kinetics at the University of Ottawa, conducting research in the learning processes of coaches and athletes; issues facing female coaches; psychological preparation for coaches and athletes, particularly within the world championship and Olympic environment; coach stress and burnout; values and ethics in sport; and the use of bioneurofeedback for enhancing the performance of coaches and athletes. She is also a consultant in sport psychology who works with many national team athletes and coaches, and has been part of seven winter and summer Canadian Olympic teams from 1988 to 2010. At the 2004 and 2008 Olympic Games, Werthner was the Canadian team consultant in sport psychology. A leader and innovator in international sport and in women and sport issues, Werthner is a 3M National Coaching Certification Level 4/5 presenter for Task #7, #8, and #17. A former Olympic track and field athlete, she represented Canada internationally from 1970 to 1981.

INDEX

Page numbers in **bold** refer to photographs.

abuse. *See* harassment and bullying
academia. *See* university and college coaches
"Actively Engaged: A Policy on Sport for Women and Girls," xxvii
advocacy, 146–63
   barriers to, 16–17
   communication skills in, 154–57
   critical questions on, 198
   definition of, 147, 150–51
   levels of organizations (Sport Systems Map), 152, 158–61
   networking and, 152, 155–61, 195–96, 213
   resources for, vii–viii, 148–49, 162
   strategies for, 151–57, 197–98
   strategies for coaches as mothers, 33–35, 197–98
   See also communications skills; networking
Anderson, Kelley, 262
androcentrism in sport, 36–55
about androcentrism, 43–45
   definition of, 37, 43
   masculinity and, 43–44, 68–69
   metaphors for, xviii–xix, 50–51, 182–83
   personal and organizational perspectives on, 44–47, 49
   research as androcentric, 43–44, 48–50
   research on issues of, 45–52, 182–83
   strategies to change, 49–54, 149–50
   theories of, 44–52
   values and, 48–54
   work-life balance and, 48–51
apprenticeships. *See* mentoring
Audet, Marie-Hélène, 262
Australia, anti-homophobia initiatives in, 86–87, 91
Australian Institute of Sport, 26–28
Ayliffe, Rhett, 28

Bandura, A., 110
Banville, Melanie, 175
Barton, Graham, 176–77
basketball coaches and athletes, **180**

Belisle, Lyndsay, 164
Béliveau, Sylvie, 263
Bessette, Frédéric, 16, 17
Biesenthal, Laryssa
    career of, 175
    CJWC articles by, 261
    coaching and motherhood, 2, 23–29
bisexuality in sport. *See* sexual
        diversity and sport
Blackstripe, 93
Boomgaardt, Mariel, 202
bottle neck, as metaphor for
        career paths, 183
Boulmerka, Hassiba, 52–53
Boyer, Kaleigh, 137
Brambell, Avery Biesenthal, 2
Brambell, Iain, 23, 25–28
Brighton Declaration on Women
    in Sport, 149–50
Brunet, Caroline, 39–40
bullying. *See* harassment and bullying
business
    business plans, 208–12
    gender differences, xv–xvi
    leadership in, xv–xvi, xx–xxiii

CAAWS. *See* Canadian Association for
        the Advancement of Women
        and Sport and Physical Activity
Callary, Bettina, 265
    on career paths for coaches, 166–79
Campbell River Skating Club, 220
Canada Games apprenticeship
        programs, 138–39, 195, 242
Canada Games Council, xxvi, 245
Canada Summer Games (2009), 164, 180
Canada Winter Games (2007),
        31, 153, 207, 225, 246
Canadian Association for the
    Advancement of Women and
    Sport and Physical Activity,
    ix–x, 59, 84, 91, 93, 245–46
Canadian Journal for Women in Coaching
    overview of, xi–xiv

selected articles in, 32,
        148–49, 259–63
Canadian Professional Coaches
        Association, 6
Canadian Ski Coaches
        Federation, 255–56
Canadian Soccer Association, 191–92
Canadian Swimming Coaches and
        Teachers Association, 256
canoe and kayak, 39–40, 176
CanoeKayak Canada, 176
Caplan, Paula and Jeremy, 43
career paths for female
        coaches, 166–201
    barriers in, xix–xx, xxii, 169–70,
        182–85, 193, 243–44, 246–47
    gender differences and, 170–73, 185
    hedgehog concept, 204–08, 215n1
    metaphors for women's careers,
        xviii–xix, 50–51, 169, 182–83
    motivation of successful
        coaches, 3–4, 17, 19, 204–08
    negotiation skills, 29, 198–99
    new coaches, 186–90
    new coaching paradigms, 192–95
    qualities of successful coaches,
        xxvii, 171–74, 186, 189, 194, 204–08
    recruitment of coaches,
        xxiv, 34, 186–90
    research areas, potential,
        183, 192, 250–52
    retention of coaches, 58–59, 190–95
    same-sex training, xxiv
    social isolation and, xxi,
        182, 184, 194
    strategies for, xxiv–xxvi, 185–99, 244
    See also advocacy; androcentrism
        in sport; coaches, female;
        mentoring; networking;
        professionalism of coaches
Carli, L., xviii–xix, 50–51, 53, 169–70
Caskey, Amy, 207
Center for the Study of Sport
        in Society, 93

China, sport system in, 262

cjwc. *See Canadian Journal for Women in Coaching*

clothing, sports, 40

coaches, female
  as social change agents, 184–85
  communities of practice, 126, 134–36, 138–39, 141
  motivation of successful, 3–4, 17, 19, 204–08
  qualities of successful, xxvii, 171–74, 186, 189, 194, 204–08
  research areas, potential, 250–52
  statistics on, xvii–xviii, 42, 58, 168–69, 178
  statistics on (nccp levels), xvii, 182
  statistics on (Olympics), xvii, 183, 247–48
  statistics on full- or part-time status, 220
  surveys of, xix–xx, 218–20, 229, 232–37
  See also gender; professionalism of coaches

coaches, male
  statistics on, 182–83, 218–19
  statistics on full- or part-time status, 220
  surveys of, xix–xx, 218–20, 229, 232–37
  See also gender

Coaches Association of British Columbia, 256

Coaches Association of Ontario, 6, 256

Coaches Association of Prince Edward Island, 256

Coaches Association of Saskatchewan, 256

Coaches of Canada, 6

Coaching Association of Canada
  apprenticeships, 138, 174–77, 195, **242**
  five-point strategy for change, 32, 245–53

mentoring programs, 129, 136, 138–42

professional development program, 174

report on status of coaches, 42, 150, 168–69, 218

research on female coaches, 247

support for maternity policies, 29–30

See also Women in Coaching program

Coaching Manitoba, 257

college coaches. *See* university and college coaches

Collins, Jim, 204, 208

Commonwealth Games apprenticeships, 138

communications skills, 100–15
  advocacy and, 154–57
  assertiveness, 103–04
  conflict management, 107–08, 111–13
  constructive feedback, 108–09
  definitions of, 102
  facilitation skills, 154, 157
  gender and, 103, 172–74
  "I" messages, 107–08, 110–11
  inclusive approaches, 53–54, 157
  listening, 105–07, 171–72
  negotiation skills, 29, 198–99
  non-verbal communication, 104–05
  receiving criticism, 109–10
  speaking clearly, 107–08, 156–57
  verbal persuasion, 110–11
  See also advocacy

communities of practice, 126, 134–36, 138–39, 141

Constantin, Jean, 5

contracts, employment. *See* employment contracts

Crane, Sarah, **180**

Crockett, Kevin, 20

Croteau, Mylène, 20

Croxon, Sheilagh

articles by, 218, 253, 261
coaching and motherhood,
    4–8, 9, 29, 30, 32
on employment contracts, 236–37
survey by, of coaches, 218
Culver, Diane
    career of, 39, 265–66
    on androcentrism in sport, 36–55
Cumpstone, Erin, 216
cycling coaches and athletes, 242

Daniels, Nina and Lisa, 7
Dankers, Arne, 35n1
David, Tracy, 190–91
Davidson, Diedre, 180
Davidson, Melody, 262
Dawson, Chad, 10
Deaf Queer Resource Center, 93
Demers, Guylaine
    career of, 266
    cjwc articles by, 260–63
    on community coaches, 149
    on homophobia in sport, 73–96
    on next generation of female
        coaches, 180–201
Devlin-Morrison, Joanne, 176
diversity, sexual. See sexual
        diversity and sport
Doan, Catriona Le May, 22
Dodge, Ann, 261
Dollard Synchro Club, 15
domestic responsibilities
Donaldson, Noel, 27
Doré, Karine, 18
Draper, Matt, 27
Dubnicoff, Tanya, 41

Eagly, A., xviii–xix, 50–51, 53, 169–70
education, coaches in. See university
        and college coaches
Égale Action, 93
Eisler, Laurie, 189–90, 193–94, 260
Elm, Steven, 35n1
employment contracts
    benefits of, 217–19
    checklist for, 237–40
    compensation in, 178,
        221–24, 230, 234–35
    definition of contract, 240n1
    duration of, 6, 233–34
    for employees and
        contractors, 219–29
    for employees and contractors,
        comparison, 219–22,
        226–29, 231, 241n5
    job descriptions, 222, 230–33
    liability, 222–23, 230
    negotiations for, 29, 198–99
    overtime, 232, 234
    performance reviews, 230, 232–33
    research areas, potential, 250–52
    specific tasks in, 228–30
    survey of coaches with,
        218–20, 229, 232–33
    termination of, 18–19, 32,
        224–26, 233–36
    See also professionalism of coaches
equipment, sports, 40

faculty coaches. See university
        and college coaches
Federation of Gay Games, 93
Feingold, A., 172–73
female coaches. See coaches, female
femininity
    androcentrism and, 44
    sexual diversity in sport
        and, 78–79, 81
feminist movement
    cultural studies, 182
    gender differences and, 47–48
    mentoring and, 134–35
    sexual diversity in sport and, 77
fencing coaches and athletes, 225
figure skating
    coaches and athletes, 137
    court case on employee/contractor
        status, 220, 226, 227

Findlay, Hilary
  career of, 266
  on contracts and contract
    negotiations, 216–41
"A Five-Point Collaborative Strategy
    for Change," 32, 245–53

Gay, Lesbian, and Straight
    Education Network, 94
Gay and Lesbian Alliance Against
    Defamation, 94
Gay and Lesbian Athletics
    Foundation, 94
Gay and Lesbian International
    Sport Association, 94
gay coaches and athletes
  coming out of, 76, 83, 89
  homophobia and, 79, 81–83
  research areas, potential, 92–93
  research on, 75, 77–79
  See also homophobia in sport;
    sexual diversity and sport
gender
  co-coaching and, 193–94
  communications styles
    and, xx, 103, 172–74
  in academic settings, xvi–xvii
  in business settings, xv–xvi, xxiii
  in employment, xvi, xix, 219, 235
  mentoring and, 131–35, 138–42
  moral development
    theories and, 42–43
  personality and, xx, 172–73
  research and, 43–45, 170–73
  stereotyping and, xx–xxi,
    xxvii, 78, 80
  theories of differences, 45–52, 170–73
  women as social change
    agents, 184–85
  See also androcentrism in sport;
    career paths for female coaches;
    sexual diversity and sport

"The Gender Structure of National
    Sport Organizations"
    (Sport Canada), 45–47
Generations for Peace Camp, 36
Germany, coaches in, 169
Gilligan, Carol, 43–44
glass ceiling metaphor for women's
    careers, xviii–xix, 50–51, 182–83
Good to Great (Collins), 204, 208
Gorman, Tobie, 175–76
government and coaching
  employment standards
    laws, 224–25, 232
  impact of Title ix on US
    sports, xviii, xxvi
  policies on maternity leave
    and support, 4, 15
  policies to support female
    coaches, xxvi–xxvii, 250
  resources for self-employed, 214
  sports organizations, 158–61
Granger, Mark, 176
Granite Club, Toronto, 7–8
Greenwald, Mark, 21, 22
Griffin, Pat, 81, 91
Groves, Kristina, 35n1, **166**

Hakim, Catherine, 170
Hall, M.A., 53
Hand, Kelly, 261
harassment and bullying, 57–72
  definitions of, 59–60
  effects of, 59, 64–65, 69
  gender harassment and,
    60, 62–66, 69
  homonegativity and, 63–64, 66, 69
  in other workplaces, 58–59, 65–68
  job insecurity and, 64, 67, 69
  masculinity and, 66, 68–69
  minority status and, 59, 66–67, 69
  physicality of sport and, 68–69
  power imbalance and, 59–60, 65, 67
  research areas, potential, 69, 250–52
  research on, 57–58, 60–67, 69

social isolation and, 60,
63–64, 66–67, 69
strategies to change, 65, 67–68
"Harassment-Free Sport:
Guidelines to Address
Homophobia and Sexuality
Discrimination in Sport," 91
Havaris, Eva, 9
Hedgehog Concept, 204–08, 215n1
Hesketh, Rae Anne, 220
heterosexuality and
homophobia, 75, 78–85
See also homophobia in sport
hockey, field, 189
hockey, ice
androcentrism and, 40
coaches and athletes, 31
gender differences in, 185
homophobia in sport, 73–96
benefits of action against, 76, 90, 92
coming out and, 63, 76,
79–80, 87–90, 92–93
definitions of, 74, 95n1
discrediting performances
and, 79, 81
femininity and, 78–79, 81
heterosexuality and, 75, 78–85
impact of, 78–80, 83–86
in education, 77–78
job insecurity and, 84–85
legal rights, 74–75, 92
masculinity and, 81–82
media coverage and, 74, 80
research areas, potential,
80, 92–93, 250–52
research on, 75, 77–83, 86–87
silence about, 73–75
sport organizations for
diversity, 93–95
sport organizations' responses
to, 78, 81, 84, 86–87, 92–93
strategies to change, 90–93

See also gay coaches and athletes;
lesbian coaches and athletes;
sexual diversity and sport
Hoogveld, Arno, 20
Hooper, Ivan, 27
Howes, Patricia, 225
Hughes, Clara, i, 35n1
Hureau, Mark, 180

In a Different Voice (Gilligan), 43–44
International Centre of Excellence, 6, 7
International Working Group on
Women and Sport, 150
intimidation. See harassment
and bullying
Inward, Laura, 116
It Takes a Team! (anti-homophobia
program), 86–87, 91, 94
IWG. See International Working
Group on Women and Sport

Jeux de la Francophonie
apprenticeship programs, 138
job insecurity
harassment and, 64, 67, 69
homophobia and, 84–85
See also employment contracts
John, Geraint, 13–14
Johnson, Elizabeth, 43

Kamphoff, C., 182
kayak. See canoe and kayak
Kayser, Samantha, 202
Kenwright, David, 176
Kerr, Gretchen
career of, 266–67
CJWC articles by, 262–63
on harassment and
bullying, 57–72, 263
Kiland, Kam, 22
Knobbs, Jennifer, 8
Kohlberg, Lawrence, 43–44

labyrinth metaphor, xix, 50–51, 169
Lachapelle, Diane, 15
Laval University, women's
    basketball team, 56
Law, Brianne, 153
Lay, Marion, 253
Le Complexe Multisport
    Saint-Eustache, 19
LeBlanc, Lynne, 36
Legal Issues in Sport: Tools and Techniques
    for the Sport Manager, 241n5
Leonard, Dorothy, 174
Lesbian and Gay Sports, 94
lesbian coaches and athletes
    coming out and, 63, 76,
        79–80, 87–90, 92–93
    impact of homonegativity
        on, 76, 83–86
    research areas, potential, 92–93
    research on, 77–81
    social isolation of, 66–67
    See also homophobia in sport;
        sexual diversity and sport
Lips, Hilary, 54
Long-Term Apprenticeship
    Program, 119
    See also Women in
        Coaching program

male coaches and athletes
    homophobia and, 81–83
    masculinity and, 44, 81–82
    survey of contracts for, 218
    See also androcentrism in sport
Map, Sport System (levels of
    organizations), 152
Marquis, Linda, 56
Marsh, Jen, 202
Marshall, Dru
    career of, 267
    cjwc articles by, 259–62
    on employment, 191, 236–37
    on mentoring, 116–45, 196

on next generation of female
    coaches, 180–01
on political advocacy, 146–63
survey by, of coaches,
    218, 229, 233–37
Marshall, Moira, 20, 22
Martel, Josée, 262
Martin, Angela, 31
masculinity
    androcentrism and, 43–44, 68–69
    homophobia and, 81–82
    See also androcentrism in sport
Matheson, Andrew, 27
Mauresmo, Amélie, 80
McCarthy, Lyall, 27–28
McLaughlin, Siobhan, 202
media coverage of sports, 44–45, 74, 80
mentoring, 116–45
    apprenticeships, 138–39, 174–77, 195
    benefits of, xxiv, 119–22,
        125–27, 132–35, 142, 213
    coaching and, 119, 135–42, 196–97
    communities of practice,
        126, 134–36, 138–39, 141
    critical questions on, 197
    definitions of, 118–20, 128–29, 133–34
    gender and, 131–35, 138–42
    organizations and, 33, 123–27, 131–42
    qualities of successful, 121–24
    research on, 136–38
    strategies for, 140–42
    structure and duration of, 128–33
    types of, 128–29, 133–34
    use in other settings,
        118–19, 130–31, 196
    See also career paths for
        female coaches
Mercier, Rose
    career of, 268
    cjwc articles by, 259–62
    on androcentrism in sport, 36–55
    on political advocacy, 146–63
    on professionalism of
        coaches, 202–15, 263

metaphors for women's careers,
xviii–xix, 50–51, 169, 182–83
Minister of National Revenue,
Moose Jaw Kinsmen Flying
Fins Inc. v., 226, 227
Minister of National Revenue,
Puri v., 220, 226, 227
Minister of National Revenue, Whistler
Mountain Ski Club v., 226, 227
Moose Jaw Kinsmen Flying Fins
Inc. v. Minister of National
Revenue, 226, 227
Morace, Carolina, 192
moral development, theories of, 43–44
Morgan, William, 52
Morrill, Adam, **137**
Morton, Shelley, **164**
Moss, Ian, 24, 25
motherhood, 2–35
advocacy for, 10, 33–35, 197–98
androcentrism and, 51
childcare benefits, 9, 16–17,
20, 22, 25, 27, 34
co-coaching and, 20, 193–94
employment contracts, 6, 27
employment issues, xxv,
4–5, 9, 12, 20, 21, 24, 194
family support and, 5, 10,
16–17, 20–22, 25–28
funding and, 12, 22–23, 30
geographic mobility and, xxii, 5, 16
government policies, 4, 15
nannies and, 17, 24–25
sport organizations and, 29–30
statistics on impact of, xxii
strategies to support,
xxv, 33–35, 194–95
work-life balance and, xxii,
10–11, 17, 19, 21, 24, 26, 28, 29
See also career paths for
female coaches
Ms. Foundation for Women, 94
Muslim culture and sports, 52–53

National Center for Lesbian Rights, 94
National Coach Workshop, 135, 195, 246
National Coaching Certification
Program
business training in, 35
facilitator program, 157
mentorships in, 5
statistics on, by level, xvii, 182
National Coaching Institute,
119, 130, 139, 174
National Collegiate Athletic
Association, 94, 193
National Team Apprenticeship
Program, 138, 174–77
NCCP. *See* National Coaching
Certification Program
negotiation skills, 29, 198–99
See also communications skills
networking
benefits of, xxiv, 152,
155–61, 195–96, 213
critical questions, 195–96
See also career paths for female
coaches; mentoring
New Zealand, synchronized
swimming, 7
Nordhagen, Christine, **146**
Norman, Leanne, 182–83
Norway's legislation on gender
equity, xxviii

Olympic Games
advocacy and, 40, 151
androcentrism and, 39–40, 45, 52–53
female coaches of medal-
winning athletes, 246–48
statistics on male and female
coaches, xvii, 183
support for, 22, 23, 158, 178
Olympic Oval, Calgary, 19–22
Online Mentor Program, 141
Ontario Rugby Union, 8, 11
OutSports, 94
Own the Podium, 22, 23, 158

Pan American Games, 18, 138–39
Parents, Families, and Friends of
        Lesbians and Gays, 94
Parfitt, Adam, 24
Pellerud, Even, 190, 192
physical abuse. *See* harassment
        and bullying
Pinker, Susan, 47–48, 53, 170
political advocacy. *See* advocacy
Positive Space Campaign, 94
post-secondary coaches. *See* university
        and college coaches
power relationships
        advocacy and, 151–57
        androcentrism and, 52–54
        harassment and imbalance
            in, 59–60, 65, 67
        See also advocacy
Price, Biz, 6, 19
professional development
        apprenticeships, 138–39, 174–77, 195
        communities of practice,
            126, 134–36, 138–39, 141
        curriculum for, 148, 161
        leadership and, 171
        levels of sport organizations
            for, 158–61
        strategies to support, 33–35
        women-only training, xxiv
        See also career paths for female
            coaches; mentoring; Women
            in Coaching program
professionalism of coaches, 202–15
        branding and, 213–14
        business plans, 208–12
        hedgehog concept of, 204–08, 215n1
        resources for support, 214
        self-employment and, 204–05
        sustainable income, 206–08
        values, mission, goals, and
            objectives, 209–11
        volunteers and, 203–04, 206, 208, 212
        work-life balance, 212–15

written plans, importance
        of, 208–09, 211–12
        See also career paths for
            female coaches
Puri, Jannine, 220
*Puri v. Minister of National
        Revenue*, 220, 226, 227
Purnell, Heather, 175
pyramid, as metaphor for
        career paths, 183

Radecki, Sophia, 242
Rail, Genevieve, 52
Reade, Ian, 194
        survey by, of coaches,
            218–20, 229, 232, 233
recruitment of coaches,
        xxiv, 34, 186–90
        See also career paths for
            female coaches
reflective practices, 171–72
*A Report on the Status of Coaches in
        Canada*, 42, 150, 168–69, 218
research areas, potential
        on career paths for female
            coaches, 183, 192, 250–52
        on harassment and bullying, 69
        on homophobia, 80, 92–93
        strategies for, 250
resource lists
        cJwc articles, 259–63
        political advocacy groups, 162
        sport organizations for
            sexual diversity, 93–95
retention of coaches
        during first five years, 58, 193
        general factors, 58–59, 193
        impact of harassment on, 58–59
        strategies for, 190–95
        See also career paths for
            female coaches
Richardson, Brian, 175
Ritchie, Kaeli, **180**
Roaf, Alan, 24

Robertson, Brenda, 261
Robertson, Sheila
   articles by, 253, 259–63
   career of, 268
   on motherhood, 149
   on women in coaching, xi–xiv
Rodionenko, Andrei, 176
role models
   benefits of, xxi, xxiv–
      xxv, 184–85, 188
   mentoring and, 118, 121, 129–30
   See also career paths for female
      coaches; mentoring
Rouge et Or women's
   basketball team, 56
rowing
   apprenticeships and, 175–76
   coaches and athletes, 2, **202**
   coaching and motherhood, 23–29
Rowing Australia, 26–27
Rowing Canada, 23–26, 175
rugby
   coaches and athletes, **xxx**
   coaching and motherhood, 8–15
Rugby Canada, 8–15
Rugby World Cup Sevens, **xxx**, 11–13

Safe Schools Coalition, 94
Safe Schools Program for Gay and
      Lesbian Students, 95
Sauvé, Denise, 18
Sawula, Lorne, 193–94
Sax, L., 172
*Seeing the Invisible, Speaking About
      the Unspoken: Addressing
      Homophobia in Sport*, 91
self-employment
   benefits of, xxii
   coaches as consultants,
      15, 204–05, 214
   See also professionalism of coaches
sexual bullying, 60
   See also harassment and bullying

sexual diversity and sport
   bisexuality and, 93
   definitions, 74, 95n1
   legal rights, 74–75
   research on, 77–81
   sports organizations for, 93–95
   strategies to support, 86–87, 90–93
   See also homophobia in sport
The Sexual Paradox (Pinker), 47–48
Sharp, Dawn-Marie
   career of, 269
   on mentoring, 116–45
   on next generation of female
      coaches, 180–201
Simard, Lise, 175–76
Sippel, Lori, **216**
ski jumping, 40, 151
skiing, downhill
   androcentrism and, 39
   coaches, **153**
   court case on employee/
      contractor status, 226, 227
soccer coaches and athletes, 190–92
social isolation
   harassment and bullying
      and, 60, 63–64, 66–67, 69
   mentoring to reduce, 122, 132
   of female coaches, xxi, 182, 184, 194
   See also mentoring; networking
social networking media, 156
softball coaches and athletes, **216**
speed skating, 21–22
   coaches and athletes, **i**, **166**
Speed Skating Canada, 19–20
Sport and Postmodern Times (Rail), 52
Sport Canada
   policies on women in sport,
      xxvii, 29–30, 190, 192, 199n1
   political advocacy, 197
   research by, on gender
      and sport, 45–46
*Sport Canada Policy on Women
      in Sport*, 199

Sport System Map (levels of
    organizations), 152, 158–61
sports clubs
    coaching and motherhood
        at, 5, 7–8, 19
sports equipment and clothing, 40
sports organizations
    anti-homophobia programs, 90–91
    apprenticeships, 138–39, 174–77, 195
    committees in, xxvi, 186–88
    communities of practice in,
        126, 134–36, 138–39, 141
    contact information for, 255–56
    for support of sexual
        diversity, 93–95
    homophobia and, 81, 86–87
    levels of organizations (Sport
        Systems Map), 152, 158–61
    maternity policies of,
        6–7, 29–30, 33–35
    mentoring and, 33, 123–27, 135–42
    negotiations with, 29, 198–99
    partnerships and
        collaboration, 248–49
    person- and organization-centred
        perspectives, 44–47, 49
    See also androcentrism in sport;
        Coaching Association of
        Canada; Sport Canada; Women
        in Coaching program
Strategic Think Tank, 193
Strong Women, Deep Closets
    (Griffin), 81, 91
Stuffco, Marian, 29
Sukunda, Adrienne, 225
Sullivan, Monique, 41
Swap, Walter, 174
swimming
    court case on employee/
        contractor status, 226, 227
Synchro Canada, 4–6, 15–19, 29
synchronized swimming
    coaches and athletes, 207

coaching and motherhood,
    4–8, 15–19

Taillon, Isabelle
    coaching and motherhood,
        6, 15–19, 30, 32
"Taking Action: A Five-Point
    Collaborative Strategy
    for Change," 245–53
Tannen, Deborah, 172
Taylor, Shaunna
    career of, 269
    on communications skills, 101–15
tennis, 80
Terry, Georgena, 40
"They Never Give Up: Once a Coach,
    Always a Coach," 32–33
Thinking Critically About Research on
    Sex and Gender (Caplan), 43
Thomson, Cindy, 262
track and field, 39, 51–52
track cycling coaches and athletes, 41
Tucker Center for Research on Girls
    and Women in Sport, 95, 184
two-spirited persons
    definition of, 95n1
    See also homophobia in sport;
        sexual diversity and sport

United Kingdom, coaching
    in, 86, 169, 182
United States
    anti-homophobia
        initiatives in, 86–87
    impact of Title IX, xviii, xxvi
    statistics on female leaders, xvi, 169
university and college coaches
    coaching and motherhood in, 19–23
    coaching positions, 19–20, 178,
        189–91, 194, 197, 218–19
    gender differences in, xvi–xvii
    gender equity policies
        in, xxvi–xxvii

mentoring and, 118, 196
sports organizations, 158–61
University of Alberta
coaching at, 189–91, 194
University of Calgary
coaching and motherhood at, 19–23
University of Victoria
soccer coaching at, 190–91
University of Western Ontario
coaching and motherhood at, 8, 10

values
advocacy and, 154, 157
androcentrism and, 52–54
business plans and, 209–10
conflict management and, 113
core values, how to identify, 209
See also work-life balance
verbal abuse. *See* harassment
and bullying
Vickers, Joan, 260
volleyball coaches and athletes,
36, 116, 189–90, 193–94
volunteer coaches
as professionals, 203–04,
206, 208, 212
benefits of contracts for, 218
motherhood and, 9
See also professionalism of coaches

Wang, Xiuli
coaching and motherhood,
i, 19–23, 35n1, **166**
Werthner, Penny
career of, 39, 49, 269
cjwc articles by, 259–61
on androcentrism in sport, 36–55
on career paths for coaches, 166–79
on communications
skills, 101–15, 149
Wesch, Natascha
coaching and motherhood,
xxx, 8–15, 30

*Whistler Mountain Ski Club v. Minister
of National Revenue,* 226, 227
Whitton, Charlotte, 173
Why Gender Matters (Sax), 172
Wilson, Erin, 8
WinSport Canada, 22, 23
Women, Men, and Power (Lips), 54
"Women in Coaching: A
Descriptive Study," 150
Women in Coaching program
apprenticeships, 138, 174–77, 195, **242**
five-point strategy for
change, 32, 245–53
mandate of, vii–viii, 5, 42
mentoring programs, 129, 138–42
networking in, 195–96
resources in, 152, 214
See also Coaching Association
of Canada
Women's Sports Foundation,
86–87, 91, 95
work-life balance
androcentrism and, 48–51
blended or balanced life, 214–15
metaphors for women's careers,
xviii–xix, 50–51, 169, 182–83
motherhood and, 10–11,
17, 19, 21, 24, 26, 28
professionalism and, 212–15
sports and, 29
See also career paths for
female coaches
*Work-Lifestyle Choices in the Twenty-
First Century* (Hakim), 170
World Conference on Women
and Sport, 149–50
World Outgames, 92
wrestling coaches and
athletes, **146, 164**

*You Just Don't Understand: Women and
Men in Conversation* (Tannen), 172

Zhao, Zonghang, 20